Cloud Design Patterns

Prescriptive Architecture Guidance for Cloud Applications

Cloud Design Patterns

Prescriptive Architecture Guidance for Cloud Applications

Alex Homer
John Sharp
Larry Brader
Masashi Narumoto
Trent Swanson

978-1-62114-036-8

Contents

GUIDANCE

Preface

This guide from the Microsoft patterns & practices group, produced with the help of many people within the developer community, provides solutions for common problems encountered when developing cloud-hosted applications.

The guide:

- Articulates the benefit of applying patterns when implementing cloud applications, especially when they will be hosted in Windows Azure.
- Discusses the problems that the patterns address, and how these relate to Windows Azure applications.
- Shows how to implement the patterns using the features of Windows Azure, emphasizing benefits and considerations.
- Depicts the big picture by showing how these patterns fit into cloud application architectures, and how they relate to other patterns.

The majority of topics described in the guide are equally relevant to all kinds of distributed systems, whether hosted on Windows Azure or on other cloud platforms.

> Our intention is not to provide a comprehensive collection of patterns. Instead, we chose what we think are useful patterns for cloud applications—taking into account the popularity of each one amongst users. Neither is this a detailed guide to the features of Windows Azure. To learn about Windows Azure see *http://windowsazure.com*.

CONTENTS OF THIS GUIDE

In conjunction with feedback from a wide representation of the developer community, we identified eight categories that encompass the most common problem areas in cloud application development.

Category	Description
Availability	Availability defines the proportion of time that the system is functional and working. It will be affected by system errors, infrastructure problems, malicious attacks, and system load. It is usually measured as a percentage of uptime. Cloud applications typically provide users with a service level agreement (SLA), which means that applications must be designed and implemented in a way that maximizes availability.
Data Management	Data management is the key element of cloud applications, and influences most of the quality attributes. Data is typically hosted in different locations and across multiple servers for reasons such as performance, scalability or availability, and this can present a range of challenges. For example, data consistency must be maintained, and data will typically need to be synchronized across different locations.

Category	Description
Design and Implementation	Good design encompasses factors such as consistency and coherence in component design and deployment, maintainability to simplify administration and development, and reusability to allow components and subsystems to be used in other applications and in other scenarios. Decisions made during the design and implementation phase have a huge impact on the quality and the total cost of ownership of cloud hosted applications and services.
Messaging	The distributed nature of cloud applications requires a messaging infrastructure that connects the components and services, ideally in a loosely coupled manner in order to maximize scalability. Asynchronous messaging is widely used, and provides many benefits, but also brings challenges such as the ordering of messages, poison message management, idempotency, and more.
Management and Monitoring	Cloud applications run in in a remote datacenter where you do not have full control of the infrastructure or, in some cases, the operating system. This can make management and monitoring more difficult than an on-premises deployment. Applications must expose runtime information that administrators and operators can use to manage and monitor the system, as well as supporting changing business requirements and customization without requiring the application to be stopped or redeployed.
Performance and Scalability	Performance is an indication of the responsiveness of a system to execute any action within a given time interval, while scalability is ability of a system either to handle increases in load without impact on performance or for the available resources to be readily increased. Cloud applications typically encounter variable workloads and peaks in activity. Predicting these, especially in a multi-tenant scenario, is almost impossible. Instead, applications should be able to scale out within limits to meet peaks in demand, and scale in when demand decreases. Scalability concerns not just compute instances, but other elements such as data storage, messaging infrastructure, and more.
Resiliency	Resiliency is the ability of a system to gracefully handle and recover from failures. The nature of cloud hosting, where applications are often multi-tenant, use shared platform services, compete for resources and bandwidth, communicate over the Internet, and run on commodity hardware means there is an increased likelihood that both transient and more permanent faults will arise. Detecting failures, and recovering quickly and efficiently, is necessary to maintain resiliency.
Security	Security is the capability of a system to prevent malicious or accidental actions outside of the designed usage, and to prevent disclosure or loss of information. Cloud applications are exposed on the Internet outside trusted on-premises boundaries, are often open to the public, and may serve untrusted users. Applications must be designed and deployed in a way that protects them from malicious attacks, restricts access to only approved users, and protects sensitive data.

For each of these categories, we created related guidance and documented common patterns designed to help developers solve problems they regularly encounter. The guide contains:

- **Twenty-four design patterns** that are useful in cloud-hosted applications. Each pattern is provided in a common format that describes the context and problem, the solution, issues and considerations for applying the pattern, and an example based on Windows Azure. Each pattern also includes links to other related patterns.
- **Two primers and eight guidance topics** that provide basic knowledge and describe good practice techniques for developing cloud-hosted applications. The format of each primer and guidance topic is designed to present this information in a relevant and informative way.
- **Ten sample applications** that demonstrate the usage of the design patterns described in this guide. You can use and adapt the source code to suit your own specific requirements.

The Design Patterns

The design patterns are allocated to one or more of the eight categories described earlier. The full list of patterns is shown in the following table.

Pattern	Categories	Description
Cache-aside		Load data on demand into a cache from a data store. This pattern can improve performance and also helps to maintain consistency between data held in the cache and the data in the underlying data store.
Circuit Breaker		Handle faults that may take a variable amount of time to rectify when connecting to a remote service or resource. This pattern can improve the stability and resiliency of an application.
Compensating Transaction		Undo the work performed by a series of steps, which together define an eventually consistent operation, if one or more of the operations fails. Operations that follow the eventual consistency model are commonly found in cloud-hosted applications that implement complex business processes and workflows.
Competing Consumers		Enable multiple concurrent consumers to process messages received on the same messaging channel. This pattern enables a system to process multiple messages concurrently to optimize throughput, to improve scalability and availability, and to balance the workload.
Compute Resource Consolidation		Consolidate multiple tasks or operations into a single computational unit. This pattern can increase compute resource utilization, and reduce the costs and management overhead associated with performing compute processing in cloud-hosted applications.
Command and Query Responsibility Segregation (CQRS)		Segregate operations that read data from operations that update data by using separate interfaces. This pattern can maximize performance, scalability, and security; support evolution of the system over time through higher flexibility; and prevent update commands from causing merge conflicts at the domain level
Event Sourcing		Use an append-only store to record the full series of events that describe actions taken on data in a domain, rather than storing just the current state, so that the store can be used to materialize the domain objects. This pattern can simplify tasks in complex domains by avoiding the requirement to synchronize the data model and the business domain; improve performance, scalability, and responsiveness; provide consistency for transactional data; and maintain full audit trails and history that may enable compensating actions.
External Configuration Store		Move configuration information out of the application deployment package to a centralized location. This pattern can provide opportunities for easier management and control of configuration data, and for sharing configuration data across applications and application instances.
Federated Identity		Delegate authentication to an external identity provider. This pattern can simplify development, minimize the requirement for user administration, and improve the user experience of the application.
Gatekeeper		Protect applications and services by using a dedicated host instance that acts as a broker between clients and the application or service, validates and sanitizes requests, and passes requests and data between them. This pattern can provide an additional layer of security, and limit the attack surface of the system.

Pattern	Categories	Description
Health Endpoint Monitoring		Implement functional checks within an application that external tools can access through exposed endpoints at regular intervals. This pattern can help to verify that applications and services are performing correctly.
Index Table		Create indexes over the fields in data stores that are frequently referenced by query criteria. This pattern can improve query performance by allowing applications to more quickly retrieve data from a data store.
Leader Election		Coordinate the actions performed by a collection of collaborating task instances in a distributed application by electing one instance as the leader that assumes responsibility for managing the other instances. This pattern can help to ensure that tasks do not conflict with each other, cause contention for shared resources, or inadvertently interfere with the work that other task instances are performing.
Materialized View		Generate prepopulated views over the data in one or more data stores when the data is formatted in a way that does not favor the required query operations. This pattern can help to support efficient querying and data extraction, and improve application performance.
Pipes and Filters		Decompose a task that performs complex processing into a series of discrete elements that can be reused. This pattern can improve performance, scalability, and reusability by allowing task elements that perform the processing to be deployed and scaled independently.
Priority Queue		Prioritize requests sent to services so that requests with a higher priority are received and processed more quickly than those of a lower priority. This pattern is useful in applications that offer different service level guarantees to individual types of client.
Queue-based Load Leveling		Use a queue that acts as a buffer between a task and a service that it invokes in order to smooth intermittent heavy loads that may otherwise cause the service to fail or the task to timeout. This pattern can help to minimize the impact of peaks in demand on availability and responsiveness for both the task and the service.
Retry		Enable an application to handle temporary failures when connecting to a service or network resource by transparently retrying the operation in the expectation that the failure is transient. This pattern can improve the stability of the application.
Runtime Reconfiguration		Design an application so that it can be reconfigured without requiring redeployment or restarting the application. This helps to maintain availability and minimize downtime.
Scheduler Agent Supervisor		Coordinate a set of actions across a distributed set of services and other remote resources, attempt to transparently handle faults if any of these actions fail, or undo the effects of the work performed if the system cannot recover from a fault. This pattern can add resiliency to a distributed system by enabling it to recover and retry actions that fail due to transient exceptions, long-lasting faults, and process failures.
Sharding		Divide a data store into a set of horizontal partitions shards. This pattern can improve scalability when storing and accessing large volumes of data.
Static Content Hosting		Deploy static content to a cloud-based storage service that can deliver these directly to the client. This pattern can reduce the requirement for potentially expensive compute instances.

Pattern	Categories	Description
Throttling		Control the consumption of resources used by an instance of an application, an individual tenant, or an entire service. This pattern can allow the system to continue to function and meet service level agreements, even when an increase in demand places an extreme load on resources.
Valet Key		Use a token or key that provides clients with restricted direct access to a specific resource or service in order to offload data transfer operations from the application code. This pattern is particularly useful in applications that use cloud-hosted storage systems or queues, and can minimize cost and maximize scalability and performance.

The Primer and Guidance Topics

The primer and guidance topics are related to specific areas of application development, as shown in the following diagram.

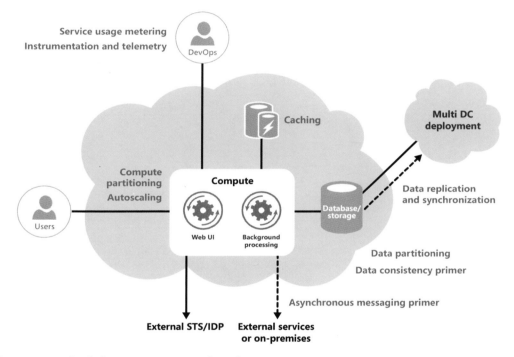

The guide contains the following primers and guidance topics.

Topic	Categories	Description
Asynchronous Messaging Primer		Messaging is a key strategy employed in many distributed environments such as the cloud. It enables applications and services to communicate and cooperate, and can help to build scalable and resilient solutions. Messaging supports asynchronous operations, enabling you to decouple a process that consumes a service from the process that implements the service.
Autoscaling Guidance		Constantly monitoring performance and scaling a system to adapt to fluctuating workloads to meet capacity targets and optimize operational cost can be a labor-intensive process. It may not be feasible to perform these tasks manually. This is where autoscaling is useful.

6

Topic	Categories	Description
Caching Guidance		Caching is a common technique that aims to improve the performance and scalability of a system by temporarily copying frequently accessed data to fast storage located close to the application. Caching is most effective when an application instance repeatedly reads the same data, especially if the original data store is slow relative to the speed of the cache, it is subject to a high level of contention, or it is far away resulting in network latency.
Compute Partitioning Guidance		When deploying an application to the cloud it may be desirable to allocate the services and components it uses in a way that helps to minimize running costs while maintaining the scalability, performance, availability, and security of the application.
Data Consistency Primer		Cloud applications typically use data that is dispersed across data stores. Managing and maintaining data consistency in this environment can become a critical aspect of the system, particularly in terms of the concurrency and availability issues that can arise. You frequently need to trade strong consistency for performance. This means that you may need to design some aspects of your solutions around the notion of eventual consistency and accept that the data that your applications use might not be completely consistent all of the time.
Data Partitioning Guidance		In many large-scale solutions, data is divided into separate partitions that can be managed and accessed separately. The partitioning strategy must be chosen carefully to maximize the benefits while minimizing adverse effects. Partitioning can help to improve scalability, reduce contention, and optimize performance.
Data Replication and Synchronization Guidance		When you deploy an application to more than one datacenter, such as cloud and on-premises locations, you must consider how you will replicate and synchronize the data each instance of the application uses in order to maximize availability and performance, ensure consistency, and minimize data transfer costs between locations.
Instrumentation and Telemetry Guidance		Most applications will include diagnostics features that generate custom monitoring and debugging information, especially when an error occurs. This is referred to as instrumentation, and is usually implemented by adding event and error handling code to the application. The process of gathering remote information that is collected by instrumentation is usually referred to as telemetry.
Multiple Datacenter Deployment Guidance		Deploying an application to more than one datacenter can provide benefits such as increased availability and a better user experience across wider geographical areas. However, there are challenges that must be resolved, such as data synchronization and regulatory limitations.
Service Metering Guidance		You may need to meter the use of applications or services in order to plan future requirements; to gain an understanding of how they are used; or to bill users, organization departments, or customers. This is a common requirement, particularly in large corporations and for independent software vendors and service providers.

The Sample Applications

Ten example applications that demonstrate the implementation of some of the patterns in this guide are available for you to download and run on your own computer or in your own Windows Azure subscription. To obtain and run the applications:

1. Go to the "Cloud Design Patterns - Sample Code" page on the Microsoft Download Center at http://aka.ms/cloud-design-patterns-sample. Download the "Cloud Design Patterns Examples.zip" file.
2. In Windows Explorer open the **Properties** for the zip file and choose **Unblock**.

3. Copy the files from the zip file to a folder near the root of your disk, such as **C:\PatternsGuide**. Do not unzip the files into your user profile folders (such as **Documents** or **Downloads**) because this will result in over-length file names.

4. Open the file **Readme.htm** in your browser. It contains information about configuring your system and the examples, running the examples locally in the Windows Azure emulator or deploying them to Windows Azure, and understanding what the examples show.

The example applications for use in conjunction with this guide are shown in the following table.

Topic	Categories	Description
Competing Consumers		This example contains two components: the Sender worker role is responsible for sending messages to a Service Bus queue, and the Receiver worker role retrieves messages from the queue and processes them. The Receiver worker role is configured to run with two instances to simulate competition between consumers.
Compute Resource Consolidation		This example shows how you can consolidate several separate and distinct tasks into a single worker role. There are no additional requirements for running this example.
External Configuration Store		This example shows a mechanism for storing configuration settings in an external store instead of using configuration files. In this example, settings are stored in Windows Azure Blob Storage. The blob containing the configuration information is monitored by an instance of the ExternalConfigurationManager class. When the ExternalConfigurationManager object detects a change in the configuration store, it notifies the application of the change.
Health Endpoint Monitoring		This example shows how you can set up a web endpoint that checks the health of dependent services by returning appropriate status codes. The endpoints are designed to be consumed by a watchdog monitoring service such as Windows Azure endpoint monitoring, but you can open and invoke the endpoint operations from a browser to see the results. You can also deploy and configure your own endpoint monitoring tool of choice to send requests to the service operations and analyze the responses received.
Leader Election		This example shows how a worker role instance can become a leader among a group of peer instances. The leader can then perform tasks that coordinate and control the other instances; these tasks should be performed by only one instance of the worker role. The leader is elected by acquiring a blob lease.
Pipes and Filters		This example contains two filters that could perform some part of the overall processing for a task. The two filters are combined into a pipeline; the output of one filter is passed as the input to the next. The filters are implemented as separate worker roles and a Windows Azure Service Bus queue provides the infrastructure that acts as the pipe.
Priority Queue		This example shows how you can implement priority queues by using Service Bus Topics and Subscriptions. A worker role is responsible for sending messages to a topic. It assigns a priority to each one. The receiving worker roles read messages from subscriptions that have the corresponding priority. In the example, The PriorityQueue.High worker role runs with two instances, whereas the PriorityQueue.Low worker runs only with one. This ensures that high priority messages are read from the queue more quickly than low priority messages.
Runtime Reconfiguration		This example shows how a change in the settings of a Cloud Service can be applied without restarting the web or worker role.

Topic	Categories	Description
Static Content Hosting		This example shows how to reference static content from a publicly accessible storage service. The example contains a Windows Azure web role, which hosts a web application that references JavaScript files and images deployed to a Windows Azure storage account. This type of content is typically deployed to the storage account as part of the application deployment process. However, to simplify the example, these files are deployed to the storage account when the application starts up.
Valet Key		This example shows how a client application can obtain a shared access signature with the necessary permissions to write directly to blob storage. For simplicity, this sample focuses on the mechanism to obtain and consume a valet key and does not show how to implement authentication or secure communications.

The samples provided for this guide are simplified to focus on and demonstrate the essential features of each pattern. They are not designed to be used in production scenarios.

MORE INFORMATION

All of the chapters include references to additional resources such as books, blog posts, and papers that will provide additional detail if you want to explore some of the topics in greater depth. For your convenience, there is a bibliography online that contains all the links so that these resources are just a click away: *http://aka.ms/cdpbibliography*.

FEEDBACK AND SUPPORT

Questions? Comments? Suggestions? To provide feedback about this guide, or to get help with any problems, please visit our Community site at *http://wag.codeplex.com*. The message board on the community site is the preferred feedback and support channel because it allows you to share your ideas, questions, and solutions with the entire community.

THE TEAM WHO BROUGHT YOU THIS GUIDE

Vision/Program Management: Masashi Narumoto
Authors: Alex Homer, John Sharp, Larry Brader, Masashi Narumoto, and Trent Swanson
Development: Julian Dominguez, Trent Swanson (Full Scale 180), Alejandro Jezierski (Southworks)
Testing: Larry Brader, Federico Boerr and Mariano Grande (Digit Factory)
Performance Testing: Carlos Farre, Naveen Pitipornvivat (Adecco)
Documentation: Alex Homer, John Sharp (Content Master Ltd)
Graphic Artists: Chris Burns (Linda Werner & Associates Inc), Kieran Phelan (Allovus Design Inc)
Editor: RoAnn Corbisier
Production: Nelly Delgado
Technical Review: Bill Wilder (Author, Cloud Architecture Patterns), Michael Wood (Cerebrata)
Contributors: Hatay Tuna, Chris Clayton, Amit Srivastava, Jason Wescott, Clemens Vasters, Abhishek Lal, Vittorio Bertocci, Boris Scholl, Conor Cunningham, Stuart Ozer, Paolo Salvatori, Shirley Wang, Saurabh Pant, Ben Ridgway, Rahul Rai, Jeremiah Talkar, Simon Gurevich, Haishi Bai, Larry Franks, Grigori Melnik, Mani Subramanian, Rohit Sharma, Christopher Bennage, Andrew Oakley, Jane Sinyagina, and Julian Dominguez, Fernando Simonazzi (Clarius Consulting), and Valery Mizonov (Full Scale 180)
Members of Microsoft Developer Guidance Advisory Council who reviewed drafts:
Carlos dos Santos, CDS Informatica Ltda; Catalin Gheorghiu, I Computer Solutions; Neil Mackenzie, Satory Global; Christopher Maneu, Deezer.com; Paulo Morgado; Bill Wagner, Bill Wagner Software LLC; and Roger Whitehead, ProSource.It

Thank you all for bringing this guide to life!

Cache-Aside Pattern

Load data on demand into a cache from a data store. This pattern can improve performance and also helps to maintain consistency between data held in the cache and the data in the underlying data store.

CONTEXT AND PROBLEM

Applications use a cache to optimize repeated access to information held in a data store. However, it is usually impractical to expect that cached data will always be completely consistent with the data in the data store. Applications should implement a strategy that helps to ensure that the data in the cache is up to date as far as possible, but can also detect and handle situations that arise when the data in the cache has become stale.

SOLUTION

Many commercial caching systems provide read-through and write-through/write-behind operations. In these systems, an application retrieves data by referencing the cache. If the data is not in the cache, it is transparently retrieved from the data store and added to the cache. Any modifications to data held in the cache are automatically written back to the data store as well.

For caches that do not provide this functionality, it is the responsibility of the applications that use the cache to maintain the data in the cache.

An application can emulate the functionality of read-through caching by implementing the cache-aside strategy. This strategy effectively loads data into the cache on demand. Figure 1 summarizes the steps in this process.

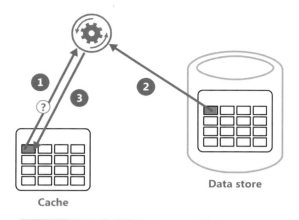

1: Determine whether the item is currently held in the cache.
2: If the item is not currently in the cache, read the item from the data store.
3: Store a copy of the item in the cache.

FIGURE 1
Using the Cache-Aside pattern to store data in the cache

If an application updates information, it can emulate the write-through strategy as follows:

1. Make the modification to the data store
2. Invalidate the corresponding item in the cache.

When the item is next required, using the cache-aside strategy will cause the updated data to be retrieved from the data store and added back into the cache.

ISSUES AND CONSIDERATIONS

Consider the following points when deciding how to implement this pattern:

- **Lifetime of Cached Data**. Many caches implement an expiration policy that causes data to be invalidated and removed from the cache if it is not accessed for a specified period. For cache-aside to be effective, ensure that the expiration policy matches the pattern of access for applications that use the data. Do not make the expiration period too short because this can cause applications to continually retrieve data from the data store and add it to the cache. Similarly, do not make the expiration period so long that the cached data is likely to become stale. Remember that caching is most effective for relatively static data, or data that is read frequently.

- **Evicting Data**. Most caches have only a limited size compared to the data store from where the data originates, and they will evict data if necessary. Most caches adopt a least-recently-used policy for selecting items to evict, but this may be customizable. Configure the global expiration property and other properties of the cache, and the expiration property of each cached item, to help ensure that the cache is cost effective. It may not always be appropriate to apply a global eviction policy to every item in the cache. For example, if a cached item is very expensive to retrieve from the data store, it may be beneficial to retain this item in cache at the expense of more frequently accessed but less costly items.

- **Priming the Cache.** Many solutions prepopulate the cache with the data that an application is likely to need as part of the startup processing. The Cache-Aside pattern may still be useful if some of this data expires or is evicted.
- **Consistency.** Implementing the Cache-Aside pattern does not guarantee consistency between the data store and the cache. An item in the data store may be changed at any time by an external process, and this change might not be reflected in the cache until the next time the item is loaded into the cache. In a system that replicates data across data stores, this problem may become especially acute if synchronization occurs very frequently.
- **Local (In-Memory) Caching.** A cache could be local to an application instance and stored in-memory. Cache-aside can be useful in this environment if an application repeatedly accesses the same data. However, a local cache is private and so different application instances could each have a copy of the same cached data. This data could quickly become inconsistent between caches, so it may be necessary to expire data held in a private cache and refresh it more frequently. In these scenarios it may be appropriate to investigate the use of a shared or a distributed caching mechanism.

WHEN TO USE THIS PATTERN

Use this pattern when:

- A cache does not provide native read-through and write-through operations.
- Resource demand is unpredictable. This pattern enables applications to load data on demand. It makes no assumptions about which data an application will require in advance.

This pattern might not be suitable:

- When the cached data set is static. If the data will fit into the available cache space, prime the cache with the data on startup and apply a policy that prevents the data from expiring.
- For caching session state information in a web application hosted in a web farm. In this environment, you should avoid introducing dependencies based on client-server affinity.

EXAMPLE

In Windows Azure you can use Windows Azure Cache to create a distributed cache that can be shared by multiple instances of an application. The **GetMyEntityAsync** method in the following code example shows an implementation of the Cache-aside pattern based on Windows Azure Cache. This method retrieves an object from the cache using the read-though approach.

An object is identified by using an integer ID as the key. The **GetMyEntityAsync** method generates a string value based on this key (the Windows Azure Cache API uses strings for key values) and attempts to retrieve an item with this key from the cache. If a matching item is found, it is returned. If there is no match in the cache, the **GetMyEntityAsync** method retrieves the object from a data store, adds it to the cache, and then returns it (the code that actually retrieves the data from the data store has been omitted because it is data store dependent). Note that the cached item is configured to expire in order to prevent it from becoming stale if it is updated elsewhere.

C#

```csharp
private DataCache cache;
...
public async Task<MyEntity> GetMyEntityAsync(int id)
{
  // Define a unique key for this method and its parameters.
  var key = string.Format("StoreWithCache_GetAsync_{0}", id);
  var expiration = TimeSpan.FromMinutes(3);
  bool cacheException = false;

  try
  {
    // Try to get the entity from the cache.
    var cacheItem = cache.GetCacheItem(key);
    if (cacheItem != null)
    {
      return cacheItem.Value as MyEntity;
    }
  }
  catch (DataCacheException)
  {
    // If there is a cache related issue, raise an exception
    // and avoid using the cache for the rest of the call.
    cacheException = true;
  }

  // If there is a cache miss, get the entity from the original store and cache it.
  // Code has been omitted because it is data store dependent.
  var entity = ...;

  if (!cacheException)
  {
    try
    {
      // Avoid caching a null value.
      if (entity != null)
      {
        // Put the item in the cache with a custom expiration time that
        // depends on how critical it might be to have stale data.
        cache.Put(key, entity, timeout: expiration);
      }
    }
    catch (DataCacheException)
    {
      // If there is a cache related issue, ignore it
      // and just return the entity.
    }
  }

  return entity;
}
```

The examples use the Windows Azure Cache API to access the store and retrieve information from the cache. For more information about the Windows Azure Cache API, see *Using Windows Azure Cache* on MSDN.

The **UpdateEntityAsync** method shown below demonstrates how to invalidate an object in the cache when the value is changed by the application. This is an example of a write-through approach. The code updates the original data store and then removes the cached item from the cache by calling the **Remove** method, specifying the key (the code for this part of the functionality has been omitted as it will be data store dependent).

The order of the steps in this sequence is important. If the item is removed before the cache is updated, there is a small window of opportunity for a client application to fetch the data (because it is not found in the cache) before the item in the data store has been changed, resulting in the cache containing stale data.

```csharp
C#
public async Task UpdateEntityAsync(MyEntity entity)
{
  // Update the object in the original data store
  await this.store.UpdateEntityAsync(entity).ConfigureAwait(false);

  // Get the correct key for the cached object.
  var key = this.GetAsyncCacheKey(entity.Id);

  // Then, invalidate the current cache object
  this.cache.Remove(key);
}

private string GetAsyncCacheKey(int objectId)
{
  return string.Format("StoreWithCache_GetAsync_{0}", objectId);
}
```

RELATED PATTERNS AND GUIDANCE

The following patterns and guidance may also be relevant when implementing this pattern:

- **Caching Guidance.** This guidance provides additional information on how you can cache data in a cloud solution, and the issues that you should consider when you implement a cache.
- **Data Consistency Primer.** Cloud applications typically use data that is dispersed across data stores. Managing and maintaining data consistency in this environment can become a critical aspect of the system, particularly in terms of the concurrency and availability issues that can arise. This primer describes the issues surrounding consistency across distributed data, and summarizes how an application can implement eventual consistency to maintain the availability of data.

MORE INFORMATION

All links in this book are accessible from the book's online bibliography available at: *http://aka.ms/cdpbibliography*.

- The article *Using Windows Azure Cache* on MSDN.

Circuit Breaker Pattern

Handle faults that may take a variable amount of time to rectify when connecting to a remote service or resource. This pattern can improve the stability and resiliency of an application.

CONTEXT AND PROBLEM

In a distributed environment such as the cloud, where an application performs operations that access remote resources and services, it is possible for these operations to fail due to transient faults such as slow network connections, timeouts, or the resources being overcommitted or temporarily unavailable. These faults typically correct themselves after a short period of time, and a robust cloud application should be prepared to handle them by using a strategy such as that described by the Retry Pattern.

However, there may also be situations where faults are due to unexpected events that are less easily anticipated, and that may take much longer to rectify. These faults can range in severity from a partial loss of connectivity to the complete failure of a service. In these situations it may be pointless for an application to continually retry performing an operation that is unlikely to succeed, and instead the application should quickly accept that the operation has failed and handle this failure accordingly.

Additionally, if a service is very busy, failure in one part of the system may lead to cascading failures. For example, an operation that invokes a service could be configured to implement a timeout, and reply with a failure message if the service fails to respond within this period. However, this strategy could cause many concurrent requests to the same operation to be blocked until the timeout period expires. These blocked requests might hold critical system resources such as memory, threads, database connections, and so on. Consequently, these resources could become exhausted, causing failure of other possibly unrelated parts of the system that need to use the same resources. In these situations, it would be preferable for the operation to fail immediately, and only attempt to invoke the service if it is likely to succeed. Note that setting a shorter timeout may help to resolve this problem, but the timeout should not be so short that the operation fails most of the time, even if the request to the service would eventually succeed.

SOLUTION

The Circuit Breaker pattern can prevent an application repeatedly trying to execute an operation that is likely to fail, allowing it to continue without waiting for the fault to be rectified or wasting CPU cycles while it determines that the fault is long lasting. The Circuit Breaker pattern also enables an application to detect whether the fault has been resolved. If the problem appears to have been rectified, the application can attempt to invoke the operation.

The purpose of the Circuit Breaker pattern is different from that of the Retry Pattern. The Retry Pattern enables an application to retry an operation in the expectation that it will succeed.The Circuit Breaker pattern prevents an application from performing an operation that is likely to fail. An application may combine these two patterns by using the Retry pattern to invoke an operation through a circuit breaker.However, the retry logic should be sensitive to any exceptions returned by the circuit breaker and abandon retry attempts if the circuit breaker indicates that a fault is not transient.

A circuit breaker acts as a proxy for operations that may fail. The proxy should monitor the number of recent failures that have occurred, and then use this information to decide whether to allow the operation to proceed, or simply return an exception immediately.

The proxy can be implemented as a state machine with the following states that mimic the functionality of an electrical circuit breaker:

- **Closed**: The request from the application is routed through to the operation. The proxy maintains a count of the number of recent failures, and if the call to the operation is unsuccessful the proxy increments this count. If the number of recent failures exceeds a specified threshold within a given time period, the proxy is placed into the **Open** state. At this point the proxy starts a timeout timer, and when this timer expires the proxy is placed into the **Half-Open** state.

The purpose of the timeout timer is to give the system time to rectify the problem that caused the failure before allowing the application to attempt to perform the operation again.

- **Open**: The request from the application fails immediately and an exception is returned to the application.
- **Half-Open**: A limited number of requests from the application are allowed to pass through and invoke the operation. If these requests are successful, it is assumed that the fault that was previously causing the failure has been fixed and the circuit breaker switches to the **Closed** state (the failure counter is reset). If any request fails, the circuit breaker assumes that the fault is still present so it reverts back to the **Open** state and restarts the timeout timer to give the system a further period of time to recover from the failure.

The **Half-Open** state is useful to prevent a recovering service from suddenly being inundated with requests. As a service recovers, it may be able to support a limited volume of requests until the recovery is complete, but while recovery is in progress a flood of work may cause the service to time out or fail again.

Figure 1 illustrates the states for one possible implementation of a circuit breaker.

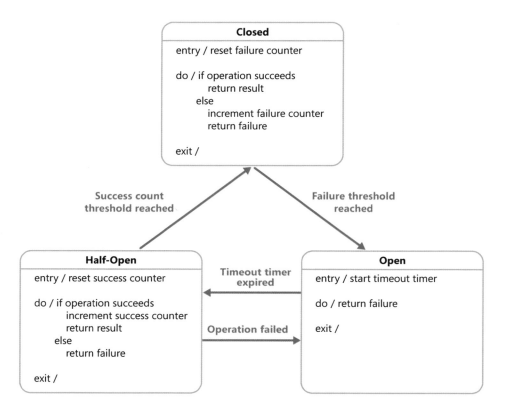

FIGURE 1
Circuit Breaker states

Note that, in Figure 1, the failure counter used by the **Closed** state is time-based. It is automatically reset at periodic intervals. This helps to prevent the circuit breaker from entering the **Open** state if it experiences occasional failures; the failure threshold that trips the circuit breaker into the **Open** state is only reached when a specified number of failures have occurred during a specified interval. The success counter used by the **Half-Open** state records the number of successful attempts to invoke the operation. The circuit breaker reverts to the **Closed** state after a specified number of consecutive operation invocations have been successful. If any invocation fails, the circuit breaker enters the **Open** state immediately and the success counter will be reset the next time it enters the **Half-Open** state.

How the system recovers is handled externally, possibly by restoring or restarting a failed component or repairing a network connection.

Implementing the circuit breaker pattern adds stability and resiliency to a system, offering stability while the system recovers from a failure and minimizing the impact of this failure on performance. It can help to maintain the response time of the system by quickly rejecting a request for an operation that is likely to fail, rather than waiting for the operation to time out (or never return). If the circuit breaker raises an event each time it changes state, this information can be used to monitor the health of the part of the system protected by the circuit breaker, or to alert an administrator when a circuit breaker trips to the **Open** state.

The pattern is customizable and can be adapted according to the nature of the possible failure. For example, you can apply an increasing timeout timer to a circuit breaker. You could place the circuit breaker in the **Open** state for a few seconds initially, and then if the failure has not been resolved increase the timeout to a few minutes, and so on. In some cases, rather than the **Open** state returning failure and raising an exception, it could be useful to return a default value that is meaningful to the application.

ISSUES AND CONSIDERATIONS

You should consider the following points when deciding how to implement this pattern:

- **Exception Handling**. An application invoking an operation through a circuit breaker must be prepared to handle the exceptions that could be raised if the operation is unavailable. The way in which such exceptions are handled will be application specific. For example, an application could temporarily degrade its functionality, invoke an alternative operation to try to perform the same task or obtain the same data, or report the exception to the user and ask them to try again later.

- **Types of Exceptions**. A request may fail for a variety of reasons, some of which may indicate a more severe type of failure than others. For example, a request may fail because a remote service has crashed and may take several minutes to recover, or failure could be caused by a timeout due to the service being temporarily overloaded. A circuit breaker may be able to examine the types of exceptions that occur and adjust its strategy depending on the nature of these exceptions. For example, it may require a larger number of timeout exceptions to trip the circuit breaker to the **Open** state compared to the number of failures due to the service being completely unavailable.

- **Logging**. A circuit breaker should log all failed requests (and possibly successful requests) to enable an administrator to monitor the health of the operation that it encapsulates.

- **Recoverability**. You should configure the circuit breaker to match the likely recovery pattern of the operation it is protecting. For example, if the circuit breaker remains in the **Open** state for a long period, it could raise exceptions even if the reason for the failure has long since been resolved. Similarly, a circuit breaker could oscillate and reduce the response times of applications if it switches from the **Open** state to the **Half-Open** state too quickly.

- **Testing Failed Operations**. In the **Open** state, rather than using a timer to determine when to switch to the **Half-Open** state, a circuit breaker may instead periodically ping the remote service or resource to determine whether it has become available again. This ping could take the form of an attempt to invoke an operation that had previously failed, or it could use a special operation provided by the remote service specifically for testing the health of the service, as described by the Health Endpoint Monitoring Pattern.

- **Manual Override**. In a system where the recovery time for a failing operation is extremely variable, it may be beneficial to provide a manual reset option that enables an administrator to forcibly close a circuit breaker (and reset the failure counter). Similarly, an administrator could force a circuit breaker into the **Open** state (and restart the timeout timer) if the operation protected by the circuit breaker is temporarily unavailable.

- **Concurrency**. The same circuit breaker could be accessed by a large number of concurrent instances of an application. The implementation should not block concurrent requests or add excessive overhead to each call to an operation.

- **Resource Differentiation**. Be careful when using a single circuit breaker for one type of resource if there might be multiple underlying independent providers. For example, in a data store that comprises multiple shards, one shard may be fully accessible while another is experiencing a temporary issue. If the error responses in these scenarios are conflated, an application may attempt to access some shards even when failure is highly likely, while access to other shards may be blocked even though it is likely to succeed.

- **Accelerated Circuit Breaking.** Sometimes a failure response can contain enough information for the circuit breaker implementation to know it should trip immediately and stay tripped for a minimum amount of time. For example, the error response from a shared resource that is overloaded could indicate that an immediate retry is not recommended and that the application should instead try again in a few minutes time.

> The HTTP protocol defines the "HTTP 503 Service Unavailable" response that can be returned if a requested service is not currently available on a particular web server. This response can include additional information, such as the anticipated duration of the delay.

- **Replaying Failed Requests**. In the **Open** state, rather than simply failing quickly, a circuit breaker could also record the details of each request to a journal and arrange for these requests to be replayed when the remote resource or service becomes available.

- **Inappropriate Timeouts on External Services**. A circuit breaker may not be able to fully protect applications from operations that fail in external services that are configured with a lengthy timeout period. If the timeout is too long, a thread running a circuit breaker may be blocked for an extended period before the circuit breaker indicates that the operation has failed. In this time, many other application instances may also attempt to invoke the service through the circuit breaker and tie up a significant number of threads before they all fail.

WHEN TO USE THIS PATTERN

Use this pattern:

- To prevent an application from attempting to invoke a remote service or access a shared resource if this operation is highly likely to fail.

This pattern might not be suitable:

- For handling access to local private resources in an application, such as in-memory data structure. In this environment, using a circuit breaker would simply add overhead to your system.

- As a substitute for handling exceptions in the business logic of your applications.

EXAMPLE

In a web application, several of the pages are populated with data retrieved from an external service. If the system implements minimal caching, most hits to each of these pages will cause a round trip to the service. Connections from the web application to the service could be configured with a timeout period (typically 60 seconds), and if the service does not respond in this time the logic in each web page will assume that the service is unavailable and throw an exception.

However, if the service fails and the system is very busy, users could be forced to wait for up to 60 seconds before an exception occurs. Eventually resources such as memory, connections, and threads could be exhausted, preventing other users from connecting to the system—even if they are not accessing pages that retrieve data from the service.

Scaling the system by adding further web servers and implementing load balancing may delay the point at which resources become exhausted, but it will not resolve the issue because user requests will still be unresponsive and all web servers could still eventually run out of resources.

Wrapping the logic that connects to the service and retrieves the data in a circuit breaker could help to alleviate the effects of this problem and handle the service failure more elegantly. User requests will still fail, but they will fail more quickly and the resources will not be blocked.

The **CircuitBreaker** class maintains state information about a circuit breaker in an object that implements the **ICircuitBreakerStateStore** interface shown in the following code.

```C#
interface ICircuitBreakerStateStore
{
  CircuitBreakerStateEnum State { get; }

  Exception LastException { get; }

  DateTime LastStateChangedDateUtc { get; }

  void Trip(Exception ex);

  void Reset();

  void HalfOpen();

  bool IsClosed { get; }
}
```

The **State** property indicates the current state of the circuit breaker, and will be one of the values **Open**, **HalfOpen**, or **Closed** as defined by the **CircuitBreakerStateEnum** enumeration. The **IsClosed** property should be true if the circuit breaker is closed, but false if it is open or half-open. The **Trip** method switches the state of the circuit breaker to the open state and records the exception that caused the change in state, together with the date and time that the exception occurred. The **LastException** and the **LastStateChangedDateUtc** properties return this information. The **Reset** method closes the circuit breaker, and the **HalfOpen** method sets the circuit breaker to half-open.

The **InMemoryCircuitBreakerStateStore** class in the example contains an implementation of the **ICircuitBreakerStateStore** interface. The **CircuitBreaker** class creates an instance of this class to hold the state of the circuit breaker.

The **ExecuteAction** method in the **CircuitBreaker** class wraps an operation (in the form of an **Action** delegate) that could fail. When this method runs, it first checks the state of the circuit breaker. If it is closed (the local **IsOpen** property, which returns true if the circuit breaker is open or half-open, is false) the **ExecuteAction** method attempts to invoke the **Action** delegate. If this operation fails, an exception handler executes the **TrackException** method, which sets the state of the circuit breaker to open by calling the **Trip** method of the **InMemoryCircuitBreakerStateStore** object. The following code example highlights this flow.

```C#
public class CircuitBreaker
{
  private readonly ICircuitBreakerStateStore stateStore =
    CircuitBreakerStateStoreFactory.GetCircuitBreakerStateStore();

  private readonly object halfOpenSyncObject = new object ();
  ...
```

```
    public bool IsClosed { get { return stateStore.IsClosed; } }

    public bool IsOpen { get { return !IsClosed; } }

    public void ExecuteAction(Action action)
    {
      ...
      if (IsOpen)
      {
        // The circuit breaker is Open.
        ... (see code sample below for details)
      }

      // The circuit breaker is Closed, execute the action.
      try
      {
        action();
      }
      catch (Exception ex)
      {
        // If an exception still occurs here, simply
        // re-trip the breaker immediately.
        this.TrackException(ex);

        // Throw the exception so that the caller can tell
        // the type of exception that was thrown.
        throw;
      }
    }

    private void TrackException(Exception ex)
    {
      // For simplicity in this example, open the circuit breaker on the first exception.
      // In reality this would be more complex. A certain type of exception, such as one
      // that indicates a service is offline, might trip the circuit breaker immediately.
      // Alternatively it may count exceptions locally or across multiple instances and
      // use this value over time, or the exception/success ratio based on the exception
      // types, to open the circuit breaker.
      this.stateStore.Trip(ex);
    }
  }
```

The following example shows the code (omitted from the previous example) that is executed if the circuit breaker is *not* closed. It first checks if the circuit breaker has been open for a period longer than the time specified by the local **OpenToHalfOpenWaitTime** field in the **CircuitBreaker** class. If this is the case, the **ExecuteAction** method sets the circuit breaker to half-open, then attempts to perform the operation specified by the **Action** delegate.

If the operation is successful, the circuit breaker is reset to the closed state. If the operation fails, it is tripped back to the open state and the time at which the exception occurred is updated so that the circuit breaker will wait for a further period before attempting to perform the operation again.

If the circuit breaker has only been open for a short time, less than the **OpenToHalfOpenWaitTime** value, the **ExecuteAction** method simply throws a **CircuitBreakerOpenException** exception and returns the error that caused the circuit breaker to transition to the open state.

Additionally, to prevent the circuit breaker from attempting to perform concurrent calls to the operation while it is half-open, it uses a lock. A concurrent attempt to invoke the operation will be handled as if the circuit breaker was open, and it will fail with an exception as described later.

```C#
...
    if (IsOpen)
    {
      // The circuit breaker is Open. Check if the Open timeout has expired.
      // If it has, set the state to HalfOpen. Another approach may be to simply
      // check for the HalfOpen state that had be set by some other operation.
      if (stateStore.LastStateChangedDateUtc + OpenToHalfOpenWaitTime < DateTime.UtcNow)
      {
        // The Open timeout has expired. Allow one operation to execute. Note that, in
        // this example, the circuit breaker is simply set to HalfOpen after being
        // in the Open state for some period of time. An alternative would be to set
        // this using some other approach such as a timer, test method, manually, and
        // so on, and simply check the state here to determine how to handle execution
        // of the action.
        // Limit the number of threads to be executed when the breaker is HalfOpen.
        // An alternative would be to use a more complex approach to determine which
        // threads or how many are allowed to execute, or to execute a simple test
        // method instead.
        bool lockTaken = false;
        try
        {
          Monitor.TryEnter(halfOpenSyncObject, ref lockTaken)
          if (lockTaken)
          {
            // Set the circuit breaker state to HalfOpen.
            stateStore.HalfOpen();

            // Attempt the operation.
            action();

            // If this action succeeds, reset the state and allow other operations.
            // In reality, instead of immediately returning to the Open state, a counter
            // here would record the number of successful operations and return the
            // circuit breaker to the Open state only after a specified number succeed.
            this.stateStore.Reset();
            return;
          }
        catch (Exception ex)
        {
          // If there is still an exception, trip the breaker again immediately.
          this.stateStore.Trip(ex);

          // Throw the exception so that the caller knows which exception occurred.
          throw;
        }
        finally
```

```
          {
            if (lockTaken)
            {
              Monitor.Exit(halfOpenSyncObject);
            }
          }
        }
      }
      // The Open timeout has not yet expired. Throw a CircuitBreakerOpen exception to
      // inform the caller that the caller that the call was not actually attempted,
      // and return the most recent exception received.
      throw new CircuitBreakerOpenException(stateStore.LastException);
    }
    ...
```

To use a **CircuitBreaker** object to protect an operation, an application creates an instance of the **Circuit-Breaker** class and invokes the **ExecuteAction** method, specifying the operation to be performed as the parameter. The application should be prepared to catch the **CircuitBreakerOpenException** exception if the operation fails because the circuit breaker is open. The following code shows an example:

```csharp
C#
var breaker = new CircuitBreaker();

try
{
  breaker.ExecuteAction(() =>
  {
    // Operation protected by the circuit breaker.
    ...
  });
}
catch (CircuitBreakerOpenException ex)
{
  // Perform some different action when the breaker is open.
  // Last exception details are in the inner exception.
  ...
}
catch (Exception ex)
{
  ...
}
```

RELATED PATTERNS AND GUIDANCE

The following patterns may also be relevant when implementing this pattern:

- **Retry Pattern**. The Retry pattern is a useful adjunct to the Circuit Breaker pattern. It describes how an application can handle anticipated temporary failures when it attempts to connect to a service or network resource by transparently retrying an operation that has previously failed in the expectation that the cause of the failure is transient.

- **Health Endpoint Monitoring Pattern**. A circuit breaker may be able to test the health of a service by sending a request to an endpoint exposed by the service. The service should return information indicating its status.

Compensating Transaction Pattern

Undo the work performed by a series of steps, which together define an eventually consistent operation, if one or more of the steps fail. Operations that follow the eventual consistency model are commonly found in cloud-hosted applications that implement complex business processes and workflows.

CONTEXT AND PROBLEM

Applications running in the cloud frequently modify data. This data may be spread across an assortment of data sources held in a variety of geographic locations. To avoid contention and improve performance in a distributed environment such as this, an application should not attempt to provide strong transactional consistency. Rather, the application should implement *eventual consistency*. In this model, a typical business operation consists of a series of autonomous steps. While these steps are being performed the overall view of the system state may be inconsistent, but when the operation has completed and all of the steps have been executed the system should become consistent again.

> The Data Consistency Primer provides more information about why distributed transactions do not scale well, and the principles that underpin the eventual consistency model.

A significant challenge in the eventual consistency model is how to handle a step that has failed irrecoverably. In this case it may be necessary to undo all of the work completed by the previous steps in the operation. However, the data cannot simply be rolled back because other concurrent instances of the application may have since changed it. Even in cases where the data has not been changed by a concurrent instance, undoing a step might not simply be a matter of restoring the original state. It may be necessary to apply various business-specific rules (see the travel website described in the Example section).

If an operation that implements eventual consistency spans several heterogeneous data stores, undoing the steps in such an operation will require visiting each data store in turn. The work performed in every data store must be undone reliably to prevent the system from remaining inconsistent.

Not all data affected by an operation that implements eventual consistency might be held in a database. In a Service Oriented Architecture (SOA) environment an operation may invoke an action in a service, and cause a change in the state held by that service. To undo the operation, this state change must also be undone. This may involve invoking the service again and performing another action that reverses the effects of the first.

SOLUTION

Implement a compensating transaction. The steps in a compensating transaction must undo the effects of the steps in the original operation. A compensating transaction might not be able to simply replace the current state with the state the system was in at the start of the operation because this approach could overwrite changes made by other concurrent instances of an application. Rather, it must be an intelligent process that takes into account any work done by concurrent instances. This process will usually be application-specific, driven by the nature of the work performed by the original operation.

A common approach to implementing an eventually consistent operation that requires compensation is to use a workflow. As the original operation proceeds, the system records information about each step and how the work performed by that step can be undone. If the operation fails at any point, the workflow rewinds back through the steps it has completed and performs the work that reverses each step. Note that a compensating transaction might not have to undo the work in the exact mirror-opposite order of the original operation, and it may be possible to perform some of the undo steps in parallel.

> This approach is similar to the Sagas strategy. A description of this strategy is available online in _Clemens Vasters' blog_.

A compensating transaction is itself an eventually consistent operation and it could also fail. The system should be able to resume the compensating transaction at the point of failure and continue. It may be necessary to repeat a step that has failed, so the steps in a compensating transaction should be defined as idempotent commands. For more information about idempotency, see _Idempotency Patterns_ on Jonathan Oliver's blog.

In some cases it may not be possible to recover from a step that has failed except through manual intervention. In these situations the system should raise an alert and provide as much information as possible about the reason for the failure.

ISSUES AND CONSIDERATIONS

Consider the following points when deciding how to implement this pattern:

- It might not be easy to determine when a step in an operation that implements eventual consistency has failed. A step might not fail immediately, but instead it could block. It may be necessary to implement some form of time-out mechanism.

- Compensation logic is not easily generalized. A compensating transaction is application-specific; it relies on the application having sufficient information to be able to undo the effects of each step in a failed operation.

- You should define the steps in a compensating transaction as idempotent commands. This enables the steps to be repeated if the compensating transaction itself fails.

- The infrastructure that handles the steps in the original operation, and the compensating transaction, must be resilient. It must not lose the information required to compensate for a failing step, and it must be able to reliably monitor the progress of the compensation logic.

- A compensating transaction does not necessarily return the data in the system to the state it was in at the start of the original operation. Instead, it compensates for the work performed by the steps that completed successfully before the operation failed.

- The order of the steps in the compensating transaction does not necessarily have to be the mirror opposite of the steps in the original operation. For example, one data store may be more sensitive to inconsistencies than another, and so the steps in the compensating transaction that undo the changes to this store should occur first.

- Placing a short-term timeout-based lock on each resource that is required to complete an operation, and obtaining these resources in advance, can help increase the likelihood that the overall activity will succeed. The work should be performed only after all the resources have been acquired. All actions must be finalized before the locks expire.

- Consider using retry logic that is more forgiving than usual to minimize failures that trigger a compensating transaction. If a step in an operation that implements eventual consistency fails, try handling the failure as a transient exception and repeat the step. Only abort the operation and initiate a compensating transaction if a step fails repeatedly or irrecoverably.

Many of the challenges and issues of implementing a compensating transaction are the same as those concerned with implementing eventual consistency. See the section "Considerations for Implementing Eventual Consistency" in the Data Consistency Primer for more information.

WHEN TO USE THIS PATTERN

Use this pattern only for operations that must be undone if they fail. If possible, design solutions to avoid the complexity of requiring compensating transactions (for more information, see the Data Consistency Primer).

EXAMPLE

A travel website enables customers to book itineraries. A single itinerary may comprise a series of flights and hotels. A customer traveling from Seattle to London and then on to Paris could perform the following steps when creating an itinerary:

1. Book a seat on flight F1 from Seattle to London.
2. Book a seat on flight F2 from London to Paris.
3. Book a seat on flight F3 from Paris to Seattle.
4. Reserve a room at hotel H1 in London.
5. Reserve a room at hotel H2 in Paris.

These steps constitute an eventually consistent operation, although each step is essentially a separate atomic action in its own right. Therefore, as well as performing these steps, the system must also record the counter operations necessary to undo each step in case the customer decides to cancel the itinerary. The steps necessary to perform the counter operations can then run as a compensating transaction if necessary.

Notice that the steps in the compensating transaction might not be the exact opposite of the original steps, and the logic in each step in the compensating transaction must take into account any business-specific rules. For example, "unbooking" a seat on a flight might not entitle the customer to a complete refund of any money paid.

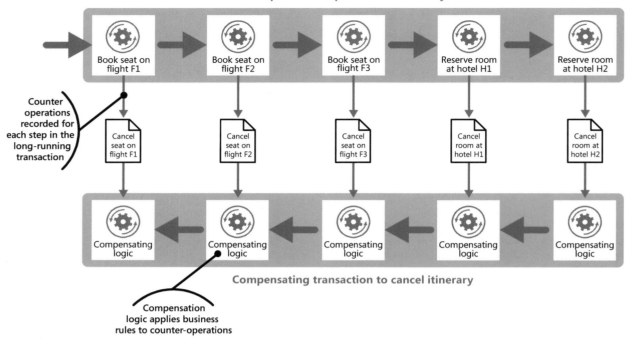

FIGURE 1
Generating a compensating transaction to undo a long-running transaction to book a travel itinerary

> It may be possible for the steps in the compensating transaction to be performed in parallel, depending on how you have designed the compensating logic for each step.

In many business solutions, failure of a single step does not always necessitate rolling the system back by using a compensating transaction. For example, if—after having booked flights F1, F2, and F3 in the travel website scenario—the customer is unable to reserve a room at hotel H1, it is preferable to offer the customer a room at a different hotel in the same city rather than cancelling the flights. The customer may still elect to cancel (in which case the compensating transaction runs and undoes the bookings made on flights F1, F2, and F3), but this decision should be made by the customer rather than by the system.

RELATED PATTERNS AND GUIDANCE

The following patterns and guidance may also be relevant when implementing this pattern:

- **Data Consistency Primer**. The Compensating Transaction pattern is frequently used to undo operations that implement the eventual consistency model. This primer provides more information on the benefits and tradeoffs of eventual consistency.

- **Scheduler-Agent-Supervisor Pattern**. This pattern describes how to implement resilient systems that perform business operations that utilize distributed services and resources. In some circumstances, it may be necessary to undo the work performed by an operation by using a compensating transaction.

- **Retry Pattern**. Compensating transactions can be expensive to perform, and it may be possible to minimize their use by implementing an effective policy of retrying failing operations by following the Retry Pattern.

MORE INFORMATION

All links in this book are accessible from the book's online bibliography available at: *http://aka.ms/cdpbibliography*.

- The article *Sagas* on Clemens Vasters' blog.
- The article *Idempotency Patterns* on Jonathan Oliver's blog.

Competing Consumers Pattern

Enable multiple concurrent consumers to process messages received on the same messaging channel. This pattern enables a system to process multiple messages concurrently to optimize throughput, to improve scalability and availability, and to balance the workload.

CONTEXT AND PROBLEM

An application running in the cloud may be expected to handle a large number of requests. Rather than process each request synchronously, a common technique is for the application to pass them through a messaging system to another service (a *consumer* service) that handles them asynchronously. This strategy helps to ensure that the business logic in the application is not blocked while the requests are being processed.

The number of requests could vary significantly over time for many reasons. A sudden burst in user activity or aggregated requests coming from multiple tenants may cause unpredictable workload. At peak hours a system might need to process many hundreds of requests per second, while at other times the number could be very small. Additionally, the nature of the work performed to handle these requests might be highly variable. Using a single instance of the consumer service might cause that instance to become flooded with requests or the messaging system may be overloaded by an influx of messages coming from the application. To handle this fluctuating workload, the system can run multiple instances of the consumer service. However these consumers must be coordinated to ensure that each message is only delivered to a single consumer. The workload also needs to be load balanced across consumers to prevent an instance from becoming a bottleneck.

SOLUTION

Use a message queue to implement the communication channel between the application and the instances of the consumer service. The application posts requests in the form of messages to the queue, and the consumer service instances receive messages from the queue and process them. This approach enables the same pool of consumer service instances to handle messages from any instance of the application. Figure 1 illustrates this architecture.

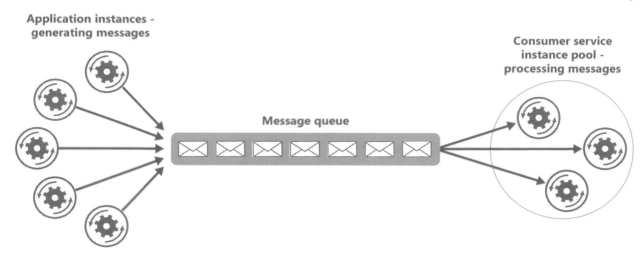

**Application instances -
generating messages**

**Consumer service
instance pool -
processing messages**

Message queue

FIGURE 1
Using a message queue to distribute work to instances of a service

This solution offers the following benefits:

- It enables an inherently load-leveled system that can handle wide variations in the volume of requests sent by application instances. The queue acts as a buffer between the application instances and the consumer service instances, which can help to minimize the impact on availability and responsiveness for both the application and the service instances (as described by the Queue-based Load Leveling Pattern). Handling a message that requires some long-running processing to be performed does not prevent other messages from being handled concurrently by other instances of the consumer service.

- It improves reliability. If a producer communicates directly with a consumer instead of using this pattern, but does not monitor the consumer, there is a high probability that messages could be lost or fail to be processed if the consumer fails. In this pattern messages are not sent to a specific service instance, a failed service instance will not block a producer, and messages can be processed by any working service instance.

- It does not require complex coordination between the consumers, or between the producer and the consumer instances. The message queue ensures that each message is delivered at least once.

- It is scalable. The system can dynamically increase or decrease the number of instances of the consumer service as the volume of messages fluctuates.

- It can improve resiliency if the message queue provides transactional read operations. If a consumer service instance reads and processes the message as part of a transactional operation, and if this consumer service instance subsequently fails, this pattern can ensure that the message will be returned to the queue to be picked up and handled by another instance of the consumer service.

ISSUES AND CONSIDERATIONS

Consider the following points when deciding how to implement this pattern:

- **Message Ordering**. The order in which consumer service instances receive messages is not guaranteed, and does not necessarily reflect the order in which the messages were created. Design the system to ensure that message processing is idempotent because this will help to eliminate any dependency on the order in which messages are handled. For more information about idempotency, see _Idempotency Patterns_ on Jonathon Oliver's blog.

> Windows Azure Service Bus Queues can implement guaranteed first-in-first-out ordering of messages by using message sessions. For more information, see *Messaging Patterns Using Sessions* on MSDN.

- **Designing Services for Resiliency**. If the system is designed to detect and restart failed service instances, it may be necessary to implement the processing performed by the service instances as idempotent operations to minimize the effects of a single message being retrieved and processed more than once.
- **Detecting Poison Messages**. A malformed message, or a task that requires access to resources that are not available, may cause a service instance to fail. The system should prevent such messages being returned to the queue, and instead capture and store the details of these messages elsewhere so that they can be analyzed if necessary.
- **Handling Results**. The service instance handling a message is fully decoupled from the application logic that generates the message, and they may not be able to communicate directly. If the service instance generates results that must be passed back to the application logic, this information must be stored in a location that is accessible to both and the system must provide some indication of when processing has completed to prevent the application logic from retrieving incomplete data.

> If you are using Windows Azure, a worker process may be able to pass results back to the application logic by using a dedicated message reply queue. The application logic must be able to correlate these results with the original message. This scenario is described in more detail in the Asynchronous Messaging Primer.

- **Scaling the Messaging System**. In a large-scale solution, a single message queue could be overwhelmed by the number of messages and become a bottleneck in the system. In this situation, consider partitioning the messaging system to direct messages from specific producers to a particular queue, or use load balancing to distribute messages across multiple message queues.
- **Ensuring Reliability of the Messaging System**. A reliable messaging system is needed to guarantee that, once the application enqueues a message, it will not be lost. This is essential for ensuring that all messages are delivered at least once.

WHEN TO USE THIS PATTERN

Use this pattern when:
- The workload for an application is divided into tasks that can run asynchronously.
- Tasks are independent and can run in parallel.
- The volume of work is highly variable, requiring a scalable solution.
- The solution must provide high availability, and must be resilient if the processing for a task fails.

This pattern may not be suitable when:
- It is not easy to separate the application workload into discrete tasks, or there is a high degree of dependence between tasks.
- Tasks must be performed synchronously, and the application logic must wait for a task to complete before continuing.
- Tasks must be performed in a specific sequence.

Some messaging systems support sessions that enable a producer to group messages together and ensure that they are all handled by the same consumer. This mechanism can be used with prioritized messages (if they are supported) to implement a form of message ordering that delivers messages in sequence from a producer to a single consumer.

EXAMPLE

Windows Azure provides storage queues and Service Bus queues that can act as a suitable mechanism for implementing this pattern. The application logic can post messages to a queue, and consumers implemented as tasks in one or more roles can retrieve messages from this queue and process them. For resiliency, a Service Bus queue enables a consumer to use **PeekLock** mode when it retrieves a message from the queue. This mode does not actually remove the message, but simply hides it from other consumers. The original consumer can delete the message when it has finished processing it. If the consumer should fail, the peek lock will time out and the message will become visible again, allowing another consumer to retrieve it.

For detailed information on using Windows Azure Service Bus queues, see *Service Bus Queues, Topics, and Subscriptions* on MSDN. For information on using Windows Azure storage queues, see *How to use the Queue Storage Service* on MSDN.

The following code shows from the **QueueManager** class in CompetingConsumers solution of the examples available for download for this guidance shows how you can create a queue by using a **QueueClient** instance in the **Start** event handler in a web or worker role.

```csharp
C#
private string queueName = ...;
private string connectionString = ...;
...

public async Task Start()
{
  // Check if the queue already exists.
  var manager = NamespaceManager.CreateFromConnectionString(this.connectionString);
  if (!manager.QueueExists(this.queueName))
  {
    var queueDescription = new QueueDescription(this.queueName);

    // Set the maximum delivery count for messages in the queue. A message
    // is automatically dead-lettered after this number of deliveries. The
    // default value for dead letter count is 10.
    queueDescription.MaxDeliveryCount = 3;

    await manager.CreateQueueAsync(queueDescription);
  }
  ...

  // Create the queue client. By default the PeekLock method is used.
  this.client = QueueClient.CreateFromConnectionString(
    this.connectionString, this.queueName);
}
```

The next code snippet shows how an application can create and send a batch of messages to the queue.

```csharp
C#
public async Task SendMessagesAsync()
{
  // Simulate sending a batch of messages to the queue.
  var messages = new List<BrokeredMessage>();

  for (int i = 0; i < 10; i++)
  {
    var message = new BrokeredMessage() { MessageId = Guid.NewGuid().ToString() };
    messages.Add(message);
  }
  await this.client.SendBatchAsync(messages);
}
```

The following code shows how a consumer service instance can receive messages from the queue by following an event-driven approach. The **processMessageTask** parameter to the **ReceiveMessages** method is a delegate that references the code to run when a message is received. This code is run asynchronously.

```csharp
C#
private ManualResetEvent pauseProcessingEvent;
...

public void ReceiveMessages(Func<BrokeredMessage, Task> processMessageTask)
{
  // Set up the options for the message pump.
  var options = new OnMessageOptions();

  // When AutoComplete is disabled it is necessary to manually
  // complete or abandon the messages and handle any errors.
  options.AutoComplete = false;
  options.MaxConcurrentCalls = 10;
  options.ExceptionReceived += this.OptionsOnExceptionReceived;

  // Use of the Service Bus OnMessage message pump.
  // The OnMessage method must be called once, otherwise an exception will occur.
  this.client.OnMessageAsync(
    async (msg) =>
    {
      // Will block the current thread if Stop is called.
      this.pauseProcessingEvent.WaitOne();

      // Execute processing task here.
      await processMessageTask(msg);
    },
    options);
}
...

private void OptionsOnExceptionReceived(object sender,
  ExceptionReceivedEventArgs exceptionReceivedEventArgs)
{
  ...
}
```

Note that autoscaling features, such as those available in Windows Azure, can be used to start and stop role instances as the queue length fluctuates. For more information, see Autoscaling Guidance. In addition, it is not necessary to maintain a one-to-one correspondence between role instances and worker processes—a single role instance can implement multiple worker processes. For more information, see the Compute Resource Consolidation Pattern.

RELATED PATTERNS AND GUIDANCE

The following patterns and guidance may be relevant when implementing this pattern:

- **Asynchronous Messaging Primer**. Message queues are an inherently asynchronous communications mechanism. If a consumer service needs to send a reply to an application, it may be necessary to implement some form of response messaging. The Asynchronous Messaging Primer provides information on how to implement request/reply messaging by using message queues.
- **Autoscaling Guidance**. It may be possible to start and stop instances of a consumer service as the length of the queue to which applications post messages varies. Autoscaling can help to maintain throughput during times of peak processing.
- **Compute Resource Consolidation Pattern**. It may be possible to consolidate multiple instances of a consumer service into a single process to reduce costs and management overhead. The Compute Resource Consolidation Pattern describes the benefits and tradeoffs of following this approach.
- **Queue-based Load Leveling Pattern**. Introducing a message queue can add resiliency to the system, enabling service instances to handle widely varying volumes of requests from application instances. The message queue effectively acts as a buffer which levels the load. The Queue-based Load Leveling Pattern describes this scenario in more detail.

MORE INFORMATION

All links in this book are accessible from the book's online bibliography available at: *http://aka.ms/cdpbibliography*.

- The article *Idempotency Patterns* is available on Jonathan Oliver's blog.
- The article *Messaging Patterns Using Sessions* on MSDN.
- The article *Service Bus Queues, Topics, and Subscriptions* on MSDN.
- The article *How to use the Queue Storage Service* on MSDN.

This pattern has a sample application associated with it. You can download the "Cloud Design Patterns – Sample Code" from the Microsoft Download Center at *http://aka.ms/cloud-design-patterns-sample*.

Compute Resource Consolidation Pattern

Consolidate multiple tasks or operations into a single computational unit. This pattern can increase compute resource utilization, and reduce the costs and management overhead associated with performing compute processing in cloud-hosted applications.

CONTEXT AND PROBLEM

A cloud application frequently implements a variety of operations. In some solutions it may make sense initially to follow the design principle of separation of concerns, and divide these operations into discrete computational units that are hosted and deployed individually (for example, as separate roles in a Windows Azure Cloud Service, separate Windows Azure Web Sites, or separate Virtual Machines). However, although this strategy can help to simplify the logical design of the solution, deploying a large number of computational units as part of the same application can increase runtime hosting costs and make management of the system more complex.

As an example, Figure 1 shows the simplified structure of a cloud-hosted solution that is implemented using more than one computational unit. Each computational unit runs in its own virtual environment. Each function has been implemented as a separate task (labeled Task A through Task E) running in its own computational unit.

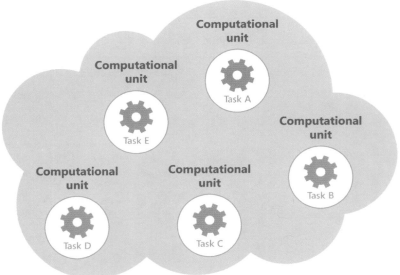

FIGURE 1
Running tasks in a cloud environment by using a set of dedicated computational units

34

Each computational unit consumes chargeable resources, even when it is idle or lightly used. Therefore, this approach may not always be the most cost-effective solution.

In Windows Azure, this concern applies to roles in a Cloud Service, Web Sites, and Virtual Machines. These items execute in their own virtual environment. Running a collection of separate roles, web sites, or virtual machines that are designed to perform a set of well-defined operations, but that need to communicate and cooperate as part of a single solution, may be an inefficient use of resources.

Solution

To help reduce costs, increase utilization, improve communication speed, and ease the management effort it may be possible to consolidate multiple tasks or operations into a single computational unit.

Tasks can be grouped according to a variety of criteria based on the features provided by the environment, and the costs associated with these features. A common approach is to look for tasks that have a similar profile concerning their scalability, lifetime, and processing requirements. Grouping these items together allows them to scale as a unit. The elasticity provided by many cloud environments enables additional instances of a computational unit to be started and stopped according to the workload. For example, Windows Azure provides autoscaling that you can apply to roles in a Cloud Service, Web Sites, and Virtual Machines. For more information, see Autoscaling Guidance.

As a counter example to show how scalability can be used to determine which operations should probably *not* be grouped together, consider the following two tasks:

- Task 1 polls for infrequent, time-insensitive messages sent to a queue.
- Task 2 handles high-volume bursts of network traffic.

The second task requires elasticity that may involve starting and stopping a large number of instances of the computational unit. Applying the same scaling to the first task would simply result in more tasks listening for infrequent messages on the same queue, and is a waste of resources.

In many cloud environments it is possible to specify the resources available to a computational unit in terms of the number of CPU cores, memory, disk space, and so on. Generally, the more resources specified, the greater the cost. For financial efficiency, it is important to maximize the amount of work an expensive computational unit performs, and not let it become inactive for an extended period.

If there are tasks that require a great deal of CPU power in short bursts, consider consolidating these into a single computational unit that provides the necessary power. However, it is important to balance this need to keep expensive resources busy against the contention that could occur if they are over-stressed. Long-running, compute-intensive tasks should probably not share the same computational unit, for example.

Issues and Considerations

Consider the following points when implementing this pattern:

- **Scalability and Elasticity**. Many cloud solutions implement scalability and elasticity at the level of the computational unit by starting and stopping instances of units. Avoid grouping tasks that have conflicting scalability requirements in the same computational unit.
- **Lifetime**. The cloud infrastructure may periodically recycle the virtual environment that hosts a computational unit. When executing many long-running tasks inside a computational unit, it may be necessary to configure the unit to prevent it from being recycled until these tasks have finished. Alternatively, design the tasks by using a check-pointing approach that enables them to stop cleanly, and continue at the point at which they were interrupted when the computational unit is restarted.

- **Release Cadence**. If the implementation or configuration of a task changes frequently, it may be necessary to stop the computational unit hosting the updated code, reconfigure and redeploy the unit, and then restart it. This process will also require that all other tasks within the same computational unit are stopped, redeployed, and restarted.

- **Security**. Tasks in the same computational unit may share the same security context and be able to access the same resources. There must be a high degree of trust between the tasks, and confidence that that one task is not going to corrupt or adversely affect another. Additionally, increasing the number of tasks running in a computational unit may increase the attack surface of the computational unit; each task is only as secure as the one with the most vulnerabilities.

- **Fault Tolerance**. If one task in a computational unit fails or behaves abnormally, it can affect the other tasks running within the same unit. For example, if one task fails to start correctly it may cause the entire startup logic for the computational unit to fail, and prevent other tasks in the same unit from running.

- **Contention**. Avoid introducing contention between tasks that compete for resources in the same computational unit. Ideally, tasks that share the same computational unit should exhibit different resource utilization characteristics. For example, two compute-intensive tasks should probably not reside in the same computational unit, and neither should two tasks that consume large amounts of memory. However, mixing a compute intensive task with a task that requires a large amount of memory may be a viable combination.

> You should consider consolidating compute resources only for a system that has been in production for a period of time so that operators and developers can monitor the system and create a *heat map* that identifies how each task utilizes differing resources. This map can be used to determine which tasks are good candidates for sharing compute resources.

- **Complexity**. Combining multiple tasks into a single computational unit adds complexity to the code in the unit, possibly making it more difficult to test, debug, and maintain.

- **Stable Logical Architecture**. Design and implement the code in each task so that it should not need to change, even if the physical environment in which task runs does change.

- **Other Strategies**. Consolidating compute resources is only one way to help reduce costs associated with running multiple tasks concurrently. It requires careful planning and monitoring to ensure that it remains an effective approach. Other strategies may be more appropriate, depending on the nature of the work being performed and the location of the users on whose behalf these tasks are running. For example, functional decomposition of the workload (as described by the Compute Partitioning Guidance) may be a better option.

When to Use this Pattern

Use this pattern for tasks that are not cost effective if they run in their own computational units. If a task spends much of its time idle, running this task in a dedicated unit can be expensive.

This pattern might not be suitable for tasks that perform critical fault-tolerant operations, or tasks that process highly-sensitive or private data and require their own security context. These tasks should run in their own isolated environment, in a separate computational unit.

EXAMPLE

When building a cloud service on Windows Azure, it's possible to consolidate the processing performed by multiple tasks into a single role. Typically this is a worker role that performs background or asynchronous processing tasks.

> In some cases it may be possible to include background or asynchronous processing tasks in the web role. This technique can help to reduce costs and simplify deployment, although it can impact the scalability and responsiveness of the public-facing interface provided by the web role. The article *Combining Multiple Azure Worker Roles into an Azure Web Role* contains a detailed description of implementing background or asynchronous processing tasks in a web role.

The role is responsible for starting and stopping the tasks. When the Windows Azure fabric controller loads a role, it raises the **Start** event for the role. You can override the **OnStart** method of the **WebRole** or **Worker-Role** class to handle this event, perhaps to initialize the data and other resources on which the tasks in this method depend.

When the **OnStart** method completes, the role can start responding to requests. You can find more information and guidance about using the **OnStart** and **Run** methods in a role in the *Application Startup Processes* section in the patterns & practices guide *Moving Applications to the Cloud*.

> Keep the code in the **OnStart** method as concise as possible. Windows Azure does not impose any limit on the time taken for this method to complete, but the role will not be able to start responding to network requests sent to it until this method completes.

When the **OnStart** method has finished, the role executes the **Run** method. At this point, the fabric controller can start sending requests to the role.

Place the code that actually creates the tasks in the **Run** method. Note that the **Run** method effectively defines the lifetime of the role instance. When this method completes, the fabric controller will arrange for the role to be shut down.

When a role shuts down or is recycled, the fabric controller prevents any more incoming requests being received from the load balancer and raises the **Stop** event. You can capture this event by overriding the **OnStop** method of the role and perform any tidying up required before the role terminates.

> Any actions performed in the **OnStop** method must be completed within five minutes (or 30 seconds if you are using the Windows Azure emulator on a local computer); otherwise the Windows Azure fabric controller assumes that the role has stalled and will force it to stop.

Figure 2 illustrates the lifecycle of a role, and the tasks and resources that it hosts. The tasks are started by the **Run** method, which then waits for the tasks to complete. The tasks themselves, which implement the business logic of the cloud service, can respond to messages posted to the role through the Windows Azure load balancer.

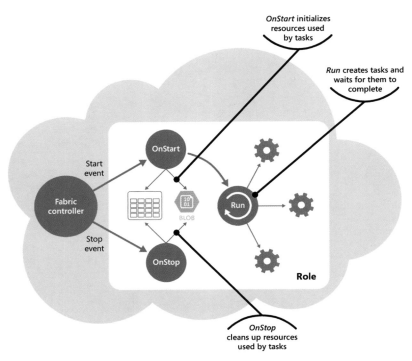

FIGURE 2
The lifecycle of tasks and resources in a role in a Windows Azure cloud service

The WorkerRole.cs file in the ComputeResourceConsolidation.Worker project shows an example of how you might implement this pattern in a Windows Azure cloud service.

> The ComputeResourceConsolidation.Worker project is part of the ComputeResourceConsolidation solution that is available for download with this guidance.

In the worker role, code that runs when the role is initialized creates the required cancellation token and a list of tasks to run.

```C#
public class WorkerRole: RoleEntryPoint
{
  // The cancellation token source used to cooperatively cancel running tasks.
  private readonly CancellationTokenSource cts = new CancellationTokenSource ();

  // List of tasks running on the role instance.
  private readonly List<Task> tasks = new List<Task>();

  // List of worker tasks to run on this role.
  private readonly List<Func<CancellationToken, Task>> workerTasks
                    = new List<Func<CancellationToken, Task>>
  {
    MyWorkerTask1,
    MyWorkerTask2
  };

  ...
}
```

The **MyWorkerTask1** and the **MyWorkerTask2** methods are provided to illustrate how to perform different tasks within the same worker role. The following code shows **MyWorkerTask1**. This is a simple task that sleeps for 30 seconds and then outputs a trace message. It repeats this process indefinitely until the task is cancelled. The code in **MyWorkerTask2** is very similar.

```csharp
C#
// A sample worker role task.
private static async Task MyWorkerTask1(CancellationToken ct)
{
  // Fixed interval to wake up and check for work and/or do work.
  var interval = TimeSpan.FromSeconds(30);

  try
  {
    while (!ct.IsCancellationRequested)
    {
      // Wake up and do some background processing if not canceled.
      // TASK PROCESSING CODE HERE
      Trace.TraceInformation("Doing Worker Task 1 Work");

      // Go back to sleep for a period of time unless asked to cancel.
      // Task.Delay will throw an OperationCanceledException when canceled.
      await Task.Delay(interval, ct);
    }
  }
  catch (OperationCanceledException)
  {
    // Expect this exception to be thrown in normal circumstances or check
    // the cancellation token. If the role instances are shutting down, a
    // cancellation request will be signaled.
    Trace.TraceInformation("Stopping service, cancellation requested");

    // Re-throw the exception.
    throw;
  }
}
```

The approach shown by the sample code is a common implementation of a background process. In a real world application you can follow this same structure, except that you should place your own processing logic in the body of the loop that waits for the cancellation request.

After the worker role has initialized the resources it uses, the **Run** method starts the two tasks concurrently, as shown here.

```csharp
C#
...
// RoleEntry Run() is called after OnStart().
// Returning from Run() will cause a role instance to recycle.
public override void Run()
{
  // Start worker tasks and add them to the task list.
  foreach (var worker in workerTasks)
    tasks.Add(worker(cts.Token));

  Trace.TraceInformation("Worker host tasks started");
  // The assumption is that all tasks should remain running and not return,
  // similar to role entry Run() behavior.
  try
  {
    Task.WaitAny(tasks.ToArray());
  }
  catch (AggregateException ex)
  {
    Trace.TraceError(ex.Message);

    // If any of the inner exceptions in the aggregate exception
    // are not cancellation exceptions then re-throw the exception.
    ex.Handle(innerEx => (innerEx is OperationCanceledException));
  }

  // If there was not a cancellation request, stop all tasks and return from Run()
  // An alternative to cancelling and returning when a task exits would be to
  // restart the task.
  if (!cts.IsCancellationRequested)
  {
    Trace.TraceInformation("Task returned without cancellation request");
    Stop(TimeSpan.FromMinutes(5));
  }
}
...
```

In this example, the **Run** method waits for tasks to be completed. If a task is canceled, the **Run** method assumes that the role is being shut down and waits for the remaining tasks to be canceled before finishing (it waits for a maximum of five minutes before terminating). If a task fails due to an expected exception, the **Run** method cancels the task.

> Note that you could implement more comprehensive monitoring and exception handling strategies in the *Run* method such as restarting tasks that have failed, or including code that enables the role to stop and start individual tasks.

The **Stop** method shown in the following code is called when the fabric controller shuts down the role instance (it is invoked from the **OnStop** method). The code stops each task gracefully by cancelling it. If any task takes more than five minutes to complete, the cancellation processing in the **Stop** method ceases waiting and the role is terminated.

```csharp
// Stop running tasks and wait for tasks to complete before returning
// unless the timeout expires.
private void Stop(TimeSpan timeout)
{
  Trace.TraceInformation("Stop called. Canceling tasks.");
  // Cancel running tasks.
  cts.Cancel();

  Trace.TraceInformation("Waiting for canceled tasks to finish and return");

  // Wait for all the tasks to complete before returning. Note that the
  // emulator currently allows 30 seconds and Windows Azure allows five
  // minutes for processing to complete.
  try
  {
    Task.WaitAll(tasks.ToArray(), timeout);
  }
  catch (AggregateException ex)
  {
    Trace.TraceError(ex.Message);

    // If any of the inner exceptions in the aggregate exception
    // are not cancellation exceptions then re-throw the exception.
    ex.Handle(innerEx => (innerEx is OperationCanceledException));
  }
}
```

RELATED PATTERNS AND GUIDANCE

The following patterns and guidance may also be relevant when implementing this pattern:

- **Autoscaling Guidance**. Autoscaling can be used to start and stop instances of service hosting computational resources, depending on the anticipated demand for processing.
- **Compute Partitioning Guidance**. This guidance describes how to allocate the services and components in a cloud service in a way that helps to minimize running costs while maintaining the scalability, performance, availability, and security of the service.

MORE INFORMATION

All links in this book are accessible from the book's online bibliography available at: _http://aka.ms/cdpbibliography_.

- The blog article _Combining Multiple Azure Worker Roles into an Azure Web Role_.
- The section _Application Startup Processes_ in the patterns & practices guide _Moving Applications to the Cloud on MSDN_.

This pattern has a sample application associated with it. You can download the "Cloud Design Patterns – Sample Code" from the Microsoft Download Center at _http://aka.ms/cloud-design-patterns-sample_.

Command and Query Responsibility Segregation (CQRS) Pattern

Segregate operations that read data from operations that update data by using separate interfaces. This pattern can maximize performance, scalability, and security; support evolution of the system over time through higher flexibility; and prevent update commands from causing merge conflicts at the domain level.

CONTEXT AND PROBLEM

In traditional data management systems, both commands (updates to the data) and queries (requests for data) are executed against the same set of entities in a single data repository. These entities may be a subset of the rows in one or more tables in a relational database such as SQL Server.

Typically, in these systems, all create, read, update, and delete (CRUD) operations are applied to the same representation of the entity. For example, a data transfer object (DTO) representing a customer is retrieved from the data store by the data access layer (DAL) and displayed on the screen. A user updates some fields of the DTO (perhaps through data binding) and the DTO is then saved back in the data store by the DAL. The same DTO is used for both the read and write operations, as shown in Figure 1.

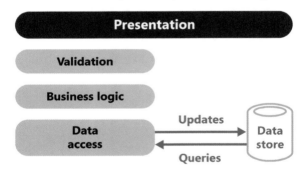

FIGURE 1
A traditional CRUD architecture

Traditional CRUD designs work well when there is only limited business logic applied to the data operations. Scaffold mechanisms provided by development tools can create data access code very quickly, which can then be customized as required.

However, the traditional CRUD approach has some disadvantages:

- It often means that there is a mismatch between the read and write representations of the data, such as additional columns or properties that must be updated correctly even though they are not required as part of an operation.

- It risks encountering data contention in a collaborative domain (where multiple actors operate in parallel on the same set of data) when records are locked in the data store, or update conflicts caused by concurrent updates when optimistic locking is used. These risks increase as the complexity and throughput of the system grows. In addition, the traditional approach can also have a negative effect on performance due to load on the data store and data access layer, and the complexity of queries required to retrieve information.

- It can make managing security and permissions more cumbersome because each entity is subject to both read and write operations, which might inadvertently expose data in the wrong context.

For a deeper understanding of the limits of the CRUD approach see "*CRUD, Only When You Can Afford It*" on MSDN.

SOLUTION

Command and Query Responsibility Segregation (CQRS) is a pattern that segregates the operations that read data (Queries) from the operations that update data (Commands) by using separate interfaces. This implies that the data models used for querying and updates are different. The models can then be isolated, as shown in Figure 2, although this is not an absolute requirement.

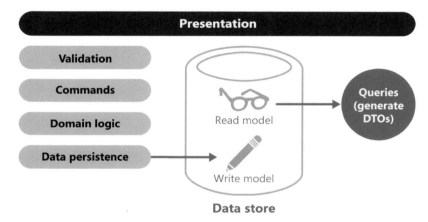

FIGURE 2
A basic CQRS architecture

Compared to the single model of the data (from which developers build their own conceptual models) that is inherent in CRUD-based systems, the use of separate query and update models for the data in CQRS-based systems considerably simplifies design and implementation. However, one disadvantage is that, unlike CRUD designs, CQRS code cannot automatically be generated by using scaffold mechanisms.

The query model for reading data and the update model for writing data may access the same physical store, perhaps by using SQL views or by generating projections on the fly. However, it is common to separate the data into different physical stores to maximize performance, scalability, and security; as shown in Figure 3.

44

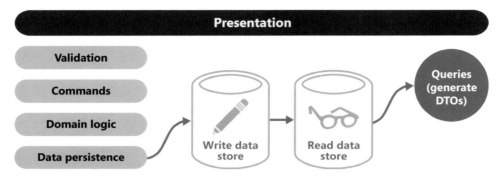

A CQRS architecture with separate read and write stores

The read store can be a read-only replica of the write store, or the read and write stores may have a different structure altogether. Using multiple read-only replicas of the read store can considerably increase query performance and application UI responsiveness, especially in distributed scenarios where read-only replicas are located close to the application instances. Some database systems, such as SQL Server, provide additional features such as failover replicas to maximize availability.

Separation of the read and write stores also allows each to be scaled appropriately to match the load. For example, read stores typically encounter a much higher load that write stores.

When the query/read model contains denormalized information (see Materialized View Pattern), performance is maximized when reading data for each of the views in an application or when querying the data in the system.

For more information about the CQRS pattern and its implementation, see the following resources:

- The patterns & practices guide _CQRS Journey_ on MSDN. In particular you should read the chapter _Introducing the Command Query Responsibility Segregation Pattern_ for a full exploration of the pattern and when it is useful, and the chapter _Epilogue: Lessons Learned_ to understand some of the issues that can arise when using this pattern.
- The post _CQRS_ by Martin Fowler, which explains the basics of the pattern and links to several other useful resources.
- Greg Young's posts on the _Code Better_ website, which explore many aspects of the CQRS pattern.

ISSUES AND CONSIDERATIONS

Consider the following points when deciding how to implement this pattern:

- Dividing the data store into separate physical stores for read and write operations can increase the performance and security of a system, but it can add considerable complexity in terms of resiliency and eventual consistency. The read model store must be updated to reflect changes to the write model store, and it may be difficult to detect when a user has issued a request based on stale read data—meaning that the operation cannot be completed.

> For a description of eventual consistency see the Data Consistency Primer.

- Consider applying CQRS to limited sections of your system where it will be most valuable, and learn from the experience.
- A typical approach to embracing eventual consistency is to use event sourcing in conjunction with CQRS so that the write model is an append-only stream of events driven by execution of commands. These events are used to update materialized views that act as the read model. For more information see the section "Event Sourcing and CQRS" below.

WHEN TO USE THIS PATTERN

This pattern is ideally suited to:

- Collaborative domains where multiple operations are performed in parallel on the same data. CQRS allows you to define commands with a sufficient granularity to minimize merge conflicts at the domain level (or any conflicts that do arise can be merged by the command), even when updating what appears to be the same type of data.

- Use with task-based user interfaces (where users are guided through a complex process as a series of steps), with complex domain models, and for teams already familiar with domain-driven design (DDD) techniques. The write model has a full command-processing stack with business logic, input validation, and business validation to ensure that everything is always consistent for each of the aggregates (each cluster of associated objects that are treated as a unit for the purpose of data changes) in the write model. The read model has no business logic or validation stack and just returns a DTO for use in a view model. The read model is eventually consistent with the write model.

- Scenarios where performance of data reads must be fine-tuned separately from performance of data writes, especially when the read/write ratio is very high, and when horizontal scaling is required. For example, in many systems the number of read operations is orders of magnitude greater that the number of write operations. To accommodate this, consider scaling out the read model, but running the write model on only one or a few instances. A small number of write model instances also helps to minimize the occurrence of merge conflicts.

- Scenarios where one team of developers can focus on the complex domain model that is part of the write model, and another less experienced team can focus on the read model and the user interfaces.

- Scenarios where the system is expected to evolve over time and may contain multiple versions of the model, or where business rules change regularly.

- Integration with other systems, especially in combination with Event Sourcing, where the temporal failure of one subsystem should not affect the availability of the others.

This pattern might not be suitable in the following situations:

- Where the domain or the business rules are simple.

- Where a simple CRUD-style user interface and the related data access operations are sufficient.

- For implementation across the whole system. There are specific components of an overall data management scenario where CQRS can be useful, but it can add considerable and often unnecessary complexity where it is not actually required.

Event Sourcing and CQRS

The CQRS pattern is often used in conjunction with the Event Sourcing pattern. CQRS-based systems use separate read and write data models, each tailored to relevant tasks and often located in physically separate stores. When used with Event Sourcing, the store of events is the write model, and this is the authoritative source of information. The read model of a CQRS-based system provides materialized views of the data, typically as highly denormalized views. These views are tailored to the interfaces and display requirements of the application, which helps to maximize both display and query performance.

Using the stream of events as the write store, rather than the actual data at a point in time, avoids update conflicts on a single aggregate and maximizes performance and scalability. The events can be used to asynchronously generate materialized views of the data that are used to populate the read store.

Because the event store is the authoritative source of information, it is possible to delete the materialized views and replay all past events to create a new representation of the current state when the system evolves, or when the read model must change. The materialized views are effectively a durable read-only cache of the data.

When using CQRS combined with the Event Sourcing pattern, consider the following:

- As with any system where the write and read stores are separate, systems based on this pattern are only eventually consistent. There will be some delay between the event being generated and the data store that holds the results of operations initiated by these events being updated.
- The pattern introduces additional complexity because code must be created to initiate and handle events, and assemble or update the appropriate views or objects required by queries or a read model. The inherent complexity of the CQRS pattern when used in conjunction with Event Sourcing can make a successful implementation more difficult, and requires relearning of some concepts and a different approach to designing systems. However, Event Sourcing can make it easier to model the domain, and makes it easier to rebuild views or create new ones because the intent of the changes in the data is preserved.
- Generating materialized views for use in the read model or projections of the data by replaying and handling the events for specific entities or collections of entities may require considerable processing time and resource usage, especially if it requires summation or analysis of values over long time periods, because all the associated events may need to be examined. This may be partially resolved by implementing snapshots of the data at scheduled intervals, such as a total count of the number of a specific action that have occurred, or the current state of an entity.

> For more information see Event Sourcing Pattern and Materialized View Pattern, and the patterns & practices guide *CQRS Journey* on MSDN. In particular you should read the chapter *Introducing Event Sourcing* for a full exploration of the pattern and how it is useful with CQRS, and the chapter *A CQRS and ES Deep Dive* to understand more—including how aggregate partitioning can be used with CQRS in Windows Azure.

EXAMPLE

The following code shows some extracts from an example of a CQRS implementation, which uses different definitions for the read and the write models. The model interfaces do not dictate any features of the underlying data stores, and they can evolve and be fine-tuned independently because these interfaces are separated.

The following code shows the read model definition.

```csharp
C#
// Query interface
namespace ReadModel
{
  public interface ProductsDao
  {
    ProductDisplay FindById(int productId);
    IEnumerable<ProductDisplay> FindByName(string name);
    IEnumerable<ProductInventory> FindOutOfStockProducts();
    IEnumerable<ProductDisplay> FindRelatedProducts(int productId);
  }

  public class ProductDisplay
  {
    public int ID { get; set; }
    public string Name { get; set; }
    public string Description { get; set; }
    public decimal UnitPrice { get; set; }
    public bool IsOutOfStock { get; set; }
    public double UserRating { get; set; }
  }
```

```csharp
public class ProductInventory
{
  public int ID { get; set; }
  public string Name { get; set; }
  public int CurrentStock { get; set; }
}
}
```

The system allows users to rate products. The application code does this by using the **RateProduct** command shown in the following code.

C#
```csharp
public interface Icommand
{
  Guid Id { get; }
}

public class RateProduct : Icommand
{
  public RateProduct()
  {
    this.Id = Guid.NewGuid();
  }
  public Guid Id { get; set; }
  public int ProductId { get; set; }
  public int rating { get; set; }
  public int UserId {get; set; }
}
```

The system uses the **ProductsCommandHandler** class to handle commands sent by the application. Clients typically send commands to the domain through a messaging system such as a queue. The command handler accepts these commands and invokes methods of the domain interface. The granularity of each command is designed to mitigate the chance of conflicting requests. The following code shows an outline of the **ProductsCommand-Handler** class.

C#
```csharp
public class ProductsCommandHandler :
    ICommandHandler<AddNewProduct>,
    ICommandHandler<RateProduct>,
    ICommandHandler<AddToInventory>,
    ICommandHandler<ConfirmItemShipped>,
    ICommandHandler<UpdateStockFromInventoryRecount>
{
  private readonly IRepository<Product> repository;

  public ProductsCommandHandler (IRepository<Product> repository)
  {
    this.repository = repository;
  }

  void Handle (AddNewProduct command)
  {
    ...
  }
```

```csharp
    void Handle (RateProduct command)
    {
      var product = repository.Find(command.ProductId);
      if (product != null)
      {
        product.RateProuct(command.UserId, command.rating);
        repository.Save(product);
      }
    }

    void Handle (AddToInventory command)
    {
      ...
    }

    void Handle (ConfirmItemsShipped command)
    {
      ...
    }

    void Handle (UpdateStockFromInventoryRecount command)
    {
      ...
    }
  }
```

The following code shows the **ProductsDomain** interface from the write model.

```csharp
C#
public interface ProductsDomain
{
  void AddNewProduct(int id, string name, string description, decimal price);
  void RateProduct(int userId int rating);
  void AddToInventory(int productId, int quantity);
  void ConfirmItemsShipped(int productId, int quantity);
  void UpdateStockFromInventoryRecount(int productId, int updatedQuantity);
}
```

Also notice how the **ProductsDomain** interface contains methods that have a meaning in the domain. Typically, in a CRUD environment these methods would have generic names such as **Save** or **Update**, and have a DTO as the only argument. The CQRS approach can be better tailored to suit the way that this organization carries out business and inventory management.

RELATED PATTERNS AND GUIDANCE

The following patterns and guidance may also be relevant when implementing this pattern:

- **Data Consistency Primer**. This guidance explains the issues that are typically encountered due to eventual consistency between the read and write data stores when using the CQRS pattern, and how these issues can be resolved.
- **Data Partitioning Guidance**. This guidance describes how the read and write data stores used in the CQRS pattern can be divided into separate partitions that can be managed and accessed separately to improve scalability, reduce contention, and optimize performance.

- **Event Sourcing Pattern**. This pattern describes in more detail how Event Sourcing can be used with the CQRS pattern to simplify tasks in complex domains; improve performance, scalability, and responsiveness; provide consistency for transactional data; and maintain full audit trails and history that may enable compensating actions.
- **Materialized View Pattern**. The read model of a CQRS implementation may contain materialized views of the write model data, or the read model may be used to generate materialized views.

More Information

All links in this book are accessible from the book's online bibliography available at: *http://aka.ms/cdpbibliography*.

- The patterns & practices guide *CQRS Journey* on MSDN.
- The article *CQRS* on Martin Fowler's blog.
- The articles by Greg Young's on the *Code Better* website.

Event Sourcing Pattern

Use an append-only store to record the full series of events that describe actions taken on data in a domain, rather than storing just the current state, so that the store can be used to materialize the domain objects. This pattern can simplify tasks in complex domains by avoiding the requirement to synchronize the data model and the business domain; improve performance, scalability, and responsiveness; provide consistency for transactional data; and maintain full audit trails and history that may enable compensating actions.

CONTEXT AND PROBLEM

Most applications work with data, and the typical approach is for the application to maintain the current state of the data by updating it as users work with the data. For example, in the traditional create, read, update, and delete (CRUD) model a typical data process will be to read data from the store, make some modifications to it, and update the current state of the data with the new values—often by using transactions that lock the data.

The CRUD approach has some limitations:

- The fact that CRUD systems perform update operations directly against a data store may hinder performance and responsiveness, and limit scalability, due to the processing overhead it requires.
- In a collaborative domain with many concurrent users, data update conflicts are more likely to occur because the update operations take place on a single item of data.
- Unless there is an additional auditing mechanism, which records the details of each operation in a separate log, history is lost.

> For a deeper understanding of the limits of the CRUD approach see "*CRUD, Only When You Can Afford It*" on MSDN.

SOLUTION

The Event Sourcing pattern defines an approach to handling operations on data that is driven by a sequence of events, each of which is recorded in an append-only store. Application code sends a series of events that imperatively describe each action that has occurred on the data to the event store, where they are persisted. Each event represents a set of changes to the data (such as AddedItemToOrder).

The events are persisted in an event store that acts as the source of truth or *system of record* (the authoritative data source for a given data element or piece of information) about the current state of the data. The event store typically publishes these events so that consumers can be notified and can handle them if needed. Consumers could, for example, initiate tasks that apply the operations in the events to other systems, or perform any other associated action that is required to complete the operation. Notice that the application code that generates the events is decoupled from the systems that subscribe to the events.

Typical uses of the events published by the event store are to maintain materialized views of entities as actions in the application change them, and for integration with external systems. For example, a system may maintain a materialized view of all customer orders that is used to populate parts of the UI. As the application adds new orders, adds or removes items on the order, and adds shipping information, the events that describe these changes can be handled and used to update the materialized view.

See the Materialized View Pattern for more information.

In addition, at any point in time it is possible for applications to read the history of events, and use it to materialize the current state of an entity by effectively "playing back" and consuming all the events related to that entity. This may occur on demand in order to materialize a domain object when handling a request, or through a scheduled task so that the state of the entity can be stored as a materialized view to support the presentation layer.

Figure 1 shows a logical overview of the pattern, including some of the options for using the event stream such as creating a materialized view, integrating events with external applications and systems, and replaying events to create projections of the current state of specific entities.

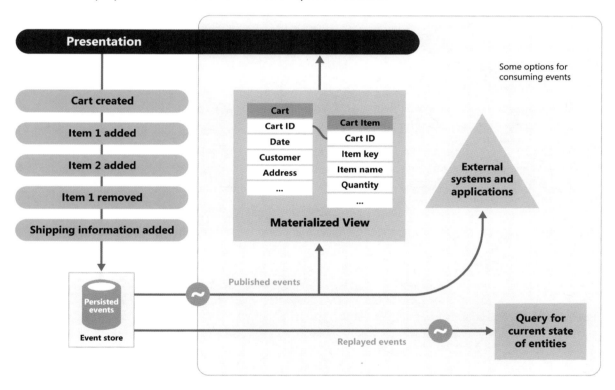

FIGURE 1
An overview and example of the Event Sourcing pattern

The Event Sourcing pattern provides many advantages, including the following:

- Events are immutable and so can be stored using an append-only operation. The user interface, workflow, or process that initiated the action that produced the events can continue, and the tasks that handle the events can run in the background. This, combined with the fact that there is no contention during the execution of transactions, can vastly improve performance and scalability for applications, especially for the presentation level or user interface.

- Events are simple objects that describe some action that occurred, together with any associated data required to describe the action represented by the event. Events do not directly update a data store; they are simply recorded for handling at the appropriate time. These factors can simplify implementation and management.

- Events typically have meaning for a domain expert, whereas the complexity of the object-relational impedance mismatch might mean that a database table may not be clearly understood by the domain expert. Tables are artificial constructs that represent the current state of the system, not the events that occurred.

- Event sourcing can help to prevent concurrent updates from causing conflicts because it avoids the requirement to directly update objects in the data store. However, the domain model must still be designed to protect itself from requests that might result in an inconsistent state.

- The append-only storage of events provides an audit trail that can be used to monitor actions taken against a data store, regenerate the current state as materialized views or projections by replaying the events at any time, and assist in testing and debugging the system. In addition, the requirement to use compensating events to cancel changes provides a history of changes that were reversed, which would not be the case if the model simply stored the current state. The list of events can also be used to analyze application performance and detect user behavior trends, or to obtain other useful business information.

- The decoupling of the events from any tasks that perform operations in response to each event raised by the event store provides flexibility and extensibility. For example, the tasks that handle events raised by the event store are aware only of the nature of the event and the data it contains. The way that the task is executed is decoupled from the operation that triggered the event. In addition, multiple tasks can handle each event. This may enable easy integration with other services and systems that need only listen for new events raised by the event store. However, the event sourcing events tend to be very low level, and it may be necessary to generate specific integration events instead.

> Event sourcing is commonly combined with the CQRS pattern by performing the data management tasks in response to the events, and by materializing views from the stored events.

ISSUES AND CONSIDERATIONS

Consider the following points when deciding how to implement this pattern:

- The system will only be eventually consistent when creating materialized views or generating projections of data by replaying events. There is some delay between an application adding events to the event store as the result of handling a request, the events being published, and consumers of the events handling them. During this period, new events that describe further changes to entities may have arrived at the event store.

> See the Data Consistency Primer for information about eventual consistency.

- The event store is the immutable source of information, and so the event data should never be updated. The only way to update an entity in order to undo a change is to add a compensating event to the event store, much as you would use a negative transaction in accounting. If the format (rather than the data) of the persisted events needs to change, perhaps during a migration, it can be difficult to combine existing events in the store with the new version. It may be necessary to iterate through all the events making changes so that they are compliant with the new format, or add new events that use the new format. Consider using a version stamp on each version of the event schema in order to maintain both the old and the new event formats.

- Multi-threaded applications and multiple instances of applications may be storing events in the event store. The consistency of events in the event store is vital, as is the order of events that affect a specific entity (the order in which changes to an entity occur affects its current state). Adding a timestamp to every event is one option that can help to avoid issues. Another common practice is to annotate each event that results from a request with an incremental identifier. If two actions attempt to add events for the same entity at the same time, the event store can reject an event that matches an existing entity identifier and event identifier.

- There is no standard approach, or ready-built mechanisms such as SQL queries, for reading the events to obtain information. The only data that can be extracted is a stream of events using an event identifier as the criteria. The event ID typically maps to individual entities. The current state of an entity can be determined only by replaying all of the events that relate to it against the original state of that entity.

- The length of each event stream can have consequences on managing and updating the system. If the streams are large, consider creating snapshots at specific intervals such as a specified number of events. The current state of the entity can be obtained from the snapshot and by replaying any events that occurred after that point in time.

> For more information about creating snapshots of data, see _Snapshot_ on Martin Fowler's Enterprise Application Architecture website and _Master-Subordinate Snapshot Replication_ on MSDN.

- Even though event sourcing minimizes the chance of conflicting updates to the data, the application must still be able to deal with inconsistencies that may arise through eventual consistency and the lack of transactions. For example, an event that indicates a reduction in stock inventory might arrive in the data store while an order for that item is being placed, resulting in a requirement to reconcile the two operations; probably by advising the customer or creating a back order.

- Event publication may be "at least once," and so consumers of the events must be idempotent. They must not reapply the update described in an event if the event is handled more than once. For example, if multiple instances of a consumer maintain an aggregate of a property of some entity, such as the total number of orders placed, only one must succeed in incrementing the aggregate when an "order placed" event occurs. While this is not an intrinsic characteristic of event sourcing, it is the usual implementation decision.

When to Use this Pattern

This pattern is ideally suited to the following scenarios:

- When you want to capture "intent," "purpose," or "reason" in the data. For example, changes to a customer entity may be captured as a series of specific event types such as **Moved home**, **Closed account**, or **Deceased**.

- When it is vital to minimize or completely avoid the occurrence of conflicting updates to data.

- When you want to record events that occur, and be able to replay them to restore the state of a system; use them to roll back changes to a system; or simply as a history and audit log. For example, when a task involves multiple steps you may need to execute actions to revert updates and then replay some steps to bring the data back into a consistent state.

- When using events is a natural feature of the operation of the application, and requires little additional development or implementation effort.
- When you need to decouple the process of inputting or updating data from the tasks required to apply these actions. This may be to improve UI performance, or to distribute events to other listeners such as other applications or services that must take some action when the events occur. An example would be integrating a payroll system with an expenses submission website so that events raised by the event store in response to data updates made in the expenses submission website are consumed by both the website and the payroll system.
- When you want flexibility to be able to change the format of materialized models and entity data if requirements change, or—when used in conjunction with CQRS—you need to adapt a read model or the views that expose the data.
- When used in conjunction with CQRS, and eventual consistency is acceptable while a read model is updated or, alternatively, the performance impact incurred in rehydrating entities and data from an event stream is acceptable.

This pattern might not be suitable in the following situations:

- Small or simple domains, systems that have little or no business logic, or non-domain systems that naturally work well with traditional CRUD data management mechanisms.
- Systems where consistency and real-time updates to the views of the data are required.
- Systems where audit trails, history, and capabilities to roll back and replay actions are not required.
- Systems where there is only a very low occurrence of conflicting updates to the underlying data. For example, systems that predominantly add data rather than updating it.

Example

A conference management system needs to track the number of completed bookings for a conference so that it can check whether there are seats still available when a potential attendee tries to make a new booking. The system could store the total number of bookings for a conference in at least two ways:

- The system could store the information about the total number of bookings as a separate entity in a database that holds booking information. As bookings are made or cancelled, the system could increment or decrement this number as appropriate. This approach is simple in theory, but can cause scalability issues if a large number of attendees are attempting to book seats during a short period of time. For example, in the last day or so prior to the booking period closing.
- The system could store information about bookings and cancellations as events held in an event store. It could then calculate the number of seats available by replaying these events. This approach can be more scalable due to the immutability of events. The system only needs to be able to read data from the event store, or to append data to the event store. Event information about bookings and cancellations is never modified.

Figure 2 shows how the seat reservation sub-system of the conference management system might be implemented by using event sourcing.

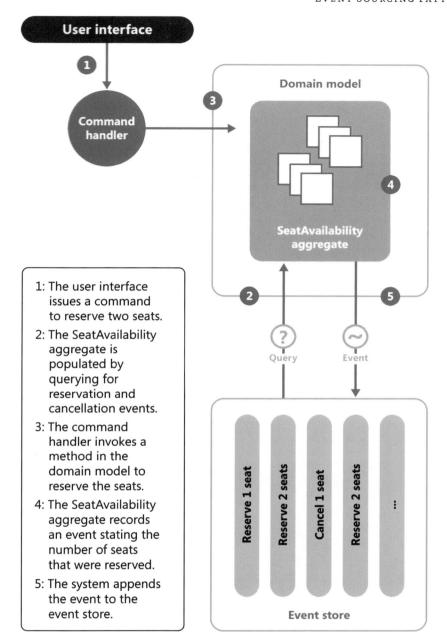

FIGURE 2
Using event sourcing to capture information about seat reservations in a conference management system

The sequence of actions for reserving two seats is as follows:

1. The user interface issues a command to reserve seats for two attendees. The command is handled by a separate command handler (a piece of logic that is decoupled from the user interface and is responsible for handling requests posted as commands).

2. An aggregate containing information about all reservations for the conference is constructed by querying the events that describe bookings and cancellations. This aggregate is called **SeatAvailability**, and is contained within a domain model that exposes methods for querying and modifying the data in the aggregate.

> Some optimizations to consider are using snapshots (so that you don't need to query and replay the full list of events to obtain the current state of the aggregate), and maintaining a cached copy of the aggregate in memory.

3. The command handler invokes a method exposed by the domain model to make the reservations.

4. The **SeatAvailability** aggregate records an event containing the number of seats that were reserved. The next time the aggregate applies events, all the reservations will be used to compute how many seats remain.

5. The system appends the new event to the list of events in the event store.

If a user wishes to cancel a seat, the system follows a similar process except that the command handler issues a command that generates a seat cancellation event and appends it to the event store

As well as providing more scope for scalability, using an event store also provides a complete history, or audit trail, of the bookings and cancellations for a conference. The events recorded in the event store are the definitive and only source of truth. There is no need to persist aggregates in any other way because the system can easily replay the events and restore the state to any point in time.

> You can find more information about this example in the chapter _Introducing Event Sourcing_ in the patterns & practices guide _CQRS Journey_ on MSDN.

Related Patterns and Guidance

The following patterns and guidance may also be relevant when implementing this pattern:

- **Command and Query Responsibility Segregation (CQRS) Pattern**. The write store that provides the immutable source of information for a CQRS implementation is often based on an implementation of the Event Sourcing pattern. The Command and Query Responsibility Segregation pattern describes how to segregate the operations that read data in an application from the operations that update data by using separate interfaces.

- **Materialized View Pattern**. The data store used in a system based on event sourcing is typically not well suited to efficient querying. Instead, a common approach is to generate pre-populated views of the data at regular intervals, or when the data changes. The Materialized View pattern shows how this can be achieved.

- **Compensating Transaction Pattern**. The existing data in an event sourcing store is not updated; instead new entries are added that transition the state of entities to the new values. To reverse a change, compensating entries are used because it is not possible to simply reverse the previous change. The Compensating Transaction pattern describes how to undo the work that was performed by a previous operation.

- **Data Consistency Primer**. When using event sourcing with a separate read store or materialized views, the read data will not be immediately consistent; instead it will be only eventually consistent. The Data Consistency Primer summarizes the issues surrounding maintaining consistency over distributed data.

- **Data Partitioning Guidance**. Data is often partitioned when using event sourcing in order to improve scalability, reduce contention, and optimize performance. The Data Partitioning Guidance describes how to divide data into discrete partitions, and the issues that can arise.

MORE INFORMATION

All links in this book are accessible from the book's online bibliography available at: _http://aka.ms/cdpbibliography_.

- The article see _"CRUD, Only When You Can Afford It"_ on MSDN.
- _Introducing Event Sourcing_ and _A CQRS and ES Deep Dive_ in the patterns & practices guide _CQRS Journey_ on MSDN.
- The post _Event Sourcing_ on Martin Fowler's blog.
- Greg Young's post _Why use Event Sourcing?_ On the _Code Better_ website.

External Configuration Store Pattern

Move configuration information out of the application deployment package to a centralized location. This pattern can provide opportunities for easier management and control of configuration data, and for sharing configuration data across applications and application instances.

CONTEXT AND PROBLEM

The majority of application runtime environments include configuration information that is held in files deployed with the application, located within the application folders. In some cases it is possible to edit these files to change the behavior of the application after it has been deployed. However, in many cases, changes to the configuration require the application to be redeployed, resulting in unacceptable downtime and additional administrative overhead.

Local configuration files also limit the configuration to a single application, whereas in some scenarios it would be useful to share configuration settings across multiple applications. Examples include database connection strings, UI theme information, or the URLs of queues and storage used by a related set of applications.

Managing changes to local configurations across multiple running instances of the application, especially in a cloud-hosted scenario, may also be challenging. It may result in instances using different configuration settings while the update is being deployed.

In addition, updates to applications and components may require changes to configuration schemas. Many configuration systems do not support different versions of configuration information.

SOLUTION

Store the configuration information in external storage, and provide an interface that can be used to quickly and efficiently read and update configuration settings. The type of external store depends on the hosting and runtime environment of the application. In a cloud-hosted scenario it is typically a cloud-based storage service, but could be a hosted database or other system.

The backing store chosen for configuration information should be fronted by a suitable interface that provides consistent and easy to use access in a controlled way that enables reuse. Ideally, it should expose the information in a correctly typed and structured format. The implementation may also need to authorize users' access in order to protect configuration data, and be flexible enough to allow multiple versions of the configuration (such as development, staging, or production, and multiple release versions of each one) to be stored.

Many built-in configuration systems read the data when the application starts up, and cache the data in memory to provide fast access and to minimize the impact on application performance. Depending on the type of backing store used, and the latency of this store, it might be advantageous to implement a caching mechanism within the external configuration store. For more information about implementing caching, see the Caching Guidance.

Figure 1 shows an overview of this pattern.

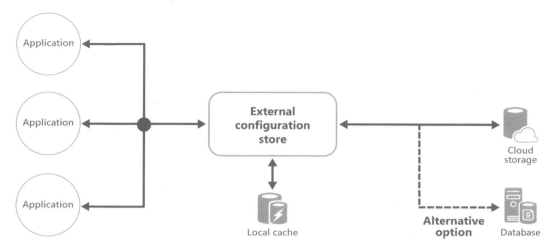

FIGURE 1
An overview of the External Configuration Store pattern with optional local cache

ISSUES AND CONSIDERATIONS

Consider the following points when deciding how to implement this pattern:

- Choose a backing store that offers acceptable performance, high availability, robustness, and can be backed up as part of the application maintenance and administration process. In a cloud-hosted application, using a cloud storage mechanism is usually a good choice to meet these requirements.

- Design the schema of the backing store to allow flexibility in the types of information it can hold. Ensure that it provides for all configuration requirements such as typed data, collections of settings, multiple versions of settings, and any other features that the applications using it may require. The schema should be easy to extend as requirements change in order to support additional settings.

- Consider the physical capabilities of the backing store, how it relates to the way that configuration information is stored, and the effects on performance. For example, storing an XML document containing configuration information will require either the configuration interface or the application to parse the document in order to read individual settings, and will make updating a setting more complicated, though caching the settings can help to offset slower read performance.

- Consider how the configuration interface will permit control of the scope and inheritance of configuration settings. For example, it may be a requirement to scope configuration settings at the organization, application, and the machine level; to support delegation of control over access to different scopes; and to prevent or allow individual applications to override settings.

- Ensure that the configuration interface can expose the configuration data in the required formats such as typed values, collections, key/value pairs, or property bags. However, consider the balance between capabilities and complexity of the API in order to make it useful and yet as easy to use as possible.

- Consider how the configuration store interface will behave when settings contain errors, or do not exist in the backing store. It may be appropriate to return default settings and log errors. Also consider aspects such as the case sensity of configuration setting keys or names, the storage and handling of binary data, and the ways that null or empty values are handled.

- Consider how you will protect the configuration data to allow access only to the appropriate users and applications. This is likely to be a feature of the configuration store interface, but it is also necessary to ensure that the data in the backing store cannot be accessed directly without the appropriate permission. Ensure strict separation between the permissions required to read and to write configuration data. Also consider whether you need to encrypt some or all of the configuration settings, and how this will be implemented within the configuration store interface.

- Keep in mind that centrally stored configurations, which change application behavior during runtime, are critically important and should be deployed, updated, and managed using the same mechanisms as deploying application code. For example, changes that can affect more than one application must be carried out using a full test and staged deployment approach to ensure that the change is appropriate for all applications that use this configuration. If an administrator simply edits a setting to update one application, it could adversely impact other applications that use the same setting.

- If an application caches configuration information, the application may need to be alerted if the configuration changes. It may be possible to implement an expiration policy over cached configuration data so that this information is automatically refreshed periodically and any changes picked up (and actioned). The Runtime Reconfiguration Pattern described elsewhere in this guide may be relevant to your scenario.

When to Use this Pattern

This pattern is ideally suited for:

- Configuration settings that are shared between multiple applications and application instances, or where a standard configuration must be enforced across multiple applications and application instances.

- Where the standard configuration system does not support all of the required configuration settings, such as storing images or complex data types.

- As a complementary store for some of the settings for applications, perhaps allowing applications to override some or all of the centrally-stored settings.

- As a mechanism for simplifying administration of multiple applications, and optionally for monitoring use of configuration settings by logging some or all types of access to the configuration store.

Example

In a Windows Azure hosted application, a typical choice for storing configuration information externally is to use Windows Azure storage. This is resilient, offers high performance, and is replicated three times with automatic failover to offer high availability. Windows Azure tables provide a key/value store with the capability to use a flexible schema for the values. Windows Azure blob storage provides a hierarchical container-based store that can hold any type of data in individually named blobs.

The following example shows how a configuration store can be implemented over Windows Azure blob storage to store and expose configuration information. The **BlobSettingsStore** class abstracts blob storage for holding configuration information, and implements the **ISettingsStore** interface shown in the following code.

This code is provided in the ExternalConfigurationStore.Cloud project in the ExternalConfigurationStore solution. This solution is available for download with this guidance.

```csharp
C#
public interface IsettingsStore
{
  string Version { get; }

  Dictionary<string, string> FindAll();

  void Update(string key, string value);
}
```

This interface defines methods for retrieving and updating configuration settings held in the configuration store, and includes a version number that can be used to detect whether any configuration settings have been modified recently. When a configuration setting is updated, the version number changes. The **BlobSettings-Store** class uses the **ETag** property of the blob to implement versioning. The **ETag** property of a blob is updated automatically each time the blob is written.

> Note that, by design, this simple solution exposes all configuration settings as string values rather than typed values.

The **ExternalConfigurationManager** class provides a wrapper around a **BlobSettingsStore** object. An application can use this class to store and retrieve configuration information. This class uses the Microsoft Reactive Extensions library to expose any changes made to the configuration through an implementation of the **IObservable** interface. If a setting is modified by calling the **SetAppSetting** method, the **Changed** event is raised and all subscribers to this event will be notified.

Note that all settings are also cached in a **Dictionary** object inside the **ExternalConfigurationManager** class for fast access. The **SetAppSetting** method updates this cache, and the **GetSetting** method that an application can use to retrieve a configuration setting reads the data from the cache (if the setting is not found in the cache, it is retrieved from the **BlobSettingsStore** object instead).

The **GetSettings** method invokes the **CheckForConfigurationChanges** method to detect whether the configuration information in blob storage has changed by examining the version number and comparing it with the current version number held by the **ExternalConfigurationManager** object. If one or more changes have occurred, the **Changed** event is raised and the configuration settings cached in the **Dictionary** object are refreshed. This is an application of the Cache-Aside Pattern.

The following code sample shows how the **Changed** event, the **SetAppSettings** method, the **GetSettings** method, and the **CheckForConfigurationChanges** method are implemented.

```csharp
C#
public class ExternalConfigurationManager : IDisposable
{
  // An abstraction of the configuration store.
  private readonly ISettingsStore settings;
  private readonly ISubject<KeyValuePair<string, string>> changed;
  ...
  private Dictionary<string, string> settingsCache;
  private string currentVersion;
  ...
  public ExternalConfigurationManager(ISettingsStore settings, ...)
```

```csharp
{
  this.settings = settings;
  ...
}
...
public IObservable<KeyValuePair<string, string>> Changed
{
  get { return this.changed.AsObservable(); }
}
...
public void SetAppSetting(string key, string value)
{
  ...
  // Update the setting in the store.
  this.settings.Update(key, value);

  // Publish the event.
  this.Changed.OnNext(
      new KeyValuePair<string, string>(key, value));

  // Refresh the settings cache.
  this.CheckForConfigurationChanges();
}

public string GetAppSetting(string key)
{
  ...
  // Try to get the value from the settings cache.
  // If there is a miss, get the setting from the settings store.
  string value;
  if (this.settingsCache.TryGetValue(key, out value))
  {
    return value;
  }

  // Check for changes and refresh the cache.
  this.CheckForConfigurationChanges();

  return this.settingsCache[key];
}
...
private void CheckForConfigurationChanges()
{
  try
  {

    // Assume that updates are infrequent. Lock to avoid
    // race conditions when refreshing the cache.
    lock (this.settingsSyncObject)
    {            {
      var latestVersion = this.settings.Version;

      // If the versions differ, the configuration has changed.
      if (this.currentVersion != latestVersion)
```

```
      {
        // Get the latest settings from the settings store and publish the changes.
        var latestSettings = this.settings.FindAll();
        latestSettings.Except(this.settingsCache).ToList().ForEach(
                          kv => this.changed.OnNext(kv));

        // Update the current version.
        this.currentVersion = latestVersion;

        // Refresh settings cache.
        this.settingsCache = latestSettings;
      }
    }
  }
  catch (Exception ex)
  {
    this.changed.OnError(ex);
  }
 }
}
```

The **ExternalConfigurationManager** class also provides a property named **Environment**. The purpose of this property is to support varying configurations for an application running in different environments, such as staging and production.

An **ExternalConfigurationManager** object can also query the **BlobSettingsStore** object periodically for any changes (by using a timer). The **StartMonitor** and **StopMonitor** methods illustrated in the code sample below start and stop the timer. The **OnTimerElapsed** method runs when the timer expires and invokes the **Check-ForConfigurationChanges** method to detect any changes and raise the **Changed** event, as described earlier.

```csharp
C#
public class ExternalConfigurationManager : IDisposable
{
  ...
  private readonly ISubject<KeyValuePair<string, string>> changed;
  private readonly Timer timer;
  private ISettingsStore settings;
  ...
  public ExternalConfigurationManager(ISettingsStore settings,
                                      TimeSpan interval, ...)
  {
    ...

    // Set up the timer.
    this.timer = new Timer(interval.TotalMilliseconds)
    {
      AutoReset = false;
    };
    this.timer.Elapsed += this.OnTimerElapsed;

    this.changed = new Subject<KeyValuePair<string, string>>();
    ...
  }
```

```
...
public void StartMonitor()
{
  if (this.timer.Enabled)
  {
    return;
  }

  lock (this.timerSyncObject)
  {
    if (this.timer.Enabled)
    {
      return;
    }
    this.keepMonitoring = true;

    // Load the local settings cache.
    this.CheckForConfigurationChanges();

    this.timer.Start();
  }
}

public void StopMonitor()
{
  lock (this.timerSyncObject)
  {
    this.keepMonitoring = false;
    this.timer.Stop();
  }
}

private void OnTimerElapsed(object sender, EventArgs e)
{
  Trace.TraceInformation(
      "Configuration Manager: checking for configuration changes.");

  try
  {
    this.CheckForConfigurationChanges();
  }
  finally
  {
    ...
    // Restart the timer after each interval.
    this.timer.Start();
    ...
  }
}
...
}
```

The **ExternalConfigurationManager** class is instantiated as a singleton instance by the **ExternalConfiguration** class shown below.

```C#
public static class ExternalConfiguration
{
  private static readonly Lazy<ExternalConfigurationManager> configuredInstance
                         = new Lazy<ExternalConfigurationManager>(
    () =>
    {
      var environment = CloudConfigurationManager.GetSetting("environment");
      return new ExternalConfigurationManager(environment);
    });

  public static ExternalConfigurationManager Instance
  {
    get { return configuredInstance.Value; }
  }
}
```

The following code is taken from the **WorkerRole** class in the ExternalConfigurationStore.Cloud project. It shows how the application uses the **ExternalConfiguration** class to read and update a setting.

```C#
public override void Run()
{
  // Start monitoring for configuration changes.
  ExternalConfiguration.Instance.StartMonitor();

  // Get a setting.
  var setting = ExternalConfiguration.Instance.GetAppSetting("setting1");
  Trace.TraceInformation("Worker Role: Get setting1, value: " + setting);

  Thread.Sleep(TimeSpan.FromSeconds(10));

  // Update a setting.
  Trace.TraceInformation("Worker Role: Updating configuration");
  ExternalConfiguration.Instance.SetAppSetting("setting1", "new value");

  this.completeEvent.WaitOne();
}
```

The following code, also from the **WorkerRole** class, shows how the application subscribes to configuration events.

```C#
public override bool OnStart()
{
  ...
  // Subscribe to the event.
  ExternalConfiguration.Instance.Changed.Subscribe(
     m => Trace.TraceInformation("Configuration has changed. Key:{0} Value:{1}",
         m.Key, m.Value),
     ex => Trace.TraceError("Error detected: " + ex.Message));
  ...
}
```

RELATED PATTERNS AND GUIDANCE

The following pattern may also be relevant when implementing this pattern:

- **Runtime Reconfiguration Pattern**. In addition to storing configuration externally, it is useful to be able to update configuration settings and have the changes applied without restarting the application. The Runtime Reconfiguration pattern describes how to design an application so that it can be reconfigured without requiring redeployment or restarting.

This pattern has a sample application associated with it. You can download the "Cloud Design Patterns – Sample Code" from the Microsoft Download Center at *http://aka.ms/cloud-design-patterns-sample*.

Federated Identity Pattern

Delegate authentication to an external identity provider. This pattern can simplify development, minimize the requirement for user administration, and improve the user experience of the application.

CONTEXT AND PROBLEM

Users typically need to work with multiple applications provided by, and hosted by different organizations with which they have a business relationship. However, these users may be forced to use specific (and different) credentials for each one. This can:

- **Cause a disjointed user experience**. Users often forget sign-in credentials when they have many different ones.
- **Expose security vulnerabilities**. When a user leaves the company the account must immediately be deprovisioned. It is easy to overlook this in large organizations.
- **Complicate user management**. Administrators must manage credentials for all of the users, and perform additional tasks such as providing password reminders.

Users will, instead, typically expect to use the same credentials for these applications.

SOLUTION

Implement an authentication mechanism that can use federated identity. Separating user authentication from the application code, and delegating authentication to a trusted identity provider, can considerably simplify development and allow users to authenticate using a wider range of identity providers (IdPs) while minimizing the administrative overhead. It also allows you to clearly decouple authentication from authorization.

The trusted identity providers may include corporate directories, on-premises federation services, other security token services (STSs) provided by business partners, or social identity providers that can authenticate users who have, for example, a Microsoft, Google, Yahoo!, or Facebook account.

Figure 1 illustrates the principles of the federated identity pattern when a client application needs to access a service that requires authentication. The authentication is performed by an identity provider (IdP), which works in concert with a security token service (STS). The IdP issues security tokens that assert information about the authenticated user. This information, referred to as *claims*, includes the user's identity, and may also include other information such as role membership and more granular access rights.

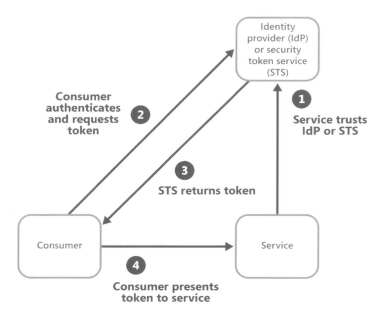

FIGURE 1
An overview of federated authentication

This model is often referred to as *claims-based access control*. Applications and services authorize access to features and functionality based on the claims contained in the token. The service that requires authentication must trust the IdP. The client application contacts the IdP that performs the authentication. If the authentication is successful, the IdP returns a token containing the claims that identify the user to the STS (note that the IdP and STS may be the same service). The STS can transform and augment the claims in the token based on predefined rules, before returning it to the client. The client application can then pass this token to the service as proof of its identity.

> In some scenarios there may be additional STSs in the chain of trust. For example, in the Windows Azure scenario described later, an on-premises STS trusts another STS that is responsible for accessing an identity provider to authenticate the user. This approach is common in enterprise scenarios where there is an on-premises STS and directory.

Federated authentication provides a standards-based solution to the issue of trusting identities across diverse domains, and can support single sign on. It is becoming more common across all types of applications, especially cloud-hosted applications, because it supports single sign on without requiring a direct network connection to identity providers. The user does not have to enter credentials for every application. This increases security because it prevents the proliferation of credentials required to access many different applications, and it also hides the user's credentials from all but the original identity provider. Applications see just the authenticated identity information contained within the token.

Federated identity also has the major advantage that management of the identity and credentials is the responsibility of the identity provider. The application or service does not need to provide identity management features. In addition, in corporate scenarios, the corporate directory does not need to know about the user (providing it trusts the identity provider), which removes all the administrative overhead of managing the user identity within the directory.

Issues and Considerations

Consider the following when designing applications that implement federated authentication:

- Authentication can be a single point of failure. If you deploy your application to multiple datacenters, consider deploying your identity management mechanism to the same datacenters in order to maintain application reliability and availability.

- Authentication mechanisms may provide facilities to configure access control based on role claims contained in the authentication token. This is often referred to as *role-based access control* (RBAC), and it may allow a more granular level of control over access to features and resources.

- Unlike a corporate directory, claims-based authentication using social identity providers does not usually provide information about the authenticated user other than an email address, and perhaps a name. Some social identity providers, such as a Microsoft account, provide only a unique identifier. The application will usually need to maintain some information on registered users, and be able to match this information to the identifier contained in the claims in the token. Typically this is done through a registration process when the user first accesses the application, and information is then injected into the token as additional claims after each authentication.

- If there is more than one identity provider configured for the STS, it must detect which identity provider the user should be redirected to for authentication. This process is referred to as *home realm discovery*. The STS may be able to do this automatically based on an email address or user name that the user provides, a subdomain of the application that the user is accessing, the user's IP address scope, or on the contents of a cookie stored in the user's browser. For example, if the user entered an email address in the Microsoft domain, such as *user*@live.com, the STS will redirect the user to the Microsoft account sign-in page. On subsequent visits, the STS could use a cookie to indicate that the last sign in was with a Microsoft account. If automatic discovery cannot determine the home realm, the STS will display a home realm discovery (HRD) page that lists the trusted identity providers, and the user must select the one they want to use.

WHEN TO USE THIS PATTERN

This pattern is ideally suited for a range of scenarios, such as:

- **Single sign on in the enterprise**. In this scenario you need to authenticate employees for corporate applications that are hosted in the cloud outside the corporate security boundary, without requiring them to sign on every time they visit an application. The user experience is the same as when using on-premises applications where they are initially authenticated when signing on to a corporate network, and from then on have access to all relevant applications without needing to sign on again.

- **Federated identity with multiple partners**. In this scenario you need to authenticate both corporate employees and business partners who do not have accounts in the corporate directory. This is common in business-to-business (B2B) applications, applications that integrate with third party services, and where companies with disparate IT systems have merged or share resources.

- **Federated identity in SaaS applications**. In this scenario independent software vendors (ISVs) provide a ready to use service for multiple clients or tenants. Each tenant will want to authenticate using a suitable identity provider. For example, business users will want to us their corporate credentials, while consumers and clients of the tenant may want to use their social identity credentials.

This pattern might not be suitable in the following situations:

- All users of the application can be authenticated by one identity provider, and there is no requirement to authenticate using any other identity provider. This is typical in business applications that use only a corporate directory for authentication, and access to this directory is available in the application directly, by using a VPN, or (in a cloud-hosted scenario) through a virtual network connection between the on-premises directory and the application.

- The application was originally built using a different authentication mechanism, perhaps with custom user stores, or does not have the capability to handle the negotiation standards used by claims-based technologies. Retrofitting claims-based authentication and access control into existing applications can be complex, and may not be cost effective.

EXAMPLE

An organization hosts a multi-tenant Software as a Service (SaaS) application in Windows Azure. The application incudes a website that tenants can use to manage the application for their own users. The application allows tenants to access the tenant's website by using a federated identity that is generated by Active Directory Federation Services (ADFS) when a user is authenticated by that organization's own Active Directory. Figure 2 shows an overview of this process.

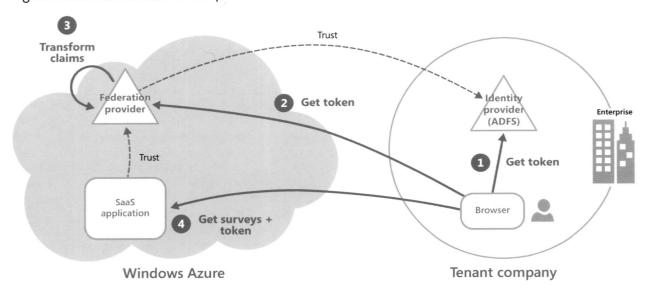

FIGURE 2
How users at a large enterprise subscriber access the application

In the scenario shown in Figure 2, tenants authenticate with their own identity provider (step 1), in this case ADFS. After successfully authenticating a tenant, ADFS issues a token. The client browser forwards this token to the SaaS application's federation provider, which trusts tokens issued by the tenant's ADFS, in order to get back a token that is valid for the SaaS federation provider (step 2). If necessary, the SaaS federation provider performs a transformation on the claims in the token into claims that the application recognizes (step 3) before returning the new token to the client browser. The application trusts tokens issued by the SaaS federation provider and uses the claims in the token to apply authorization rules (step 4).

Tenants will not need to remember separate credentials to access the application, and an administrator at the tenant's company will be able to configure in its own ADFS the list of users that can access the application.

RELATED PATTERNS AND GUIDANCE

At this time, there are no related patterns and guidance.

MORE INFORMATION

All links in this book are accessible from the book's online bibliography available at:
http://aka.ms/cdpbibliography.

For more information on the federated authentication technologies you can use in Windows Azure applications, see the following:

- *Windows Azure Active Directory* on the Windows Azure website.
- *Active Directory Domain Services* on MSDN.
- *Active Directory Federation Services* on MSDN.
- *Windows Identity Foundation* on MSDN.
- *Developing Multi-Tenant Web Applications with Windows Azure AD* on MSDN.

For comprehensive information about claims-based identity and federated authentication see:

- *Federated Identity: Scenarios, Architecture, and Implementation* on MSDN.
- *Federated Identity Patterns in a Service-Oriented World* in the Architecture Journal.

Gatekeeper Pattern

Protect applications and services by using a dedicated host instance that acts as a broker between clients and the application or service, validates and sanitizes requests, and passes requests and data between them. This can provide an additional layer of security, and limit the attack surface of the system.

CONTEXT AND PROBLEM

Applications expose their functionality to clients by accepting and processing requests. In cloud-hosted scenarios, applications expose endpoints to which clients connect, and typically include the code to handle the requests from clients. This code may perform authentication and validation, some or all request processing, and is likely to accesses storage and other services on behalf of the client.

If a malicious user is able to compromise the system and gain access to application's hosting environment, the security mechanisms it uses such as credentials and storage keys, and the services and data it accesses, are exposed. As a result, the malicious user may be able to gain unrestrained access to sensitive information and other services.

SOLUTION

To minimize the risk of clients gaining access to sensitive information and services, decouple hosts or tasks that expose public endpoints from the code that processes requests and accesses storage. This can be achieved by using a façade or a dedicated task that interacts with clients and then hands off the request (perhaps through a decoupled interface) to the hosts or tasks that will handle the request. Figure 1 shows a high-level view of this approach.

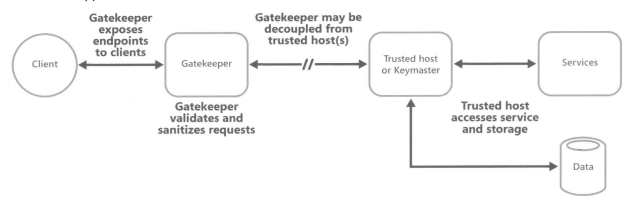

FIGURE 1
High level overview of this pattern

The gatekeeper pattern may be used simply to protect storage, or it may be used as a more comprehensive façade to protect all of the functions of the application. The important factors are:

- **Controlled validation**. The Gatekeeper validates all requests, and rejects those that do not meet validation requirements.
- **Limited risk and exposure**. The Gatekeeper does not have access to the credentials or keys used by the trusted host to access storage and services. If the Gatekeeper is compromised, the attacker does not obtain access to these credentials or keys.
- **Appropriate security**. The Gatekeeper runs in a limited privilege mode, whereas the remainder of the application runs in the full trust mode required to access storage and services. If the Gatekeeper is compromised, it cannot directly access the application services or data.

This pattern effectively acts like a firewall in a typical network topography. It allows the Gatekeeper to examine requests and make a decision about whether to pass the request on to the trusted host (sometimes called the Keymaster) that performs the required tasks. This decision will typically require the Gatekeeper to validate and sanitize the request content before passing it on to the trusted host.

ISSUES AND CONSIDERATIONS

Consider the following points when deciding how to implement this pattern:

- Ensure that the trusted hosts to which the Gatekeeper passes requests expose only internal or protected endpoints, and connect only to the Gatekeeper. The trusted hosts should not expose any external endpoints or interfaces.
- The Gatekeeper must run in a limited privilege mode. Typically this means running the Gatekeeper and the trusted host in separate hosted services or virtual machines.
- The Gatekeeper should not perform any processing related to the application or services, or access any data. Its function is purely to validate and sanitize requests. The trusted hosts may need to perform additional validation of requests, but the core validation should be performed by the Gatekeeper.
- Use a secure communication channel (HTTPS, SSL, or TLS) between the Gatekeeper and the trusted hosts or tasks where this is possible. However, some hosting environments may not support HTTPS on internal endpoints.
- Adding the extra layer to the application to implement the Gatekeeper pattern is likely to have some impact on performance of the application due to the additional processing and network communication it requires.
- The Gatekeeper instance could be a single point of failure. To minimize the impact of a failure, consider deploying additional instances and using an autoscaling mechanism to ensure sufficient capacity to maintain availability.

WHEN TO USE THIS PATTERN

This pattern is ideally suited for:

- Applications that handle sensitive information, expose services that must have high a degree of protection from malicious attacks, or perform mission-critical operations that must not be disrupted.
- Distributed applications where it is necessary to perform request validation separately from the main tasks, or to centralize this validation to simplify maintenance and administration.

EXAMPLE

In a cloud-hosted scenario, this pattern can be implemented by decoupling the Gatekeeper role or virtual machine from the trusted roles and services in an application by using an internal endpoint, a queue, or storage as an intermediate communication mechanism. Figure 2 shows the basic principle when using an internal endpoint.

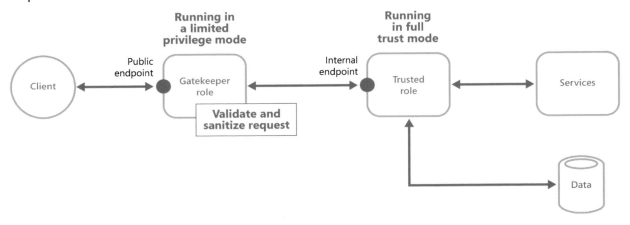

FIGURE 2
An example of the pattern using Cloud Services web and worker roles

RELATED PATTERNS AND GUIDANCE

The following pattern may also be relevant when implementing this pattern:

- **Valet Key Pattern**. When communicating between the Gatekeeper and trusted roles it is good practice to enhance security by using keys or tokens that limit permissions for accessing resources. The Valet Key pattern describes how to use a token or key that provides clients with restricted direct access to a specific resource or service.

Health Endpoint Monitoring Pattern

Implement functional checks within an application that external tools can access through exposed endpoints at regular intervals. This pattern can help to verify that applications and services are performing correctly

CONTEXT AND PROBLEM

It is good practice—and often a business requirement—to monitor web applications, and middle-tier and shared services, to ensure that they are available and performing correctly. However, it is more difficult to monitor services running in the cloud than it is to monitor on-premises services. For example, you do not have full control of the hosting environment, and the services typically depend on other services provided by platform vendors and others.

There are also many factors that affect cloud-hosted applications such as network latency, the performance and availability of the underlying compute and storage systems, and the network bandwidth between them. The service may fail entirely or partially due to any of these factors. Therefore, you must verify at regular intervals that the service is performing correctly to ensure the required level of availability—which might be part of your Service Level Agreement (SLA).

SOLUTION

Implement health monitoring by sending requests to an endpoint on the application. The application should perform the necessary checks, and return an indication of its status.

A health monitoring check typically combines two factors: the checks (if any) performed by the application or service in response to the request to the health verification endpoint, and analysis of the result by the tool or framework that is performing the health verification check. The response code indicates the status of the application and, optionally, any components or services it uses. The latency or response time check is performed by the monitoring tool or framework. Figure 1 shows an overview of the implementation of this pattern.

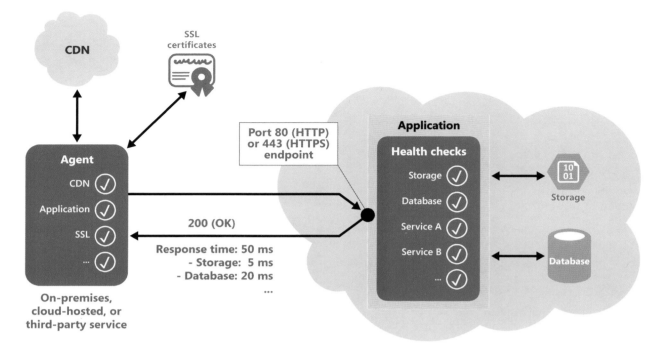

FIGURE 1
Overview of the pattern

Additional checks that might be carried out by the health monitoring code in the application include:

- Checking cloud storage or a database for availability and response time.
- Checking other resources or services located within the application, or located elsewhere but used by the application.

Several existing services and tools are available for monitoring web applications by submitting a request to a configurable set of endpoints, and evaluating the results against a set of configurable rules. It is relatively easy to create a service endpoint whose sole purpose is to perform some functional tests on the system.

Typical checks that can be performed by the monitoring tools include:

- Validating the response code. For example, an HTTP Response of 200 (OK) indicates that the application responded without error. The monitoring system might also check for other response codes to give a more comprehensive indication of the result.
- Checking the content of the response to detect errors, even when a 200 (OK) status code is returned. This can detect errors that affect only a section of the returned web page or service response. For example, checking the title of a page or looking for a specific phrase that indicates the correct page was returned.
- Measuring the response time, which indicates a combination of the network latency and the time that the application took to execute the request. An increasing value may indicate an emerging problem with the application or network.
- Checking resources or services located outside the application, such as a content delivery network used by the application to deliver content from global caches.
- Checking for expiration of SSL certificates.

- Measuring the response time of a DNS lookup for the URL of the application in order to measure DNS latency and DNS failures.
- Validating the URL returned by the DNS lookup to ensure correct entries. This can help to avoid malicious request redirection through a successful attack on the DNS server.

It is also useful, where possible, to run these checks from different on-premises or hosted locations to measure and compare response times from different places. Ideally you should monitor applications from locations that are close to customers in order to get an accurate view of the performance from each location. In addition to providing a more robust checking mechanism, the results may influence the choice of deployment location for the application—and whether to deploy it in more than one datacenter.

Tests should also be run against all the service instances that customers use to ensure the application is working correctly for all customers. For example, if customer storage is spread across more than one storage account, the monitoring process must check all of these.

ISSUES AND CONSIDERATIONS

Consider the following points when deciding how to implement this pattern:

- How to validate the response. For example, is just a single a 200 (OK) status code sufficient to verify the application is working correctly? While this provides the most basic measure of application availability, and is the minimum implementation of this pattern, it provides little information about the operations, trends, and possible upcoming issues in the application.

> Make sure that the application does correctly return a 200 status code only when the target resource is found and processed. In some scenarios, such as when using a master page to host the target web page, the server may send back a 200 OK status code instead of a 404 Not Found code, even when the target content page was not found.

- The number of endpoints to expose for an application. One approach is to expose at least one endpoint for the core services the application uses and another for ancillary or lower priority services, allowing different levels of importance to be assigned to each monitoring result. Also consider exposing more endpoints, such as one for each core service, to provide additional monitoring granularity. For example, a health verification check might check the database, storage, and an external geocoding service an application uses; each requiring a different level of uptime and response time. The application may still be healthy if the geocoding service, or some other background task, is unavailable for a few minutes.
- Whether to use the same endpoint for monitoring as is used for general access, but to a specific path designed for health verification checks; for example, /HealthCheck/{GUID}/ on the general access endpoint. This allows some functional tests within the application to be executed by the monitoring tools, such as adding a new user registration, signing in, and placing a test order, while also verifying that the general access endpoint is available.
- The type of information to collect in the service in response to monitoring requests, and how to return this information. Most existing tools and frameworks look only at the HTTP status code that the endpoint returns. To return and validate additional information it may be necessary to create a custom monitoring utility or service.
- How much information to collect. Performing excessive processing during the check may overload the application and impact other users, and the time it takes may exceed the timeout of the monitoring system so that it marks the application as unavailable. Most applications include instrumentation such as error handlers and performance counters that log performance and detailed error information, and this may be sufficient instead of returning additional information from a health verification check.

- How to configure security for the monitoring endpoints to protect them from public access; which might expose the application to malicious attacks, risk the exposure of sensitive information, or attract denial of service (DoS) attacks. Typically this should be done in the application configuration so that it can be updated easily without restarting the application. Consider using one or more of the following techniques:
    - Secure the endpoint by requiring authentication. This may be achieved by using an authentication security key in the request header or by passing credentials with the request, provided that the monitoring service or tool supports authentication.
    - Use an obscure or hidden endpoint. For example, expose the endpoint on a different IP address to that used by the default application URL, configure the endpoint on a non-standard HTTP port, and/or use a complex path to the test page. It is usually possible to specify additional endpoint addresses and ports in the application configuration, and add entries for these endpoints to the DNS server if required to avoid having to specify the IP address directly.
    - Expose a method on an endpoint that accepts a parameter such as a key value or an operation mode value. Depending on the value supplied for this parameter when a request is received the code can perform a specific test or set of tests, or return a 404 (Not Found) error if the parameter value is not recognized. The recognized parameter values could be set in the application configuration.

> DoS attacks are likely to have less impact on a separate endpoint that performs basic functional tests without compromising the operation of the application. Ideally, avoid using a test that might expose sensitive information. If you must return any information that might be useful to an attacker, consider how you will protect the endpoint and the data from unauthorized access. In this case just relying on obscurity is not sufficient. You should also consider using an HTTPS connection and encrypting any sensitive data, although this will increase the load on the server.

- How to access an endpoint that is secured using authentication. Not all tools and frameworks can be configured to include credentials with the health verification request. For example, Windows Azure built-in health verification features cannot provide authentication credentials. Some third party alternatives that can are *Pingdom*, *Panopta*, *NewRelic*, and *Statuscake*.
- How to ensure that the monitoring agent is performing correctly. One approach is to expose an endpoint that simply returns a value from the application configuration or a random value that can be used to test the agent.

> Also ensure that the monitoring system performs checks on itself, such as a self-test and built-in test, to avoid it issuing false positive results.

WHEN TO USE THIS PATTERN

This pattern is ideally suited for:

- Monitoring websites and web applications to verify availability.
- Monitoring websites and web applications to check for correct operation.

- Monitoring middle-tier or shared services to detect and isolate a failure that could disrupt other applications.
- To complement existing instrumentation within the application, such as performance counters and error handlers. Health verification checking does not replace the requirement for logging and auditing in the application. Instrumentation can provide valuable information for an existing framework that monitors counters and error logs to detect failures or other issues. However, it cannot provide information if the application is unavailable.

EXAMPLE

The following code examples, taken from the **HealthCheckController** class in the **HealthEndpointMonitoring. Web** project that is included in the samples you can download for this guide, demonstrates exposing an endpoint for performing a range of health checks.

The **CoreServices** method, shown below, performs a series of checks on services used in the application. If all of the tests execute without error, the method returns a 200 (OK) status code. If any of the tests raises an exception, the method returns a 500 (Internal Error) status code. The method could optionally return additional information when an error occurs, if the monitoring tool or framework is able to make use of it.

```csharp
C#
public ActionResult CoreServices()
{
  try
  {
    // Run a simple check to ensure the database is available.
    DataStore.Instance.CoreHealthCheck();

    // Run a simple check on our external service.
    MyExternalService.Instance.CoreHealthCheck();
  }
  catch (Exception ex)
  {
    Trace.TraceError("Exception in basic health check: {0}", ex.Message);

    // This can optionally return different status codes based on the exception.
    // Optionally it could return more details about the exception.
    // The additional information could be used by administrators who access the
    // endpoint with a browser, or using a ping utility that can display the
    // additional information.
    return new HttpStatusCodeResult((int)HttpStatusCode.InternalServerError);
  }
  return new HttpStatusCodeResult((int)HttpStatusCode.OK);
}
```

The **ObscurePath** method shows how you can read a path from the application configuration and use it as the endpoint for tests. This example also shows how you can accept an ID as a parameter and use it to check for valid requests.

```csharp
C#
public ActionResult ObscurePath(string id)
{
  // The id could be used as a simple way to obscure or hide the endpoint.
  // The id to match could be retrieved from configuration and, if matched,
  // perform a specific set of tests and return the result. It not matched it
  // could return a 404 Not Found status.

  // The obscure path can be set through configuration in order to hide the endpoint.
  var hiddenPathKey = CloudConfigurationManager.GetSetting("Test.ObscurePath");

  // If the value passed does not match that in configuration, return 403 "Not Found".
  if (!string.Equals(id, hiddenPathKey))
  {
    return new HttpStatusCodeResult((int)HttpStatusCode.NotFound);
  }

  // Else continue and run the tests...
  // Return results from the core services test.
  return this.CoreServices();
}
```

The **TestResponseFromConfig** method shows how you can expose an endpoint that performs a check for a specified configuration setting value.

```csharp
C#
public ActionResult TestResponseFromConfig()
{
  // Health check that returns a response code set in configuration for testing.
  var returnStatusCodeSetting = CloudConfigurationManager.GetSetting(
                                            "Test.ReturnStatusCode");

  int returnStatusCode;

  if (!int.TryParse(returnStatusCodeSetting, out returnStatusCode))
  {
    returnStatusCode = (int)HttpStatusCode.OK;
  }

  return new HttpStatusCodeResult(returnStatusCode);
}
```

Monitoring Endpoints in Windows Azure Hosted Applications

Some options for monitoring endpoints in Windows Azure applications are:

- Use the built-in features of Windows Azure, such as the Management Services or Traffic Manager.
- Use a third party service or a framework such as Microsoft System Center Operations Manager.
- Create a custom utility or a service that runs on your own or on a hosted server.

> Even though Windows Azure provides a reasonably comprehensive set of monitoring options, you may decide to use additional services and tools to provide extra information.

Windows Azure Management Services provides a comprehensive built-in monitoring mechanism built around alert rules. The Alerts section of the Management Services page in the Windows Azure management portal allows you to configure up to ten alert rules per subscription for your services. These rules specify a condition and a threshold value for a service such as CPU load, or the number of requests or errors per second, and the service can automatically send email notifications to addresses you define in each rule.

The conditions you can monitor vary depending on the hosting mechanism you choose for your application (such as Web Sites, Cloud Services, Virtual Machines, or Mobile Services), but all of these include the capability to create an alert rule that uses a web endpoint you specify in the settings for your service. This endpoint should respond in a timely way so that the alert system can detect that the application is operating correctly.

> For more information about creating monitoring alerts, see _Management Services_ on MSDN.

If you host your application in Windows Azure Cloud Services web and worker roles or Virtual Machines, you can take advantage of one of the built-in services in Windows Azure called Traffic Manager. Traffic Manager is a routing and load-balancing service that can distribute requests to specific instances of your Cloud Services hosted application based on a range of rules and settings.

In addition to routing requests, Traffic Manager pings a URL, port, and relative path you specify on a regular basis to determine which instances of the application defined in its rules are active and are responding to requests. If it detects a status code 200 (OK) it marks the application as available, any other status code causes Traffic Manager to mark the application as offline. You can view the status in the Traffic Manager console, and configure the rule to reroute requests to other instances of the application that are responding.

However, keep in mind that Traffic Manager will only wait ten seconds to receive a response from the monitoring URL. Therefore, you should ensure that your health verification code executes within this timescale, allowing for network latency for the round trip from Traffic Manager to your application and back again.

> For more information about using Windows Traffic Manager to monitor your applications, see _Windows Azure Traffic Manager_ on MSDN. Traffic Manager is also discussed in Multiple Datacenter Deployment Guidance.

RELATED PATTERNS AND GUIDANCE

The following guidance may also be relevant when implementing this pattern:

- **Instrumentation and Telemetry Guidance**. Checking the health of services and components is typically done by probing, but it is also useful to have the appropriate information in place to monitor application performance and detect events that occur at runtime. This data can be transmitted back to monitoring tools to provide an additional feature for health monitoring. The Instrumentation and Telemetry guidance explores the process of gathering remote diagnostics information that is collected by instrumentation in applications.

MORE INFORMATION

All links in this book are accessible from the book's online bibliography available at: _http://aka.ms/cdpbibliography_.

- Third-party tools _Pingdom_, _Panopta_, _NewRelic_, and _Statuscake_.
- The article _Management Services_ on MSDN.
- The article _Windows Azure Traffic Manager_ on MSDN.

This pattern has a sample application associated with it. You can download the "Cloud Design Patterns – Sample Code" from the Microsoft Download Center at _http://aka.ms/cloud-design-patterns-sample_.

Index Table Pattern

Create indexes over the fields in data stores that are frequently referenced by query criteria. This pattern can improve query performance by allowing applications to more quickly locate the data to retrieve from a data store.

CONTEXT AND PROBLEM

Many data stores organize the data for a collection of entities by using the primary key. An application can use this key to locate and retrieve data. Figure 1 shows an example of a data store holding customer information. The primary key is the Customer ID.

Primary Key (Customer ID)	Customer Data
1	LastName: Smith, Town: Redmond, ...
2	LastName: Jones, Town: Seattle, ...
3	LastName: Robinson, Town: Portland, ...
4	LastName: Brown, Town: Redmond, ...
5	LastName: Smith, Town: Chicago, ...
6	LastName: Green, Town: Redmond, ...
7	LastName: Clarke, Town: Portland, ...
8	LastName: Smith, Town: Redmond, ...
9	LastName: Jones, Town: Chicago, ...
...	...
1000	LastName: Clarke, Town: Chicago, ...
...	...

FIGURE 1
Customer information organized by the primary key (Customer ID)

While the primary key is valuable for queries that fetch data based on the value of this key, an application might not be able to use the primary key if it needs to retrieve data based on some other field. In the Customers example, an application cannot use the Customer ID primary key to retrieve customers if it queries data solely by specifying criteria that reference the value of some other attribute, such as the town in which the customer is located. To perform a query such as this may require the application to fetch and examine every customer record, and this could be a slow process.

Many relational database management systems support secondary indexes. A secondary index is a separate data structure that is organized by one or more non-primary (secondary) key fields, and it indicates where the data for each indexed value is stored. The items in a secondary index are typically sorted by the value of the secondary keys to enable fast lookup of data. These indexes are usually maintained automatically by the database management system.

You can create as many secondary indexes as are required to support the different queries that your application performs. For example, in a Customers table in a relational database where the customer ID is the primary key, it may be beneficial to add a secondary index over the town field if the application frequently looks up customers by the town in which they reside.

However, although secondary indexes are a common feature of relational systems, most NoSQL data stores used by cloud applications do not provide an equivalent feature.

SOLUTION

If the data store does not support secondary indexes, you can emulate them manually by creating your own *index tables*. An index table organizes the data by a specified key. Three strategies are commonly used for structuring an index table, depending on the number of secondary indexes that are required and the nature of the queries that an application performs:

- Duplicate the data in each index table but organize it by different keys (complete denormalization). Figure 2 shows index tables that organize the same customer information by Town and LastName:

Secondary Key (Town)	Customer Data
Chicago	ID: 5, LastName: Smith, Town: Chicago, ...
Chicago	ID: 9, LastName: Jones, Town: Chicago, ...
Chicago	ID: 1000, LastName: Clarke, Town: Chicago, ...
...	...
Portland	ID: 3, LastName: Robinson, Town: Portland, ...
Portland	ID: 7, LastName: Clarke, Town: Portland, ...
Redmond	ID: 1, LastName: Smith, Town: Redmond, ...
Redmond	ID: 4, LastName: Brown, Town: Redmond, ...
Redmond	ID: 6, LastName: Green, Town: Redmond, ...
Redmond	ID: 8, LastName: Smith, Town: Redmond, ...
Seattle	ID: 2, LastName: Jones, Town: Seattle, ...
...	...

Secondary Key (LastName)	Customer Data
Brown	ID: 4, LastName: Brown, Town: Redmond, ...
Clarke	ID: 7, LastName: Clarke, Town: Portland, ...
Clarke	ID: 1000, LastName: Clarke, Town: Chicago, ...
Green	ID: 6, LastName: Green, Town: Redmond, ...
Jones	ID: 2, LastName: Jones, Town: Seattle, ...
Jones	ID: 9, LastName: Jones, Town: Chicago, ...
...	...
Robinson	ID: 3, LastName: Robinson, Town: Portland, ...
Smith	ID: 1, LastName: Smith, Town: Redmond, ...
Smith	ID: 5, LastName: Smith, Town: Chicago, ...
Smith	ID: 8, LastName: Smith, Town: Redmond, ...
...	...

FIGURE 2
Index tables implementing secondary indexes for customer data. The data is duplicated in each index table.

This strategy may be appropriate if the data is relatively static compared to the number of times it is queried by using each key. If the data is more dynamic, the processing overhead of maintaining each index table may become too great for this approach to be useful. Additionally, if the volume of data is very large, the amount of space required to store the duplicate data will be significant.

- Create normalized index tables organized by different keys and reference the original data by using the primary key rather than duplicating it, as shown in Figure 3. The original data is referred to as a *fact table*:

Fact Table

Secondary Key (Town)	Customer Reference (ID)
Chicago	ID: 5
Chicago	ID: 9
Chicago	ID: 1000
...	...
Portland	ID: 3
Portland	ID: 7
Redmond	ID: 1
Redmond	ID: 4
Redmond	ID: 6
Redmond	ID: 8
Seattle	ID: 2
...	...

Index Table

Primary Key (Customer ID)	Customer Data
1	LastName: Smith, Town: Redmond, ...
2	LastName: Jones, Town: Seattle, ...
3	LastName: Robinson, Town: Portland, ...
4	LastName: Brown, Town: Redmond, ...
5	LastName: Smith, Town: Chicago, ...
6	LastName: Green, Town: Redmond, ...
7	LastName: Clarke, Town: Portland, ...
8	LastName: Smith, Town: Redmond, ...
9	LastName: Jones, Town: Chicago, ...
...	...
1000	LastName: Clarke, Town: Chicago, ...
...	...

Index Table

Secondary Key (LastName)	Customer Reference (ID)
Brown	ID: 4
Clarke	ID: 7
Clarke	ID: 1000
Green	ID: 6
Jones	ID: 2
Jones	ID: 9
...	...
Robinson	ID: 3
Smith	ID: 1
Smith	ID: 5
Smith	ID: 8
...	...

FIGURE 3
Index tables implementing secondary indexes for customer data. The data is referenced by each index table.

This technique saves space and reduces the overhead of maintaining duplicate data. The disadvantage is that an application has to perform two lookup operations to find data by using a secondary key (find the primary key for the data in the index table, and then look up the data in the fact table by using the primary key).

- Create partially normalized index tables organized by different keys that duplicate frequently retrieved fields. Reference the original data to access less frequently accessed fields. Figure 4 shows this structure.

Fact Table

Index Table

Secondary Key (Town)	Customer Reference (ID) and commonly queried data
Chicago	ID: 5, LastName: Smith
Chicago	ID: 9, LastName: Jones
Chicago	ID: 1000, LastName: Clarke
...	...
Portland	ID: 3, LastName: Robinson
Portland	ID: 7, LastName: Clarke
Redmond	ID: 1, LastName: Smith
Redmond	ID: 4, LastName: Brown
Redmond	ID: 6, LastName: Green
Redmond	ID: 8, LastName: Smith
Seattle	ID: 2, LastName: Jones
...	...

Primary Key (Customer ID)	Customer Data
1	LastName: Smith, Town: Redmond, ...
2	LastName: Jones, Town: Seattle, ...
3	LastName: Robinson, Town: Portland, ...
4	LastName: Brown, Town: Redmond, ...
5	LastName: Smith, Town: Chicago, ...
6	LastName: Green, Town: Redmond, ...
7	LastName: Clarke, Town: Portland, ...
8	LastName: Smith, Town: Redmond, ...
9	LastName: Jones, Town: Chicago, ...
...	...
1000	LastName: Clarke, Town: Chicago, ...
...	...

Index Table

Secondary Key (LastName)	Customer Reference (ID) and commonly queried data
Brown	ID: 4, Town: Redmond
Clarke	ID: 7, Town: Portland
Clarke	ID: 1000, Town: Chicago
Green	ID: 6, Town: Redmond
Jones	ID: 2, Town: Seattle
Jones	ID: 9, Town: Chicago
...	...
Robinson	ID: 3, Town: Portland
Smith	ID: 1, Town: Redmond
Smith	ID: 5, Town: Chicago
Smith	ID: 8, Town: Redmond
...	...

FIGURE 4
Index tables implementing secondary indexes for customer data. Commonly accessed data is duplicated in each index table.

Using this technique, you can strike a balance between the first two approaches. The data for common queries can be retrieved quickly by using a single lookup, while the space and maintenance overhead is not as great as duplicating the entire data set.

If an application frequently queries data by specifying a combination of values (for example, "Find all customers that live in Redmond and that have a last name of Smith"), you could implement the keys to the items in the index table as a concatenation of the Town attribute and the LastName attribute, as shown in Figure 5. The keys are sorted by Town, and then by LastName for records that have the same value for Town.

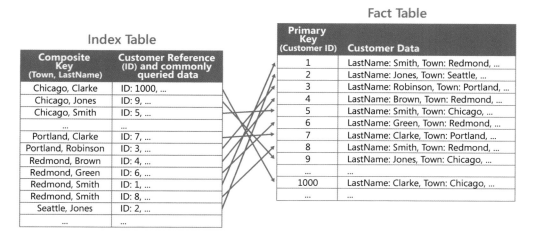

FIGURE 5
An index table based on composite keys

Index tables can speed up query operations over sharded data, and are especially useful where the shard key is hashed. Figure 6 shows an example where the shard key is a hash of the Customer ID. The index table can organize data by the non-hashed value (Town and LastName), and provide the hashed shard key as the lookup data. This can save the application from repeatedly calculating hash keys (which may be an expensive operation) if it needs to retrieve data that falls within a range, or it needs to fetch data in order of the non-hashed key. For example, a query such as "Find all customers that live in Redmond" can be quickly resolved by locating the matching items in the index table (which are all stored in a contiguous block), and then following the references to the customer data by using the shard keys stored in the index table.

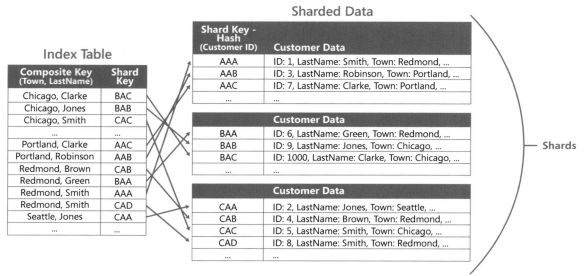

FIGURE 6
An index table providing quick look up for sharded data

Issues and Considerations

Consider the following points when deciding how to implement this pattern:

- The overhead of maintaining secondary indexes can be significant. You must analyze and understand the queries that your application uses. Only create index tables where they are likely to be used regularly. Do not create speculative index tables to support queries that an application does not perform, or that an application performs only very occasionally.

- Duplicating data in an index table can add a significant overhead in terms of storage costs and the effort required to maintain multiple copies of data.

- Implementing an index table as a normalized structure that references the original data may require an application to perform two lookup operations to find data. The first operation searches the index table to retrieve the primary key, and the second uses the primary key to fetch the data.

- If a system incorporates a number of index tables over very large data sets, it can be difficult to maintain consistency between index tables and the original data. It might be possible to design the application around the eventual consistency model. For example, to insert, update, or delete data, an application could post a message to a queue and let a separate task perform the operation and maintain the index tables that reference this data asynchronously. For more information about implementing eventual consistency, see the Data Consistency Primer.

> Windows Azure storage tables support transactional updates for changes made to data held in the same partition (referred to as *entity group transactions*). If you can store the data for a fact table and one or more index tables in the same partition, you may be able to use this feature to help ensure consistency.

- Index tables may themselves be partitioned or sharded.

When to Use this Pattern

Use this pattern to improve query performance when an application frequently needs to retrieve data by using a key other than the primary (or shard) key.

This pattern might not be suitable when:

- Data is volatile. An index table may become out of date very quickly, rendering it ineffective or making the overhead of maintaining the index table greater than any savings made by using it.

- A field selected as the secondary key for an index table is very non-discriminating and can only have a small set of values (for example, gender).

- The balance of the data values for a field selected as the secondary key for an index table are highly skewed. For example, if 90% of the records contain the same value in a field, then creating and maintaining an index table to look up data based on this field may exert more overhead than scanning sequentially through the data. However, if queries very frequently target values that lie in the remaining 10%, this index may be useful. You must understand the queries that your application is performing, and how frequently they are performed.

Example

Windows Azure storage tables provide a highly scalable key/value data store for applications running in the cloud. Applications store and retrieve data values by specifying a key. The data values can contain multiple fields, but the structure of a data item is opaque to table storage, which simply handles a data item as an array of bytes.

Windows Azure storage tables also support sharding. The sharding key comprises two elements, a partition key and a row key. Items that have the same partition key are stored in the same partition (shard), and the items are stored in row key order within a shard. Table storage is optimized for performing range queries that fetch data falling within a contiguous range of row key values within a partition. If you are building cloud applications that store information in Windows Azure tables, you should structure your data with this feature in mind.

For example, consider an application that stores information about movies. The application frequently queries movies by genre (Action, Documentary, Historical, Comedy, Drama, and so on). You could create a Windows Azure table with partitions for each genre by using the genre as the partition key, and specifying the movie name as the row key, as shown in Figure 7.

Partition Key (Genre)	Row Key (Movie Name)	Movie Data
Action	Action Movie 1	Starring Actors: [Fred, Bert], Director: Sid, Date Released 1/1/2013, ...
Action	Action Movie 2	Starring Actors: [Mary, Fred], Director: Harry, Date Released 2/2/2013, ...
Action	Action Movie 3	Starring Actors: [Bill, Ted], Director: Sid, Date Released 3/3/2013, ...
...	...	...

Partition Key (Genre)	Row Key (Movie Name)	Movie Data
Comedy	Comedy Movie 1	Starring Actor: Harry, Director: Sid, Date Released 4/1/2013, ...
Comedy	Comedy Movie 2	Starring Actors: [Alice, Anne], Director: Fred, Date Released 2/1/2013, ...
Comedy	Comedy Movie 3	Starring Actors: [Bert, Bill], Director: Harry, Date Released 3/5/2013, ...
...	...	...

Partition Key (Genre)	Row Key (Movie Name)	Movie Data
Drama	Drama Movie 1	Starring Actor: Keith, Director: Fred, Date Released 1/1/2013, ...
Drama	Drama Movie 2	Starring Actor: Susan, Director: Harry, Date Released 4/5/2013, ...
Drama	Drama Movie 3	Starring Actors: [Keith, Susan], Director: Fred, Date Released 1/8/2013, ...
...	...	...

— Shards

FIGURE 7
Movie data stored in a Windows Azure Table, partitioned by genre and sorted by movie name

This approach is less effective if the application also needs to query movies by starring actor. In this case, you can create a separate Windows Azure table that acts as an index table. The partition key is the actor and the row key is the movie name. The data for each actor will be stored in separate partitions. If a movie stars more than one actor, the same movie will occur in multiple partitions.

You can duplicate the movie data in the values held by each partition by adopting the first approach described in the Solution section above. However, it is likely that each movie will be replicated several times (once for each actor), so it may be more efficient to partially denormalize the data to support the most common queries (such as the names of the other actors) and enable an application to retrieve any remaining details by including the partition key necessary to find the complete information in the genre partitions. This approach is described by the third option in the Solution section. Figure 8 depicts this approach.

Genre can be combined with
the movie name to find the
complete details for each
movie in the genre
partitions

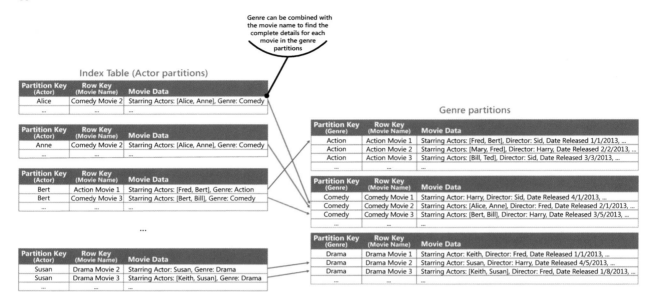

Index Table (Actor partitions)

Partition Key (Actor)	Row Key (Movie Name)	Movie Data
Alice	Comedy Movie 2	Starring Actors: [Alice, Anne], Genre: Comedy
...	...	...

Partition Key (Actor)	Row Key (Movie Name)	Movie Data
Anne	Comedy Movie 2	Starring Actors: [Alice, Anne], Genre: Comedy
...	...	...

Partition Key (Actor)	Row Key (Movie Name)	Movie Data
Bert	Action Movie 1	Starring Actors: [Fred, Bert], Genre: Action
Bert	Comedy Movie 3	Starring Actors: [Bert, Bill], Genre: Comedy
...	...	...

...

Partition Key (Actor)	Row Key (Movie Name)	Movie Data
Susan	Drama Movie 2	Starring Actor: Susan, Genre: Drama
Susan	Drama Movie 3	Starring Actors: [Keith, Susan], Genre: Drama
...	...	...

Genre partitions

Partition Key (Genre)	Row Key (Movie Name)	Movie Data
Action	Action Movie 1	Starring Actors: [Fred, Bert], Director: Sid, Date Released 1/1/2013, ...
Action	Action Movie 2	Starring Actors: [Mary, Fred], Director: Harry, Date Released 2/2/2013, ...
Action	Action Movie 3	Starring Actors: [Bill, Ted], Director: Sid, Date Released 3/3/2013, ...
...	...	...

Partition Key (Genre)	Row Key (Movie Name)	Movie Data
Comedy	Comedy Movie 1	Starring Actor: Harry, Director: Sid, Date Released 4/1/2013, ...
Comedy	Comedy Movie 2	Starring Actors: [Alice, Anne], Director: Fred, Date Released 2/1/2013, ...
Comedy	Comedy Movie 3	Starring Actors: [Bert, Bill], Director: Harry, Date Released 3/5/2013, ...
...	...	...

Partition Key (Genre)	Row Key (Movie Name)	Movie Data
Drama	Drama Movie 1	Starring Actor: Keith, Director: Fred, Date Released 1/1/2013, ...
Drama	Drama Movie 2	Starring Actor: Susan, Director: Harry, Date Released 4/5/2013, ...
Drama	Drama Movie 3	Starring Actors: [Keith, Susan], Director: Fred, Date Released 1/8/2013, ...
...	...	...

FIGURE 8
Actor partitions acting as index tables for movie data

RELATED PATTERNS AND GUIDANCE

The following patterns and guidance may also be relevant when implementing this pattern:

- **Data Consistency Primer**. An index table must be maintained as the data that it indexes changes. In the cloud, it may not be possible or appropriate to perform operations that update an index as part of the same transaction that modifies the data—an eventually consistent approach may be more suitable. This primer provides information on the issues surrounding eventual consistency.

- **Sharding Pattern**. The Index Table pattern is frequently used in conjunction with data partitioned by using shards. The Sharding pattern provides more information on how to divide a data store into a set of shards.

- **Materialized View Pattern**. Instead of indexing data to support queries that summarize data, it may be more appropriate to create a materialized view of the data. This pattern describes how to support efficient summary queries by generating pre-populated views over data.

Leader Election Pattern

Coordinate the actions performed by a collection of collaborating task instances in a distributed application by electing one instance as the leader that assumes responsibility for managing the other instances. This pattern can help to ensure that task instances do not conflict with each other, cause contention for shared resources, or inadvertently interfere with the work that other task instances are performing.

Context and Problem

A typical cloud application consists of many tasks acting in a coordinated manner. These tasks could all be instances running the same code and requiring access to the same resources, or they might be working together in parallel to perform the individual parts of a complex calculation.

The task instances might run autonomously for much of the time, but it may also be necessary to coordinate the actions of each instance to ensure that they don't conflict, cause contention for shared resources, or inadvertently interfere with the work that other task instances are performing. For example:

- In a cloud-based system that implements horizontal scaling, multiple instances of the same task could be running simultaneously with each instance servicing a different user. If these instances write to a shared resource, it may be necessary to coordinate their actions to prevent each instance from blindly overwriting the changes made by the others.
- If the tasks are performing individual elements of a complex calculation in parallel, the results will need to be aggregated when they all complete.

Because the task instances are all peers, there is no natural leader that can act as the coordinator or aggregator.

Solution

A single task instance should be elected to act as the leader, and this instance should coordinate the actions of the other subordinate task instances. If all of the task instances are running the same code, they could all be capable of acting as the leader. Therefore, the election process must be managed carefully to prevent two or more instances taking over the leader role at the same time.

The system must provide a robust mechanism for selecting the leader. This mechanism must be able to cope with events such as network outages or process failures. In many solutions, the subordinate task instances monitor the leader through some type of heartbeat mechanism, or by polling. If the designated leader terminates unexpectedly, or a network failure renders the leader inaccessible by the subordinate task instances, it will be necessary for them to elect a new leader.

There are several strategies available for electing a leader amongst a set of tasks in a distributed environment, including:

- Selecting the task instance with the lowest-ranked instance or process ID.
- Racing to obtain a shared distributed mutex. The first task instance that acquires the mutex is the leader. However, the system must ensure that, if the leader terminates or becomes disconnected from the rest of the system, the mutex is released to allow another task instance to become the leader.
- Implementing one of the common leader election algorithms such as the _Bully Algorithm_ or the _Ring Algorithm_. These algorithms are relatively straightforward, but there are also a number of more sophisticated techniques available. These algorithms assume that each candidate participating in the election has a unique ID, and that they can communicate with the other candidates in a reliable manner.

ISSUES AND CONSIDERATIONS

Consider the following points when deciding how to implement this pattern:

- The process of electing a leader should be resilient to transient and persistent failures.
- It must be possible to detect when the leader has failed or has become otherwise unavailable (perhaps due to a communications failure). The speed at which such detection is required will be system dependent. Some systems may be able to function for a short while without a leader, during which time a transient fault that caused the leader to become unavailable may have been rectified. In other cases, it may be necessary to detect leader failure immediately and trigger a new election.
- In a system that implements horizontal autoscaling, the leader could be terminated if the system scales back and shuts down some of the computing resources.
- Using a shared distributed mutex introduces a dependency on the availability of the external service that provides the mutex. This service may constitute a single point of failure. If this service should become unavailable for any reason, the system will not be able to elect a leader.
- Using a single dedicated process as the leader is a relatively straightforward approach. However, if the process fails there may be a significant delay while it is restarted, and the resultant latency may affect the performance and response times of other processes if they are waiting for the leader to coordinate an operation.
- Implementing one of the leader election algorithms manually provides the greatest flexibility for tuning and optimizing the code.

WHEN TO USE THIS PATTERN

Use this pattern when the tasks in a distributed application, such as a cloud-hosted solution, require careful coordination and there is no natural leader.

> Avoid making the leader a bottleneck in the system. The purpose of the leader is to coordinate the work performed by the subordinate tasks, and it does not necessarily have to participate in this work itself—although it should be capable of doing so if the task is not elected as the leader.

This pattern might not be suitable:

- If there is a natural leader or dedicated process that can always act as the leader. For example, it may be possible to implement a singleton process that coordinates the task instances. If this process fails or becomes unhealthy, the system can shut it down and restart it.
- If the coordination between tasks can be easily achieved by using a more lightweight mechanism. For example, if several task instances simply require coordinated access to a shared resource, a preferable solution might be to use optimistic or pessimistic locking to control access to that resource.
- If a third-party solution is more appropriate. For example, the Windows Azure HDInsight service (based on Apache Hadoop) uses the services provided by Apache Zookeeper to coordinate the map/reduce tasks that aggregate and summarize data. It's also possible to install and configure Zookeeper

on a Windows Azure Virtual Machine and integrate it into your own solutions, or use the Zookeeper prebuilt virtual machine image available from Microsoft Open Technologies. For more information, see *Apache Zookeeper on Windows Azure* on the Microsoft Open Technologies website.

EXAMPLE

The **DistributedMutex** project in the **LeaderElection** solution included in the sample code available for this guide shows how to use a lease on a Windows Azure storage blob to provide a mechanism for implementing a shared distributed mutex. This mutex can be used to elect a leader amongst a group of role instances in a Windows Azure cloud service. The first role instance to acquire the lease is elected the leader, and remains the leader until it releases the lease or until it is unable to renew the lease. Other role instances can continue to monitor the blob lease in the event that the leader is no longer available.

A blob lease is an exclusive write lock over a blob. A single blob can be the subject of a maximum of one lease at any one point in time. A role instance can request a lease over a specified blob, and it will be granted the lease if no other lease over the same blob is currently held by this or any other role instance, otherwise the request will throw an exception.

To reduce the possibility that a faulted role instance retains the lease indefinitely, specify a lifetime for the lease. When this expires, the lease becomes available. However, while a role instance holds the lease it can request that the lease is renewed, and it will be granted the lease for a further period of time. The role instance can continually repeat this process if it wishes to retain the lease.

For more information on how to lease a blob, see *Lease Blob (REST API)* on MSDN.

The **BlobDistributedMutex** class in the example contains the **RunTaskWhenMutexAquired** method that enables a role instance to attempt to obtain a lease over a specified blob. The details of the blob (the name, container, and storage account) are passed to the constructor in a **BlobSettings** object when the **BlobDistributed-Mutex** object is created (this object is a simple struct that is included in the sample code). The constructor also accepts a **Task** that references the code that the role instance should run if it successfully acquires the lease over the blob and is elected the leader. Note that the code that handles the low-level details of obtaining the lease is implemented in a separate helper class named **BlobLeaseManager**.

```C#
public class BlobDistributedMutex
{
  ...
  private readonly BlobSettings blobSettings;
  private readonly Func<CancellationToken, Task> taskToRunWhenLeaseAcquired;
  ...

  public BlobDistributedMutex(BlobSettings blobSettings,
          Func<CancellationToken, Task> taskToRunWhenLeaseAquired)
  {
    this.blobSettings = blobSettings;
    this.taskToRunWhenLeaseAquired = taskToRunWhenLeaseAquired;
  }

  public async Task RunTaskWhenMutexAcquired(CancellationToken token)
  {
    var leaseManager = new BlobLeaseManager(blobSettings);
    await this.RunTaskWhenBlobLeaseAcquired(leaseManager, token);
  }
  ...
```

The **RunTaskWhenMutexAquired** method in the code sample above invokes the **RunTaskWhenBlobLease-Acquired** method shown in the following code sample to actually acquire the lease. The **RunTaskWhen-BlobLeaseAcquired** method runs asynchronously. If the lease is successfully acquired, the role instance has been elected the leader. The purpose of the **taskToRunWhenLeaseAcquired** delegate is to perform the work that coordinates the other role instances. If the lease is not acquired, another role instance has been elected as the leader and the current role instance remains a subordinate. Note that the **TryAcquireLeaseOrWait** method is a helper method that uses the **BlobLeaseManager** object to obtain the lease.

```csharp
C#
...
    private async Task RunTaskWhenBlobLeaseAcquired(
        BlobLeaseManager leaseManager, CancellationToken token)
    {
        while (!token.IsCancellationRequested)
        {
            // Try to acquire the blob lease.
            // Otherwise wait for a short time before trying again.
            string leaseId = await this.TryAquireLeaseOrWait(leaseManager, token);

            if (!string.IsNullOrEmpty(leaseId))
            {
                // Create a new linked cancellation token source so that if either the
                // original token is cancelled or the lease cannot be renewed, the
                // leader task can be cancelled.
                using (var leaseCts =
                    CancellationTokenSource.CreateLinkedTokenSource(new[] { token }))
                {
                    // Run the leader task.
                    var leaderTask = this.taskToRunWhenLeaseAquired.Invoke(leaseCts.Token);
                    ...
                }
            }
        }
    }
...
```

The task started by the leader also executes asynchronously. While this task is running, the **RunTaskWhen-BlobLeaseAquired** method shown in the following code sample periodically attempts to renew the lease. This action helps to ensure that the role instance remains the leader. In the sample solution, the delay between renewal requests is less than the time specified for the duration of the lease in order to prevent another role instance from being elected the leader. If the renewal fails for any reason, the task is cancelled.

If the lease fails to be renewed or the task is cancelled (possibly as a result of the role instance shutting down), the lease is released. At this point, this or another role instance might be elected as the leader. The code extract below shows this part of the process.

```C#
...
  private async Task RunTaskWhenBlobLeaseAcquired(
    BlobLeaseManager leaseManager, CancellationToken token)
  {
    while (...)
    {
      ...
      if (...)
      {
        ...
        using (var leaseCts = ...)
        {
          ...
          // Keep renewing the lease in regular intervals.
          // If the lease cannot be renewed, then the task completes.
          var renewLeaseTask =
            this.KeepRenewingLease(leaseManager, leaseId, leaseCts.Token);

          // When any task completes (either the leader task itself or when it could
          // not renew the lease) then cancel the other task.
          await CancelAllWhenAnyCompletes(leaderTask, renewLeaseTask, leaseCts);
        }
      }
    }
    ...
  }
```

The **KeepRenewingLease** method is another helper method that uses the **BlobLeaseManager** object to renew the lease. The **CancelAllWhenAnyCompletes** method cancels the tasks specified as the first two parameters.

Figure 1 illustrates the functions of the **BlobDistributedMutex** class.

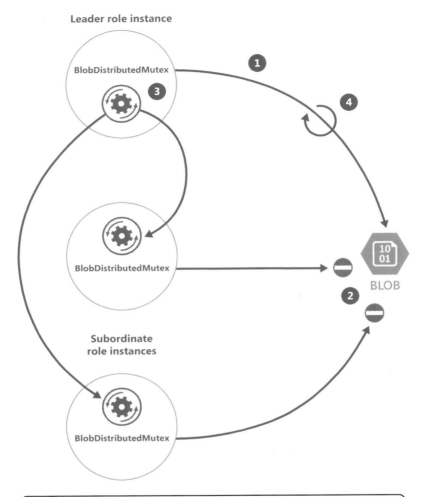

Leader role instance

BlobDistributedMutex

**Subordinate
role instances**

BlobDistributedMutex

BlobDistributedMutex

BlobDistributedMutex

BLOB

1: A role instance calls the *RunTaskWhenMutexAcquired* method of a
   BlobDistibutedMutex object and is granted the lease over the blob.
   The role instance is elected the leader.
2: Other role instances call the *RunTaskWhenMutexAcquired* method
   and are blocked.
3: The *RunTaskWhenMutexAcquired* method in the leader runs a task
   that coordinates the work of the subordinate role instances.
4: The *RunTaskWhenMutexAcquired* method in the leader periodically
   renews the lease.

FIGURE 1
Using the BlobDistributedMutex class to elect a leader and run a task that coordinates operations

The following code example shows how to use the **BlobDistributedMutex** class in a worker role. This code
obtains a lease over a blob named **MyLeaderCoordinatorTask** in the **leases** container in development storage,
and specifies that the code defined in the **MyLeaderCoordinatorTask** method should run if the role instance
is elected the leader.

```csharp
C#
var settings = new BlobSettings(CloudStorageAccount.DevelopmentStorageAccount,
  "leases", "MyLeaderCoordinatorTask");
var cts = new CancellationTokenSource();
var mutex = new BlobDistributedMutex(settings, MyLeaderCoordinatorTask);
mutex.RunTaskWhenMutexAcquired(this.cts.Token);
...

// Method that runs if the role instance is elected the leader
private static async Task MyLeaderCoordinatorTask(CancellationToken token)
{
  ...
}
```

Note the following points about the sample solution:

- The blob is a potential single point of failure. If the blob service becomes unavailable, or the blob is inaccessible, the leader will be unable to renew the lease and no other role instance will be able to obtain the lease. In this case, no role instance will be able to act as the leader. However, the blob service is designed to be resilient, so complete failure of the blob service is considered to be extremely unlikely.
- If the task being performed by the leader stalls, the leader might continue to renew the lease, preventing any other role instance from obtaining the lease and taking over the leader role in order to coordinate tasks. In the real world, the health of the leader should be checked at frequent intervals.
- The election process is non-deterministic. You cannot make any assumptions about which role instance will obtain the blob lease and become the leader.
- The blob used as the target of the blob lease should not be used for any other purpose. If a role instance attempts to store data in this blob, this data will not be accessible unless the role instance is the leader and holds the blob lease.

RELATED PATTERNS AND GUIDANCE

The following guidance may also be relevant when implementing this pattern:

- **Autoscaling Guidance**. It may be possible to start and stop instances of the task hosts as the load on the application varies. Autoscaling can help to maintain throughput and performance during times of peak processing.
- **Compute Partitioning Guidance**. This guidance describes how to allocate tasks to hosts in a cloud service in a way that helps to minimize running costs while maintaining the scalability, performance, availability, and security of the service.

MORE INFORMATION

All links in this book are accessible from the book's online bibliography available at:
http://aka.ms/cdpbibliography.

- The *Task-based Asynchronous Pattern* on MSDN.
- An example illustrating the *Bully Algorithm*.
- An example illustrating the *Ring Algorithm*.
- The article *Apache Zookeeper on Windows Azure* on the Microsoft Open Technologies website.
- The article *Lease Blob (REST API)* on MSDN.

This pattern has a sample application associated with it. You can download the "Cloud Design Patterns – Sample Code" from the Microsoft Download Center at *http://aka.ms/cloud-design-patterns-sample*.

Materialized View Pattern

Generate prepopulated views over the data in one or more data stores when the data is formatted in a way that does not favor the required query operations. This pattern can help to support efficient querying and data extraction, and improve application performance.

CONTEXT AND PROBLEM

When storing data, the priority for developers and data administrators is often focused on how the data is stored, as opposed to how it is read. The chosen storage format is usually closely related to the format of the data, requirements for managing data size and data integrity, and the kind of store in use. For example, when using NoSQL Document store, the data is often represented as a series of aggregates, each of which contains all of the information for that entity.

However, this may have a negative effect on queries. When a query requires only a subset of the data from some entities, such as a summary of orders for several customers without all of the order details, it must extract all of the data for the relevant entities in order to obtain the required information.

SOLUTION

To support efficient querying, a common solution is to generate, in advance, a view that materializes the data in a format most suited to the required results set. The Materialized View pattern describes generating prepopulated views of data in environments where the source data is not in a format that is suitable for querying, where generating a suitable query is difficult, or where query performance is poor due to the nature of the data or the data store.

These materialized views, which contain only data required by a query, allow applications to quickly obtain the information they need. In addition to joining tables or combining data entities, materialized views may include the current values of calculated columns or data items, the results of combining values or executing transformations on the data items, and values specified as part of the query. A materialized view may even be optimized for just a single query.

A key point is that a materialized view and the data it contains is completely disposable because it can be entirely rebuilt from the source data stores. A materialized view is never updated directly by an application, and so it is effectively a specialized cache.

When the source data for the view changes, the view must be updated to include the new information. This may occur automatically on an appropriate schedule, or when the system detects a change to the original data. In other cases it may be necessary to regenerate the view manually.

Figure 1 shows an example of how the Materialized View pattern might be used.

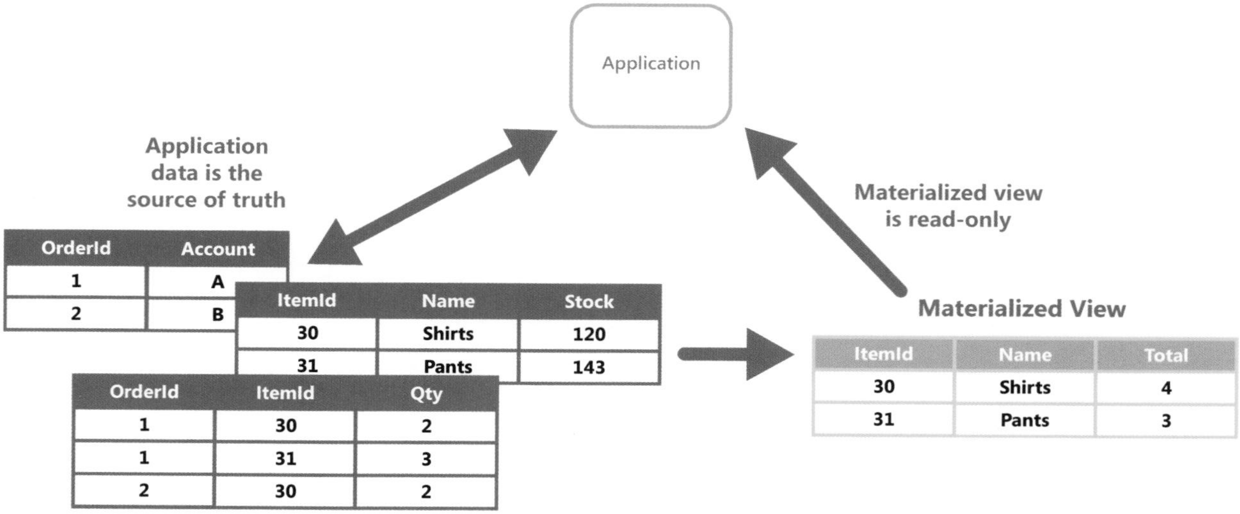

FIGURE 1
The Materialized View pattern

ISSUES AND CONSIDERATIONS

Consider the following points when deciding how to implement this pattern:

- Consider how and when the view will be updated. Ideally it will be regenerated in response to an event indicating a change to the source data, although in some circumstances this may lead to excessive overheads if the source data changes rapidly. Alternatively, consider using a scheduled task, an external trigger, or a manual action to initiate regeneration of the view.

- In some systems, such as when using the Event Sourcing Pattern to maintain a store of only the events that modified the data, materialized views may be necessary. Prepopulating views by examining all events to determine the current state may be the only way to obtain information from the event store. In cases other than when using Event Sourcing it is necessary to gauge the advantages that a materialized view may offer. Materialized views tend to be specifically tailored to one, or a small number of queries. If many queries must be used, maintaining materialized views may result in unacceptable storage capacity requirements and storage cost.

- Consider the impact on data consistency when generating the view, and when updating the view if this occurs on a schedule. If the source data is changing at the point when the view is generated, the copy of the data in the view may not be fully consistent with the original data.

- Consider where you will store the view. The view does not have to be located in the same store or partition as the original data. It could be a subsets from a few different partitions combined.

- If the view is transient and is used only to improve query performance by reflecting the current state of the data, or to improve scalability, it may be stored in cache or in a less reliable location. It can be rebuilt if lost.
- When defining a materialized view, maximize its value by adding data items or columns to the view based on computation or transformation of existing data items, on values passed in the query, or on combinations of these values where this is appropriate.
- Where the storage mechanism supports it, consider indexing the materialized view to further maximize performance. Most relational databases support indexing for views, as do Big Data solutions based on Apache Hadoop.

WHEN TO USE THIS PATTERN

This pattern is ideally suited for:

- Creating materialized views over data that is difficult to query directly, or where queries must be very complex in order to extract data that is stored in a normalized, semi-structured, or unstructured way.
- Creating temporary views that can dramatically improve query performance, or can act directly as source views or data transfer objects (DTOs) for the UI, for reporting, or for display.
- Supporting occasionally connected or disconnected scenarios where connection to the data store is not always available. The view may be cached locally in this case.
- Simplifying queries and exposing data for experimentation in a way that does not require knowledge of the source data format. For example, by joining different tables in one or more databases, or one or more domains in NoSQL stores, and then formatting the data to suit its eventual use.
- Providing access to specific subsets of the source data that, for security or privacy reasons, should not be generally accessible, open to modification, or fully exposed to users.
- Bridging the disjoint when using different data stores based on their individual capabilities. For example, by using a cloud store that is efficient for writing as the reference data store, and a relational database that offers good query and read performance to hold the materialized views.

This pattern might not be suitable in the following situations:

- The source data is simple and easy to query.
- The source data changes very quickly, or can be accessed without using a view. The processing overhead of creating views may be avoidable in these cases.
- Consistency is a high priority. The views may not always be fully consistent with the original data.

EXAMPLE

Figure 2 shows an example of using the Materialized View pattern. Data in the Order, OrderItem, and Customer tables in separate partitions in a Windows Azure storage account are combined to generate a view containing the total sales value for each product in the Electronics category, together with a count of the number of customers who made purchases of each item.

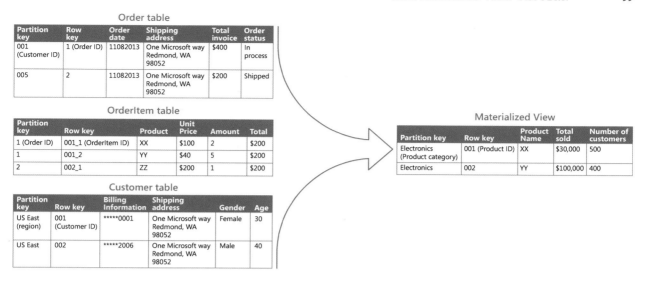

FIGURE 2
Using the Materialized View pattern to generate a summary of sales

Creating this materialized view requires complex queries. However, by exposing the query result as material-ized view, users can easily obtain the results and use them directly or incorporate them in another query. The view is likely to be used in a reporting system or dashboard, and so can be updated on a scheduled basis such as weekly.

Although this example utilizes Windows Azure table storage, many relational database management systems also provide native support for materialized views.

RELATED PATTERNS AND GUIDANCE

The following patterns and guidance may also be relevant when implementing this pattern:

- **Data Consistency Primer**. It is necessary to maintain the summary information held in a materialized view so that it reflects the underlying data values. As the data values change, it may not be feasible to update the summary data in real time, and instead an eventually consistent approach must be adopted. The Data Consistency Primer summarizes the issues surrounding maintaining consistency over distrib-uted data, and describes the benefits and tradeoffs of different consistency models.

- **Command and Query Responsibility Segregation (CQRS) Pattern**. You may be able to use this pat-tern to update the information in a materialized view by responding to events that occur when the un-derlying data values change.

- **Event Sourcing Pattern**. You can use this pattern in conjunction with the CQRS pattern to maintain the information in a materialized view. When the data values on which a materialized view is based are modified, the system can raise events that describe these modifications and save them in an event store.

- **Index Table Pattern**. The data in a materialized view is typically organized by a primary key, but que-ries may need to retrieve information from this view by examining data in other fields. You can use the Index Table Pattern to create secondary indexes over data sets for data stores that do not support na-tive secondary indexes.

Pipes and Filters Pattern

Decompose a task that performs complex processing into a series of discrete elements that can be reused. This pattern can improve performance, scalability, and reusability by allowing task elements that perform the processing to be deployed and scaled independently.

CONTEXT AND PROBLEM

An application may be required to perform a variety of tasks of varying complexity on the information that it processes. A straightforward but inflexible approach to implementing this application could be to perform this processing as monolithic module. However, this approach is likely to reduce the opportunities for refactoring the code, optimizing it, or reusing it if parts of the same processing are required elsewhere within the application.

Figure 1 illustrates the issues with processing data by using the monolithic approach. An application receives and processes data from two sources. The data from each source is processed by a separate module that performs a series of tasks to transform this data, before passing the result to the business logic of the application.

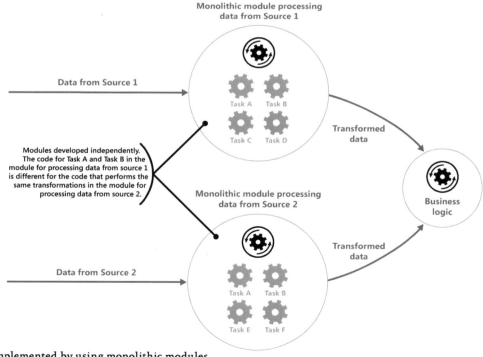

FIGURE 1
A solution implemented by using monolithic modules

100

Some of the tasks that the monolithic modules perform are functionally very similar, but the modules have been designed separately. The code that implements the tasks is closely coupled within a module, and this code has been developed with little or no thought given to reuse or scalability.

However, the processing tasks performed by each module, or the deployment requirements for each task, could change as business requirements are amended. Some tasks might be compute-intensive and could benefit from running on powerful hardware, while others might not require such expensive resources. Furthermore, additional processing might be required in the future, or the order in which the tasks performed by the processing could change. A solution is required that addresses these issues, and increases the possibilities for code reuse.

Solution

Decompose the processing required for each stream into a set of discrete components (or *filters*), each of which performs a single task. By standardizing the format of the data that each component receives and emits, these filters can be combined together into a pipeline. This helps to avoid duplicating code, and makes it easy to remove, replace, or integrate additional components if the processing requirements change. Figure 2 shows an example of this structure.

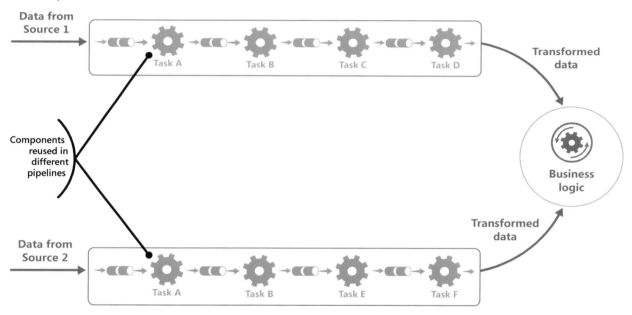

FIGURE 2
A solution implemented by using pipes and filters

The time taken to process a single request depends on the speed of the slowest filter in the pipeline. It is possible that one or more filters could prove to be a bottleneck, especially if a large number of requests appear in a stream from a particular data source. A key advantage of the pipeline structure is that it provides opportunities for running parallel instances of slow filters, enabling the system to spread the load and improve throughput.

The filters that comprise a pipeline can run on different machines, enabling them to be scaled independently and can take advantage of the elasticity that many cloud environments provide. A filter that is computationally intensive can run on high performance hardware, while other less demanding filters can be hosted on commodity (cheaper) hardware. The filters do not even have to be in the same data center or geographical location, which allows each element in a pipeline to run in an environment that is close to the resources it requires.

Figure 3 shows an example applied to the pipeline for the data from Source 1.

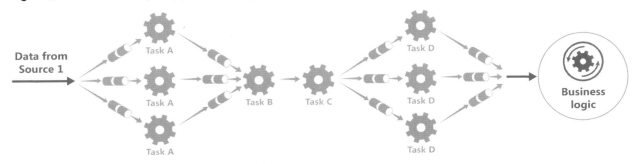

FIGURE 3
Load-balancing components in a pipeline

If the input and output of a filter are structured as a stream, it may be possible to perform the processing for each filter in parallel. The first filter in the pipeline can commence its work and start to emit its results, which are passed directly on to the next filter in the sequence before the first filter has completed its work.

Another benefit is the resiliency that this model can provide. If a filter fails or the machine it is running on is no longer available, the pipeline may be able to reschedule the work the filter was performing and direct this work to another instance of the component. Failure of a single filter does not necessarily result in failure of the entire pipeline.

Using the Pipes and Filters pattern in conjunction with the Compensating Transaction Pattern can provide an alternative approach to implementing distributed transactions. A distributed transaction can be broken down into separate compensable tasks, each of which can be implemented by using a filter that also implements the Compensating Transaction pattern. The filters in a pipeline can be implemented as separate hosted tasks running close to the data that they maintain.

ISSUES AND CONSIDERATIONS

You should consider the following points when deciding how to implement this pattern:

- **Complexity**. The increased flexibility that this pattern provides can also introduce complexity, especially if the filters in a pipeline are distributed across different servers.
- **Reliability**. Use an infrastructure that ensures data flowing between filters in a pipeline will not be lost.
- **Idempotency**. If a filter in a pipeline fails after receiving a message and the work is rescheduled to another instance of the filter, part of the work may have already been completed. If this work updates some aspect of the global state (such as information stored in a database), the same update could be repeated. A similar issue might arise if a filter fails after posting its results to the next filter in the pipeline, but before indicating that it has completed its work successfully. In these cases, the same work could be repeated by another instance of the filter, causing the same results to be posted twice. This could result in subsequent filters in the pipeline processing the same data twice. Therefore filters in a pipeline should be designed to be idempotent. For more information see _Idempotency Patterns_ on Jonathan Oliver's blog.
- **Repeated messages**. If a filter in a pipeline fails after posting a message to the next stage of the pipeline, another instance of the filter may be run (as described by the idempotency consideration above), and it will post a copy of the same message to the pipeline. This could cause two instances of the same message to be passed to the next filter. To avoid this, the pipeline should detect and eliminate duplicate messages.

> If you are implementing the pipeline by using message queues (such as Windows Azure Service Bus queues), the message queuing infrastructure may provide automatic duplicate message detection and removal.

- **Context and state**. In a pipeline, each filter essentially runs in isolation and should not make any assumptions about how it was invoked. This means that each filter must be provided with sufficient context with which it can perform its work. This context may comprise a considerable amount of state information.

WHEN TO USE THIS PATTERN

Use this pattern when:

- The processing required by an application can easily be decomposed into a set of discrete, independent steps.
- The processing steps performed by an application have different scalability requirements.

> It may be possible to group filters that should scale together in the same process. For more information, see the Compute Resource Consolidation Pattern.

- Flexibility is required to allow reordering of the processing steps performed by an application, or the capability to add and remove steps.
- The system can benefit from distributing the processing for steps across different servers.
- A reliable solution is required that minimizes the effects of failure in a step while data is being processed.

This pattern might not be suitable when:

- The processing steps performed by an application are not independent, or they must be performed together as part of the same transaction.
- The amount of context or state information required by a step makes this approach inefficient. It may be possible to persist state information to a database instead, but do not use this strategy if the additional load on the database causes excessive contention.

EXAMPLE

You can use a sequence of message queues to provide the infrastructure required to implement a pipeline. An initial message queue receives unprocessed messages. A component implemented as a filter task listens for a message on this queue, performs its work, and then posts the transformed message to the next queue in the sequence. Another filter task can listen for messages on this queue, process them, post the results to another queue, and so on until the fully transformed data appears in the final message in the queue.

FIGURE 4
Implementing a pipeline by using message queues

If you are building a solution on Windows Azure you can use Service Bus queues to provide a reliable and scalable queuing mechanism. The **ServiceBusPipeFilter** class shown below provides an example. It demonstrates how you can implement a filter that receives input messages from a queue, processes these messages, and posts the results to another queue.

The **ServiceBusPipeFilter** class is defined in the PipesAndFilters.Shared project in the PipesAndFilters solution. This sample code is available is available for download with this guidance.

```csharp
C#
public class ServiceBusPipeFilter
{
  ...
  private readonly string inQueuePath;
  private readonly string outQueuePath;
  ...
  private QueueClient inQueue;
  private QueueClient outQueue;
  ...

  public ServiceBusPipeFilter(..., string inQueuePath, string outQueuePath = null)
  {
     ...
     this.inQueuePath = inQueuePath;
     this.outQueuePath = outQueuePath;
  }

  public void Start()
  {
    ...
    // Create the outbound filter queue if it does not exist.
    ...
    this.outQueue = QueueClient.CreateFromConnectionString(...);

    ...
    // Create the inbound and outbound queue clients.
    this.inQueue = QueueClient.CreateFromConnectionString(...);
  }

  public void OnPipeFilterMessageAsync(
    Func<BrokeredMessage, Task<BrokeredMessage>> asyncFilterTask, ...)
  {
    ...

    this.inQueue.OnMessageAsync(
      async (msg) =>
    {
      ...
      // Process the filter and send the output to the
      // next queue in the pipeline.
      var outMessage = await asyncFilterTask(msg);

      // Send the message from the filter processor
      // to the next queue in the pipeline.
      if (outQueue != null)
      {
        await outQueue.SendAsync(outMessage);
      }
```

```
          // Note: There is a chance that the same message could be sent twice
          // or that a message may be processed by an upstream or downstream
          // filter at the same time.
          // This would happen in a situation where processing of a message was
          // completed, it was sent to the next pipe/queue, and then failed
          // to complete when using the PeekLock method.
          // Idempotent message processing and concurrency should be considered
          // in a real-world implementation.
        },
      options);
    }

    public async Task Close(TimeSpan timespan)
    {
      // Pause the processing threads.
      this.pauseProcessingEvent.Reset();

      // There is no clean approach for waiting for the threads to complete
      // the processing. This example simply stops any new processing, waits
      // for the existing thread to complete, then closes the message pump
      // and finally returns.
      Thread.Sleep(timespan);

      this.inQueue.Close();
      ...
    }

    ...
}
```

The **Start** method in the **ServiceBusPipeFilter** class connects to a pair of input and output queues, and the **Close** method disconnects from the input queue. The **OnPipeFilterMessageAsync** method performs the actual processing of messages; the **asyncFilterTask** parameter to this method specifies the processing to be performed. The **OnPipeFilterMessageAsync** method waits for incoming messages on the input queue, runs the code specified by the **asyncFilterTask** parameter over each messages as it arrives, and posts the results to the output queue. The queues themselves are specified by the constructor.

The sample solution implements filters in a set of worker roles. Each worker role can be scaled independently, depending on the complexity of the business processing that it performs or the resources that it requires to perform this processing. Additionally, multiple instances of each worker role can be run in parallel to improve throughput.

The following code shows a Windows Azure worker role named **PipeFilterARoleEntry**, which is defined in the **PipeFilterA** project in the sample solution.

```csharp
C#
public class PipeFilterARoleEntry : RoleEntryPoint
{
  ...
  private ServiceBusPipeFilter pipeFilterA;

  public override bool OnStart()
  {
    ...
    this.pipeFilterA = new ServiceBusPipeFilter(
      ...,
      Constants.QueueAPath,
      Constants.QueueBPath);

    this.pipeFilterA.Start();
    ...
  }

  public override void Run()
  {
    this.pipeFilterA.OnPipeFilterMessageAsync(async (msg) =>
    {
      // Clone the message and update it.
      // Properties set by the broker (Deliver count, enqueue time, ...)
      // are not cloned and must be copied over if required.
      var newMsg = msg.Clone();

      await Task.Delay(500); // DOING WORK

      Trace.TraceInformation("Filter A processed message:{0} at {1}",
        msg.MessageId, DateTime.UtcNow);

      newMsg.Properties.Add(Constants.FilterAMessageKey, "Complete");

      return newMsg;
    });

    ...
  }

  ...
}
```

This role contains a **ServiceBusPipeFilter** object. The **OnStart** method in the role connects to the queues for receiving input messages and posting output messages (the names of the queues are defined in the **Constants** class). The **Run** method invokes the **OnPipeFilterMessagesAsync** method to perform some processing on each message that is received (in this example, the processing is simulated by waiting for a short period of time). When processing is complete, a new message is constructed containing the results (in this case, the input message is simply augmented with a custom property), and this message is posted to the output queue.

The sample code contains another worker role named **PipeFilterBRoleEntry** in the **PipeFilterB** project. This role is similar to **PipeFilterARoleEntry** except that it performs different processing in the **Run** method. In the example solution, these two roles are combined to construct a pipeline; the output queue for the **PipeFilterARoleEntry** role is the input queue for the **PipeFilterBRoleEntry** role.

The sample solution also provides two further roles named **InitialSenderRoleEntry** (in the InitialSender project) and **FinalReceiverRoleEntry** (in the FinalReceiver project). The **InitialSenderRoleEntry** role provides the initial message in the pipeline. The **OnStart** method connects to a single queue and the **Run** method posts a method to this queue. This queue is the input queue used by the **PipeFilterARoleEntry** role, so posting a message to this queue causes the message to be received and processed by the **PipeFilterARoleEntry** role. The processed message then passes through the **PipeFilterBRoleEntry** role.

The input queue for the **FinalReceiveRoleEntry** role is the output queue for the **PipeFilterBRoleEntry** role. The **Run** method in the **FinalReceiveRoleEntry** role, shown below, receives the message and performs some final processing. Then it writes the values of the custom properties added by the filters in the pipeline to the trace output.

```csharp
public class FinalReceiverRoleEntry : RoleEntryPoint
{
  ...
  // Final queue/pipe in the pipeline from which to process data.
  private ServiceBusPipeFilter queueFinal;

  public override bool OnStart()
  {
    ...
    // Set up the queue.
    this.queueFinal = new ServiceBusPipeFilter(...,Constants.QueueFinalPath);
    this.queueFinal.Start();
    ...
  }

  public override void Run()
  {
    this.queueFinal.OnPipeFilterMessageAsync(
      async (msg) =>
      {
        await Task.Delay(500); // DOING WORK

        // The pipeline message was received.
        Trace.TraceInformation(
          "Pipeline Message Complete - FilterA:{0} FilterB:{1}",
          msg.Properties[Constants.FilterAMessageKey],
          msg.Properties[Constants.FilterBMessageKey]);

        return null;
      });
    ...
  }
  ...
}
```

RELATED PATTERNS AND GUIDANCE

The following patterns and guidance may also be relevant when implementing this pattern:

- **Competing Consumers Pattern**. A pipeline can contain multiple instances of one or more filters. This approach is useful for running parallel instances of slow filters, enabling the system to spread the load and improve throughput. Each instance of a filter will compete for input with the other instances; two instances of a filter should not be able to process the same data. The Competing Consumers pattern provides more information on this approach.

- **Compute Resource Consolidation Pattern**. It may be possible to group filters that should scale together into the same process. The Compute Resource Consolidation pattern provides more information about the benefits and tradeoffs of this strategy.

- **Compensating Transaction Pattern**. A filter can be implemented as an operation that can be reversed, or that has a compensating operation that restores the state to a previous version in the event of a failure. The Compensating Transaction pattern explains how this type of operation may be implemented in order to maintain or achieve eventual consistency.

MORE INFORMATION

All links in this book are accessible from the book's online bibliography available at: *http://aka.ms/cdpbibliography*.

- The article *Idempotency Patterns* on Jonathan Oliver's blog.

This pattern has a sample application associated with it. You can download the "Cloud Design Patterns – Sample Code" from the Microsoft Download Center at *http://aka.ms/cloud-design-patterns-sample*.

Priority Queue Pattern

Prioritize requests sent to services so that requests with a higher priority are received and processed more quickly than those of a lower priority. This pattern is useful in applications that offer different service level guarantees to individual clients.

CONTEXT AND PROBLEM

Applications may delegate specific tasks to other services; for example, to perform background processing or to integrate with other applications or services. In the cloud, a message queue is typically used to delegate tasks to background processing. In many cases the order in which requests are received by a service is not important. However, in some cases it may be necessary to prioritize specific requests. These requests should be processed earlier than others of a lower priority that may have been sent previously by the application.

SOLUTION

A queue is usually a first-in, first-out (FIFO) structure, and consumers typically receive messages in the same order that they were posted to the queue. However, some message queues support priority messaging; the application posting a message can assign a priority to a message and the messages in the queue are automatically reordered so that messages with a higher priority will be received before those of a lower priority. Figure 1 illustrates a queue that provides priority messaging.

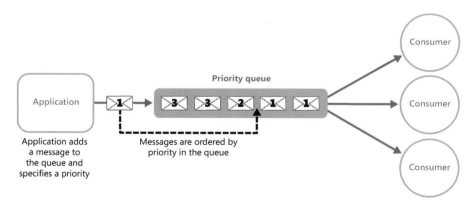

FIGURE 1
Using a queuing mechanism that supports message prioritization

> Most message queue implementations support multiple consumers (following the Competing Consumers Pattern), and the number of consumer processes can be scaled up or down as demand dictates.

In systems that do not support priority-based message queues, an alternative solution is to maintain a separate queue for each priority. The application is responsible for posting messages to the appropriate queue. Each queue can have a separate pool of consumers. Higher priority queues can have a larger pool of consumers running on faster hardware than lower priority queues. Figure 2 shows this approach.

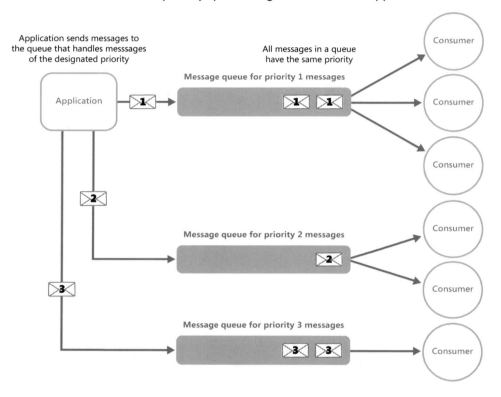

FIGURE 2
Using separate message queues for each priority

A variation on this strategy is to have a single pool of consumers that check for messages on high priority queues first, and then only start to fetch messages from lower priority queues if no higher priority messages are waiting. There are some semantic differences between a solution that uses a single pool of consumer processes (either with a single queue that supports messages with different priorities or with multiple queues that each handle messages of a single priority), and a solution that uses multiple queues with a separate pool for each queue.

In the single pool approach, higher priority messages will always be received and processed before lower priority messages. In theory, messages that have a very low priority may be continually superseded and might never be processed. In the multiple pool approach, lower priority messages will always be processed, just not as quickly as those of a higher priority (depending on the relative size of the pools and the resources that they have available).

Using a priority queuing mechanism can provide the following advantages:

- It allows applications to meet business requirements that necessitate prioritization of availability or performance, such as offering different levels of service to specific groups of customers.

- It can help to minimize operational costs. In the single queue approach, you can scale back the number of consumers if necessary. High priority messages will still be processed first (although possibly more slowly), and lower priority messages may be delayed for longer. If you have implemented the multiple message queue approach with separate pools of consumers for each queue, you can reduce the pool of consumers for lower priority queues, or even suspend processing for some very low priority queues by halting all the consumers that listen for messages on those queues.

- The multiple message queue approach can help to maximize application performance and scalability by partitioning messages based on processing requirements. For example, vital tasks can be prioritized to be handled by receivers that run immediately while less important background tasks can be handled by receivers that are scheduled to run at less busy periods.

ISSUES AND CONSIDERATIONS

Consider the following points when deciding how to implement this pattern:

- Define the priorities in the context of the solution. For example, "high priority" could mean that messages should be processed within ten seconds. Identify the requirements for handling high priority items, and what other resources must be allocated to meet these criteria.

- Decide if all high priority items must be processed before any lower priority items. If the messages are being processed by a single pool of consumers, it may be necessary to provide a mechanism that can preempt and suspend a task that is handling a low priority message if a higher priority message becomes available.

- In the multiple queue approach, when using a single pool of consumer processes that listen on all queues rather than a dedicated consumer pool for each queue, the consumer must apply an algorithm that ensures it always services messages from higher priority queues before those from lower priority queues.

- Monitor the speed of processing on high and low priority queues to ensure that messages in these queues are processed at the expected rates.

- If you need to guarantee that low priority messages will be processed, it may be necessary to implement the multiple message queue approach with multiple pools of consumers. Alternatively, in a queue that supports message prioritization, it may be possible to dynamically increase the priority of a queued message as it ages. However, this approach depends on the message queue providing this feature.

- Using a separate queue for each message priority works best for systems that have a small number of well-defined priorities.

- Message priorities may be determined logically by the system. For example, rather than having explicit high and low priority messages, they could be designated as "fee paying customer", or "non-fee paying customer." Depending on your business model, your system might allocate more resources to processing messages from fee paying customers than non-fee paying ones.

- There may be a financial and processing cost associated with checking a queue for a message (some commercial messaging systems charge a small fee each time a message is posted or retrieved, and each time a queue is queried for messages). This cost will be increased when checking multiple queues.

- It may be possible to dynamically adjust the size of a pool of consumers based on the length of the queue that the pool is servicing. For more information, see the Autoscaling Guidance.

WHEN TO USE THIS PATTERN

This pattern is ideally suited to scenarios where:

- The system must handle multiple tasks that might have different priorities.
- Different users or tenants should be served with different priority.

EXAMPLE

Windows Azure does not provide a queuing mechanism that natively support automatic prioritization of messages through sorting. However, it does provide Windows Azure Service Bus topics and subscriptions, which support a queuing mechanism that provides message filtering, together with a wide range of flexible capabilities that make it ideal for use in almost all priority queue implementations.

A Windows Azure solution can implement a Service Bus topic to which an application can post messages, in the same way as a queue. Messages can contain metadata in the form of application-defined custom properties. Service Bus subscriptions can be associated with the topic, and these subscriptions can filter messages based on their properties. When an application sends a message to a topic, the message is directed to the appropriate subscription from where it can be read by a consumer. Consumer processes can retrieve messages from a subscription using the same semantics as a message queue (a subscription is a logical queue).

Figure 3 illustrates a solution using Windows Azure Service Bus topics and subscriptions.

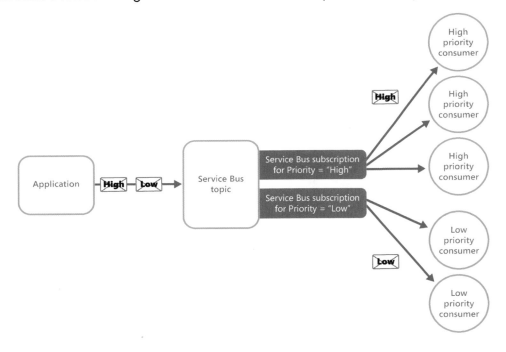

FIGURE 3
Implementing a priority queue with Windows Azure Service Bus topics and subscriptions

In Figure 3 the application creates several messages and assigns a custom property called **Priority** in each message with a value, either **High** or **Low**. The application posts these messages to a topic. The topic has two associated subscriptions, which both filter messages by examining the **Priority** property. One subscription accepts messages where the **Priority** property is set to **High**, and the other accepts messages where the **Priority** property is set to **Low**. A pool of consumers reads messages from each subscription. The high priority subscription has a larger pool, and these consumers might be running on more powerful (and expensive) computers with more resources available than the consumers in the low priority pool.

Note that there is nothing special about the designation of high and low priority messages in this example. These are simply labels specified as properties in each message, and are used to direct messages to a specific subscription. If additional priorities are required, it is relatively easy to create further subscriptions and pools of consumer processes to handle these priorities.

The PriorityQueue solution in the code available with this guidance contains an implementation of this approach. This solution contains two worker roles projects named PriorityQueue.High and PriorityQueue.Low. These two worker roles inherit from a class called **PriorityWorkerRole** which contains the functionality for connecting to a specified subscription in the **OnStart** method.

The PriorityQueue.High and PriorityQueue.Low worker roles connect to different subscriptions, defined by their configuration settings. An administrator can configure different numbers of each role to be run; typically there will be more instances of the PriorityQueue.High worker role than the PriorityQueue.Low worker role.

The **Run** method in the **PriorityWorkerRole** class arranges for the virtual **ProcessMessage** method (also defined in the **PriorityWorkerRole** class) to be executed for each message received on the queue. The following code shows the **Run** and **ProcessMessage** methods. The **QueueManager** class, defined in the PriorityQueue.Shared project, provides helper methods for using Windows Azure Service Bus queues.

```csharp
C#
public class PriorityWorkerRole : RoleEntryPoint
{
  private QueueManager queueManager;
  ...

  public override void Run()
  {
    // Start listening for messages on the subscription.
    var subscriptionName = CloudConfigurationManager.GetSetting("SubscriptionName");
    this.queueManager.ReceiveMessages(subscriptionName, this.ProcessMessage);
    ...;
  }
  ...

  protected virtual async Task ProcessMessage(BrokeredMessage message)
  {
    // Simulating processing.
    await Task.Delay(TimeSpan.FromSeconds(2));
  }
}
```

The PriorityQueue.High and PriorityQueue.Low worker roles both override the default functionality of the **ProcessMessage** method. The code below shows the **ProcessMessage** method for the PriorityQueue.High worker role.

```C#
protected override async Task ProcessMessage(BrokeredMessage message)
{
  // Simulate message processing for High priority messages.
  await base.ProcessMessage(message);
  Trace.TraceInformation("High priority message processed by " +
    RoleEnvironment.CurrentRoleInstance.Id + " MessageId: " + message.MessageId);
}
```

When an application posts messages to the topic associated with the subscriptions used by the PriorityQueue.High and PriorityQueue.Low worker roles, it specifies the priority by using the **Priority** custom property, as shown in the following code example. This code (which is implemented in the **WorkerRole** class in the PriorityQueue.Sender project), uses the **SendBatchAsync** helper method of the **QueueManager** class to post messages to a topic in batches.

```C#
// Send a low priority batch.
var lowMessages = new List<BrokeredMessage>();

for (int i = 0; i < 10; i++)
{
  var message = new BrokeredMessage() { MessageId = Guid.NewGuid().ToString() };
  message.Properties["Priority"] = Priority.Low;
  lowMessages.Add(message);
}

this.queueManager.SendBatchAsync(lowMessages).Wait();
...

// Send a high priority batch.
var highMessages = new List<BrokeredMessage>();

for (int i = 0; i < 10; i++)
{
  var message = new BrokeredMessage() { MessageId = Guid.NewGuid().ToString() };
  message.Properties["Priority"] = Priority.High;
  highMessages.Add(message);
}

this.queueManager.SendBatchAsync(highMessages).Wait();
```

RELATED PATTERNS AND GUIDANCE

The following patterns and guidance may also be relevant when implementing this pattern:

- **Asynchronous Messaging Primer**. A consumer service processing a request may need to send a reply to the instance of the application that posted the request. The Asynchronous Messaging Primer provides more information on the strategies that can be used to implement request/response messaging.

- **Competing Consumers Pattern**. To increase the throughput of the queues, it's possible to have multiple consumers that listen on the same queue, and process the tasks in parallel. These consumers will compete for messages, but only one should be able to process each message. The Competing Consumers pattern provides more information on the benefits and tradeoffs of implementing this approach.
- **Throttling Pattern**. You can implement throttling by using queues. Priority messaging can be used to ensure that requests from critical applications, or applications being run by high-value customers, are given precedence over requests from less important applications.
- **Autoscaling Guidance**. It may be possible to scale the size of the pool of consumer processes handling a queue depending on the length of the queue. This strategy can help to improve performance, especially for pools handling high priority messages.

MORE INFORMATION

All links in this book are accessible from the book's online bibliography available at: *http://aka.ms/cdpbibliography*.

- The article *Priority Queue Pattern* on the Cloud Design Pattern website.
- The article *Enterprise Integration Patterns with Service Bus* on Abhishek Lal's blog.

This pattern has a sample application associated with it. You can download the "Cloud Design Patterns – Sample Code" from the Microsoft Download Center at *http://aka.ms/cloud-design-patterns-sample*.

Queue-Based Load Leveling Pattern

Use a queue that acts as a buffer between a task and a service that it invokes in order to smooth intermittent heavy loads that may otherwise cause the service to fail or the task to time out. This pattern can help to minimize the impact of peaks in demand on availability and responsiveness for both the task and the service.

CONTEXT AND PROBLEM

Many solutions in the cloud involve running tasks that invoke services. In this environment, if a service is subjected to intermittent heavy loads, it can cause performance or reliability issues

A service could be a component that is part of the same solution as the tasks that utilize it, or it could be a third-party service providing access to frequently used resources such as a cache or a storage service. If the same service is utilized by a number of tasks running concurrently, it can be difficult to predict the volume of requests to which the service might be subjected at any given point in time.

It is possible that a service might experience peaks in demand that cause it to become overloaded and unable to respond to requests in a timely manner. Flooding a service with a large number of concurrent requests may also result in the service failing if it is unable to handle the contention that these requests could cause.

SOLUTION

Refactor the solution and introduce a queue between the task and the service. The task and the service run asynchronously. The task posts a message containing the data required by the service to a queue. The queue acts as a buffer, storing the message until it is retrieved by the service. The service retrieves the messages from the queue and processes them. Requests from a number of tasks, which can be generated at a highly variable rate, can be passed to the service through the same message queue. Figure 1 shows this structure.

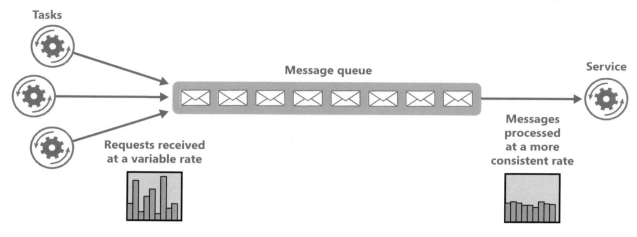

FIGURE 1
Using a queue to level the load on a service

The queue effectively decouples the tasks from the service, and the service can handle the messages at its own pace irrespective of the volume of requests from concurrent tasks. Additionally, there is no delay to a task if the service is not available at the time it posts a message to the queue.

This pattern provides the following benefits:

- It can help to maximize availability because delays arising in services will not have an immediate and direct impact on the application, which can continue to post messages to the queue even when the service is not available or is not currently processing messages.

- It can help to maximize scalability because both the number of queues and the number of services can be varied to meet demand.

- It can help to control costs because the number of service instances deployed needs only to be sufficient to meet average load rather than the peak load.

> Some services may implement throttling if demand reaches a threshold beyond which the system could fail. Throttling may reduce the functionality available. You might be able to implement load leveling with these services to ensure that this threshold is not reached.

ISSUES AND CONSIDERATIONS

Consider the following points when deciding how to implement this pattern:

- It is necessary to implement application logic that controls the rate at which services handle messages to avoid overwhelming the target resource. Avoid passing spikes in demand to the next stage of the system. Test the system under load to ensure that it provides the required leveling, and adjust the number of queues and the number of service instances that handle messages to achieve this.

- Message queues are a one-way communication mechanism. If a task expects a reply from a service, it may be necessary to implement a mechanism that the service can use to send a response. For more information, see the Asynchronous Messaging Primer.

- You must be careful if you apply autoscaling to services that are listening for requests on the queue because this may result in increased contention for any resources that these services share, and diminish the effectiveness of using the queue to level the load.

118

WHEN TO USE THIS PATTERN

This pattern is ideally suited to any type of application that uses services that may be subject to overloading.

This pattern might not be suitable if the application expects a response from the service with minimal latency.

EXAMPLE

A Windows Azure web role stores data by using a separate storage service. If a large number of instances of the web role run concurrently, it is possible that the storage service could be overwhelmed and be unable to respond to requests quickly enough to prevent these requests from timing out or failing. Figure 2 highlights this issue.

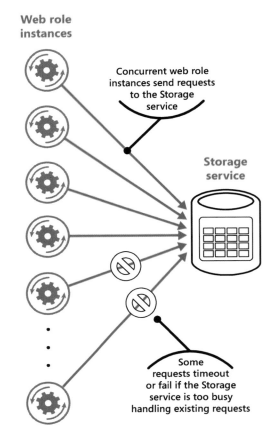

FIGURE 2
A service being overwhelmed by a large number of concurrent requests from instances of a web role

To resolve this issue, you can use a queue to level the load between the web role instances and the storage service. However, the storage service is designed to accept synchronous requests and cannot be easily modified to read messages and manage throughput. Therefore, you can introduce a worker role to act as a proxy service that receives requests from the queue and forwards them to the storage service. The application logic in the worker role can control the rate at which it passes requests to the storage service to prevent the storage service from being overwhelmed. Figure 3 shows this solution.

Web role
instances

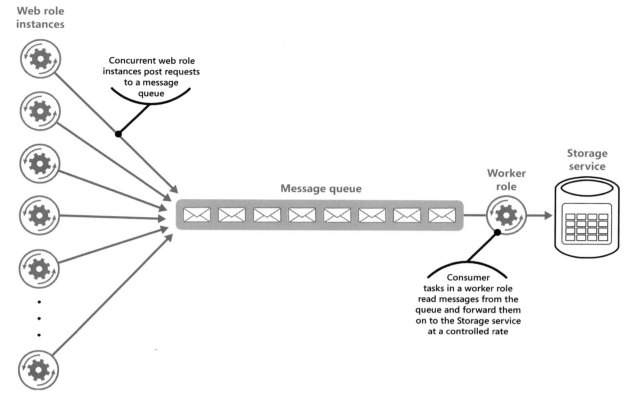

FIGURE 3
Using a queue and a worker role to level the load between instances of the web role and the service

RELATED PATTERNS AND GUIDANCE

The following patterns and guidance may also be relevant when implementing this pattern:

- **Asynchronous Messaging Primer**. Message queues are an inherently asynchronous communications mechanism. It may be necessary to redesign the application logic in a task if it is adapted from communicating directly with a service to using a message queue. Similarly, it may be necessary to refactor a service to accept requests from a message queue (alternatively, it may be possible to implement a proxy service, as described in the example).
- **Competing Consumers Pattern**. It may be possible to run multiple instances of a service, each of which act as a message consumer from the load-leveling queue. You can use this approach to adjust the rate at which messages are received and passed to a service.
- **Throttling Pattern**. A simple way to implement throttling with a service is to use queue-based load-leveling and route all requests to a service through a message queue. The service can process requests at a rate that ensures resources required by the service are not exhausted, and to reduce the amount of contention that could occur.

MORE INFORMATION

All links in this book are accessible from the book's online bibliography available at: _http://aka.ms/cdpbibliography_.

For more information about choosing a messaging and queuing mechanism in Windows Azure applications see:

- The articles _Queue Service Concepts_ and _Service Bus_ on the MSDN website.

Retry Pattern

Enable an application to handle anticipated, temporary failures when it attempts to connect to a service or network resource by transparently retrying an operation that has previously failed in the expectation that the cause of the failure is transient. This pattern can improve the stability of the application.

CONTEXT AND PROBLEM

An application that communicates with elements running in the cloud must be sensitive to the transient faults that can occur in this environment. Such faults include the momentary loss of network connectivity to components and services, the temporary unavailability of a service, or timeouts that arise when a service is busy.

These faults are typically self-correcting, and if the action that triggered a fault is repeated after a suitable delay it is likely to be successful. For example, a database service that is processing a large number of concurrent requests may implement a throttling strategy that temporarily rejects any further requests until its workload has eased. An application attempting to access the database may fail to connect, but if it tries again after a suitable delay it may succeed.

SOLUTION

In the cloud, transient faults are not uncommon and an application should be designed to handle them elegantly and transparently, minimizing the effects that such faults might have on the business tasks that the application is performing.

If an application detects a failure when it attempts to send a request to a remote service, it can handle the failure by using the following strategies:

- If the fault indicates that the failure is not transient or is unlikely to be successful if repeated (for example, an authentication failure caused by providing invalid credentials is unlikely to succeed no matter how many times it is attempted), the application should abort the operation and report a suitable exception.
- If the specific fault reported is unusual or rare, it may have been caused by freak circumstances such as a network packet becoming corrupted while it was being transmitted. In this case, the application could retry the failing request again immediately because the same failure is unlikely to be repeated and the request will probably be successful.
- If the fault is caused by one of the more commonplace connectivity or "busy" failures, the network or service may require a short period while the connectivity issues are rectified or the backlog of work is cleared. The application should wait for a suitable time before retrying the request.

For the more common transient failures, the period between retries should be chosen so as to spread requests from multiple instances of the application as evenly as possible. This can reduce the chance of a busy service continuing to be overloaded. If many instances of an application are continually bombarding a service with retry requests, it may take the service longer to recover.

If the request still fails, the application can wait for a further period and make another attempt. If necessary, this process can be repeated with increasing delays between retry attempts until some maximum number of requests have been attempted and failed. The delay time can be increased incrementally, or a timing strategy such as exponential back-off can be used, depending on the nature of the failure and the likelihood that it will be corrected during this time.

Figure 1 illustrates this pattern. If the request is unsuccessful after a predefined number of attempts, the application should treat the fault as an exception and handle it accordingly.

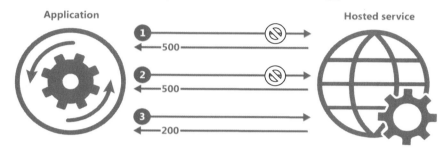

1: Application invokes operation on hosted service. The request fails, and the service host responds with HTTP response code 500 (internal server error).
2: Application waits for a short interval and tries again. The request still fails with HTTP response code 500.
3: Application waits for a longer interval and tries again. The request succeeds with HTTP response code 200 (OK).

FIGURE 1
Invoking an operation in a hosted service using the Retry pattern

The application should wrap all attempts to access a remote service in code that implements a retry policy matching one of the strategies listed above. Requests sent to different services can be subject to different policies, and some vendors provide libraries that encapsulate this approach. These libraries typically implement policies that are parameterized, and the application developer can specify values for items such as the number of retries and the time between retry attempts.

The code in an application that detects faults and retries failing operations should log the details of these failures. This information may be useful to operators. If a service is frequently reported as unavailable or busy, it is often because the service has exhausted its resources. You may be able to reduce the frequency with which these faults occur by scaling out the service. For example, if a database service is continually overloaded, it may be beneficial to partition the database and spread the load across multiple servers.

Windows Azure provides extensive support for the Retry pattern. The patterns & practices *Transient Fault Handling Block* enables an application to handle transient faults in many Windows Azure services using a range of retry strategies. The Microsoft *Entity Framework version 6* provides facilities for retrying database operations. Additionally, many of the Windows Azure Service Bus and Windows Azure Storage APIs implement retry logic transparently.

Issues and Considerations

You should consider the following points when deciding how to implement this pattern:

- The retry policy should be tuned to match the business requirements of the application and the nature of the failure. It may be better for some noncritical operations to fail fast rather than retry several times and impact the throughput of the application. For example, in an interactive web application that attempts to access a remote service, it may be better to fail after a smaller number of retries with only a short delay between retry attempts, and display a suitable message to the user (for example, "please try again later") to prevent the application from becoming unresponsive. For a batch application, it may be more appropriate to increase the number of retry attempts with an exponentially increasing delay between attempts.

- A highly aggressive retry policy with minimal delay between attempts, and a large number of retries, could further degrade a busy service that is running close to or at capacity. This retry policy could also affect the responsiveness of the application if it is continually attempting to perform a failing operation rather than doing useful work.

- If a request still fails after a significant number of retries, it may be better for the application to prevent further requests going to the same resource for a period and simply report a failure immediately. When the period expires, the application may tentatively allow one or more requests through to see whether they are successful. For more details of this strategy, see the Circuit Breaker Pattern.

- The operations in a service that are invoked by an application that implements a retry policy may need to be idempotent. For example, a request sent to a service may be received and processed successfully but, due to a transient fault, it may be unable to send a response indicating that the processing has completed. The retry logic in the application might then attempt to repeat the request on the assumption that the first request was not received.

- A request to a service may fail for a variety of reasons and raise different exceptions, depending on the nature of the failure. Some exceptions may indicate a failure that could be resolved very quickly, while others may indicate that the failure is longer lasting. It may be beneficial for the retry policy to adjust the time between retry attempts based on the type of the exception.

- Consider how retrying an operation that is part of a transaction will affect the overall transaction consistency. It may be useful to fine tune the retry policy for transactional operations to maximize the chance of success and reduce the need to undo all the transaction steps.

- Ensure that all retry code is fully tested against a variety of failure conditions. Check that it does not severely impact the performance or reliability of the application, cause excessive load on services and resources, or generate race conditions or bottlenecks.

- Implement retry logic only where the full context of a failing operation is understood. For example, if a task that contains a retry policy invokes another task that also contains a retry policy, this extra layer of retries can add long delays to the processing. It may be better to configure the lower-level task to fail fast and report the reason for the failure back to the task that invoked it. This higher-level task can then decide how to handle the failure based on its own policy.

- It is important to log all connectivity failures that prompt a retry so that underlying problems with the application, services, or resources can be identified.

- Investigate the faults that are most likely to occur for a service or a resource to discover if they are likely to be long lasting or terminal. If this is the case, it may be better to handle the fault as an exception. The application can report or log the exception, and then attempt to continue either by invoking an alternative service (if there is one available), or by offering degraded functionality. For more information on how to detect and handle long-lasting faults, see the Circuit Breaker Pattern.

WHEN TO USE THIS PATTERN

Use this pattern:

- When an application could experience transient faults as it interacts with a remote service or accesses a remote resource. These faults are expected to be short lived, and repeating a request that has previously failed could succeed on a subsequent attempt.

This pattern might not be suitable:

- When a fault is likely to be long lasting, because this can affect the responsiveness of an application. The application may simply be wasting time and resources attempting to repeat a request that is most likely to fail.
- For handling failures that are not due to transient faults, such as internal exceptions caused by errors in the business logic of an application.
- As an alternative to addressing scalability issues in a system. If an application experiences frequent "busy" faults, it is often an indication that the service or resource being accessed should be scaled up.

EXAMPLE

This example illustrates an implementation of the Retry pattern. The **OperationWithBasicRetryAsync** method, shown below, invokes an external service asynchronously through the **TransientOperationAsync** method (the details of this method will be specific to the service and are omitted from the sample code).

```csharp
private int retryCount = 3;
...

public async Task OperationWithBasicRetryAsync()
{
  int currentRetry = 0;

  for (; ;)
  {
    try
    {
      // Calling external service.
      await TransientOperationAsync();

      // Return or break.
      break;
    }
    catch (Exception ex)
    {
      Trace.TraceError("Operation Exception");

      currentRetry++;

      // Check if the exception thrown was a transient exception
      // based on the logic in the error detection strategy.
      // Determine whether to retry the operation, as well as how
      // long to wait, based on the retry strategy.
      if (currentRetry > this.retryCount || !IsTransient(ex))
      {
        // If this is not a transient error
        // or we should not retry re-throw the exception.
        throw;
      }
    }
```

```
      // Wait to retry the operation.
      // Consider calculating an exponential delay here and
      // using a strategy best suited for the operation and fault.
      Await.Task.Delay();
    }
  }

  // Async method that wraps a call to a remote service (details not shown).
  private async Task TransientOperationAsync()
  {
    ...
  }
```

The statement that invokes this method is encapsulated within a **try/catch** block wrapped in a **for** loop. The **for** loop exits if the call to the **TransientOperationAsync** method succeeds without throwing an exception. If the **TransientOperationAsync** method fails, the **catch** block examines the reason for the failure, and if it is deemed to be a transient error the code waits for a short delay before retrying the operation.

The **for** loop also tracks the number of times that the operation has been attempted, and if the code fails three times the exception is assumed to be more long lasting. If the exception is not transient or it is longlasting, the catch handler throws an exception. This exception exits the **for** loop and should be caught by the code that invokes the **OperationWithBasicRetryAsync** method.

The **IsTransient** method, shown below, checks for a specific set of exceptions that are relevant to the environment in which the code is run. The definition of a transient exception may vary according to the resources being accessed and the environment in which the operation is being performed.

```C#
private bool IsTransient(Exception ex)
{
  // Determine if the exception is transient.
  // In some cases this may be as simple as checking the exception type, in other
  // cases it may be necessary to inspect other properties of the exception.
  if (ex is OperationTransientException)
    return true;

  var webException = ex as WebException;
  if (webException != null)
  {
    // If the web exception contains one of the following status values
    // it may be transient.
    return new[] {WebExceptionStatus.ConnectionClosed,
                  WebExceptionStatus.Timeout,
                  WebExceptionStatus.RequestCanceled }.
          Contains(webException.Status);
  }

  // Additional exception checking logic goes here.
  return false;
}
```

RELATED PATTERNS AND GUIDANCE

The following pattern may also be relevant when implementing this pattern:

- **Circuit Breaker Pattern**. The Retry Pattern is ideally suited to handling transient faults. If a failure is expected to be more long lasting, it may be more appropriate to implement the Circuit Breaker Pattern. The Retry Pattern can also be used in conjunction with a circuit breaker to provide a comprehensive approach to handling faults.

MORE INFORMATION

All links in this book are accessible from the book's online bibliography available at: *http://aka.ms/cdpbibliography*.

- The *Transient Fault Handling Application Block* on MSDN.
- The article *Connection Resiliency / Retry Logic (EF6 onwards)* on MSDN.

Runtime Reconfiguration Pattern

Design an application so that it can be reconfigured without requiring redeployment or restarting the application. This helps to maintain availability and minimize downtime.

CONTEXT AND PROBLEM

A primary aim for important applications such as commercial and business websites is to minimize downtime and the consequent interruption to customers and users. However, at times it is necessary to reconfigure the application to change specific behavior or settings while it is deployed and in use. Therefore, it is an advantage for the application to be designed in such a way as to allow these configuration changes to be applied while it is running, and for the components of the application to detect the changes and apply them as soon as possible.

Examples of the kinds of configuration changes to be applied might be adjusting the granularity of logging to assist in debugging a problem with the application, swapping connection strings to use a different data store, or turning on or off specific sections or functionality of the application.

SOLUTION

The solution for implementing this pattern depends on the features available in the application hosting environment. Typically, the application code will respond to one or more events that are raised by the hosting infrastructure when it detects a change to the application configuration. This is usually the result of uploading a new configuration file, or in response to changes in the configuration through the administration portal or by accessing an API.

Code that handles the configuration change events can examine the changes and apply them to the components of the application. It is necessary for these components to detect and react to the changes, and so the values they use will usually be exposed as writable properties or methods that the code in the event handler can set to new values or execute. From this point, the components should use the new values so that the required changes to the application behavior occur.

If it is not possible for the components to apply the changes at runtime, it will be necessary to restart the application so that these changes are applied when the application starts up again. In some hosting environments it may be possible to detect these types of changes, and indicate to the environment that the application must be restarted. In other cases it may be necessary to implement code that analyses the setting changes and forces an application restart when necessary.

Figure 1 shows an overview of this pattern.

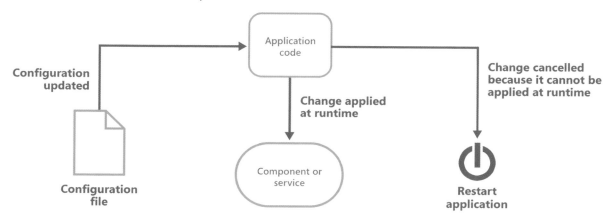

FIGURE 1
A basic overview of this pattern

Most environments expose events raised in response to configuration changes. In those that do not, a polling mechanism that regularly checks for changes to the configuration and applies these changes will be necessary. It may also be necessary to restart the application if the changes cannot be applied at runtime. For example, it may be possible to compare the date and time of a configuration file at preset intervals, and run code to apply the changes when a newer version is found. Another approach would be to incorporate a control in the administration UI of the application, or expose a secured endpoint that can be accessed from outside the application, that executes code that reads and applies the updated configuration.

Alternatively, the application could react to some other change in the environment. For example, occurrences of a specific runtime error might change the logging configuration to automatically collect additional information, or the code could use the current date to read and apply a theme that reflects the season or a special event.

ISSUES AND CONSIDERATIONS

Consider the following points when deciding how to implement this pattern:

- The configuration settings must be stored outside of the deployed application so that they can be updated without requiring the entire package to be redeployed. Typically the settings are stored in a configuration file, or in an external repository such as a database or online storage. Access to the runtime configuration mechanism should be strictly controlled, as well as strictly audited when used.

- If the hosting infrastructure does not automatically detect configuration change events, and expose these events to the application code, you must implement an alternative mechanism to detect and apply the changes. This may be through a polling mechanism, or by exposing an interactive control or endpoint that initiates the update process.

- If you need to implement a polling mechanism, consider how often checks for updates to the configuration should take place. A long polling interval will mean that changes might not be applied for some time. A short interval might adversely affect operation by absorbing available compute and I/O resources.

- If there is more than one instance of the application, additional factors should be considered, depending on how changes are detected. If changes are detected automatically through events raised by the hosting infrastructure, these changes may not be detected by all instances of the application at the same time. This means that some instances will be using the original configuration for a period while others will use the new settings. If the update is detected through a polling mechanism, this must communicate the change to all instances in order to maintain consistency.

- Some configuration changes may require the application to be restarted, or even require the hosting server to be rebooted. You must identify these types of configuration settings and perform the appropriate action for each one. For example, a change that requires the application to be restarted might do this automatically, or it might be the responsibility of the administrator to initiate the restart at a suitable time when the application is not under excessive load and other instances of the application can handle the load.

- Plan for a staged rollout of updates and confirm they are successful, and that the updated application instances are performing correctly, before applying the update to all instances. This can prevent a total outage of the application should an error occur. Where the update requires a restart or a reboot of the application, particularly where the application has a significant start up or warm up time, use a staged rollout approach to prevent multiple instances being offline at the same time.

- Consider how you will roll back configuration changes that cause issues, or that result in failure of the application. For example, it should be possible to roll back a change immediately instead of waiting for a polling interval to detect the change.

- Consider how the location of the configuration settings might affect application performance. For example, you should handle the error that will occur if the external store you use is unavailable when the application starts, or when configuration changes are to be applied—perhaps by using a default configuration or by caching the settings locally on the server and reusing these values while retrying access to the remote data store.

- Caching can help to reduce delays if a component needs to repeatedly access configuration settings. However, when the configuration changes, the application code will need to invalidate the cached settings, and the component must use the updated settings.

When to Use this Pattern

This pattern is ideally suited for:

- Applications for which you must avoid all unnecessary downtime, while still being able to apply changes to the application configuration.

- Environments that expose events raised automatically when the main configuration changes. Typically this is when a new configuration file is detected, or when changes are made to an existing configuration file.

- Applications where the configuration changes often and the changes can be applied to components without requiring the application to be restarted, or without requiring the hosting server to be rebooted.

This pattern might not be suitable if the runtime components are designed so they can be configured only at initialization time, and the effort of updating those components cannot be justified in comparison to restarting the application and enduring a short downtime.

Example

Windows Azure Cloud Services roles detect and expose two events that are raised when the hosting environment detects a change to the **ServiceConfiguration.cscfg** files:

- **RoleEnvironment.Changing**. This event is raised after a configuration change is detected, but before it is applied to the application. You can handle the event to query the changes and to cancel the runtime reconfiguration. If you cancel the change, the web or worker role will be restarted automatically so that the new configuration is used by the application.

- **RoleEnvironment.Changed**. This event is raised after the application configuration has been applied. You can handle the event to query the changes that were applied.

When you cancel a change in the **RoleEnvironment.Changing** event you are indicating to Windows Azure that a new setting cannot be applied while the application is running, and that it must be restarted in order to use the new value. Effectively you will cancel a change only if your application or component cannot react to the change at runtime, and requires a restart in order to use the new value.

For more information see *RoleEnvironment.Changing Event* and *Use the RoleEnvironment.Changing Event* on MSDN.

To handle the **RoleEnvironment.Changing** and **RoleEnvironment.Changed** events you will typically add a custom handler to the event. For example, the following code from the **Global.asax.cs** class in the **Runtime Reconfiguration** solution of the examples you can download for this guide shows how to add a custom function named **RoleEnvironment_Changed** to the event hander chain. This is from the Global.asax.cs file of the example.

The examples for this pattern are in the RuntimeReconfiguration.Web project of the RuntimeReconfiguration solution.

```csharp
C#
protected void Application_Start(object sender, EventArgs e)
{
  ConfigureFromSetting(CustomSettingName);
  RoleEnvironment.Changed += this.RoleEnvironment_Changed;
}
```

In a web or worker role you can use similar code in the **OnStart** event handler of the role to handle the **RoleEnvironment.Changing** event. This is from the WebRole.cs file of the example.

```csharp
C#
public override bool OnStart()
{
  // Add the trace listener. The web role process is not configured by web.config.
  Trace.Listeners.Add(new DiagnosticMonitorTraceListener());

  RoleEnvironment.Changing +=   this.RoleEnvironment_Changing;
  return base.OnStart();
}
```

Be aware that, in the case of web roles, the **OnStart** event handler runs in a separate process from the web application process itself. This is why you will typically handle the **RoleEnvironment.Changed** event handler in the **Global.asax** file so that you can update the runtime configuration of your web application, and the **RoleEnvironment.Changing** event in the role itself. In the case of a worker role, you can subscribe to both the **RoleEnvironment.Changing** and **RoleEnvironment.Changed** events within the **OnStart** event handler.

You can store custom configuration settings in the service configuration file, in a custom configuration file, in a database such as Windows Azure SQL Database or SQL Server in a Virtual Machine, or in Windows Azure blob or table storage. You will need to create code that can access the custom configuration settings and apply these to the application—typically by setting the properties of components within the application.

For example, the following custom function reads the value of a setting, whose name is passed as a parameter, from the Windows Azure service configuration file and then applies it to the current instance of a runtime component named **SomeRuntimeComponent**. This is from the Global.asax.cs file of the example

```csharp
private static void ConfigureFromSetting(string settingName)
{
  var value = RoleEnvironment.GetConfigurationSettingValue(settingName);
  SomeRuntimeComponent.Instance.CurrentValue = value;
}
```

Some configuration settings, such as those for Windows Identity Framework, cannot be stored in the Windows Azure service configuration file and must be in the **App.config** or **Web.config** file.

In Windows Azure, some configuration changes are detected and applied automatically. This includes the configuration of the Widows Azure diagnostics system in the **Diagnostics.wadcfg** file, which specifies the types of information to collect and how to persist the log files. Therefore, it is only necessary to write code that handles the custom settings you add to the service configuration file. Your code should either:

- Apply the custom settings from an updated configuration to the appropriate components of your application at runtime so that their behavior reflects the new configuration.
- Cancel the change to indicate to Windows Azure that the new value cannot be applied at runtime, and that the application must be restarted in order for the change to be applied.

For example, the following code from the **WebRole.cs** class in the **Runtime Reconfiguration** solution of the examples you can download for this guide shows how you can use the **RoleEnvironment.Changing** event to cancel the update for all settings except the ones that can be applied at runtime without requiring a restart. This example allows a change to the settings named "CustomSetting" to be applied at runtime without restarting the application (the component that uses this setting will be able to read the new value and change its behavior accordingly at runtime). Any other change to the configuration will automatically cause the web or worker role to restart.

```csharp
private void RoleEnvironment_Changing(object sender,
                         RoleEnvironmentChangingEventArgs e)
{
  var changedSettings = e.Changes.OfType<RoleEnvironmentConfigurationSettingChange>()
                         .Select(c => c.ConfigurationSettingName).ToList();
  Trace.TraceInformation("Changing notification. Settings being changed: "
                    + string.Join(", ", changedSettings));

  if (changedSettings
    .Any(settingName => !string.Equals(settingName, CustomSettingName,
                         StringComparison.Ordinal)))
  {
    Trace.TraceInformation("Cancelling dynamic configuration change (restarting).");

    // Setting this to true will restart the role gracefully. If Cancel is not
    // set to true, and the change is not handled by the application, the
    // application will not use the new value until it is restarted (either
    // manually or for some other reason).
    e.Cancel = true;
  }
  Else
  {
    Trace.TraceInformation("Handling configuration change without restarting. ");
  }
}
```

This approach demonstrates good practice because it ensures that a change to any setting that the application code is not aware of (and so cannot be sure that it can be applied at runtime) will cause a restart. If any one of the changes is cancelled, the role will be restarted.

Updates that are not cancelled in the **RoleEnvironment.Changing** event handler can then be detected and applied to the application components after the new configuration has been accepted by the Windows Azure framework. For example, the following code in the **Global.asax** file of the example solution handles the **RoleEnvironment.Changed** event. It examines each configuration setting and, when it finds the setting named "CustomSetting", calls a function (shown earlier) that applies the new setting to the appropriate component in the application.

```csharp
C#
private void RoleEnvironment_Changed(object sender,
                                RoleEnvironmentChangedEventArgs e)
{
  Trace.TraceInformation("Updating instance with new configuration settings.");

  foreach (var settingChange in
          e.Changes.OfType<RoleEnvironmentConfigurationSettingChange>())
  {
    if (string.Equals(settingChange.ConfigurationSettingName,
                  CustomSettingName,
                  StringComparison.Ordinal))
    {
      // Execute a function to update the configuration of the component.
      ConfigureFromSetting(CustomSettingName );
    }
  }
}
```

Note that if you fail to cancel a configuration change, but do not apply the new value to your application component, then the change will not take effect until the next time that the application is restarted. This may lead to unpredictable behavior, particularly if the hosting role instance is restarted automatically by Windows Azure as part of its regular maintenance operations—at which point the new setting value will be applied.

RELATED PATTERNS AND GUIDANCE

The following pattern may also be relevant when implementing this pattern:

- **External Configuration Store Pattern**. Moving configuration information out of the application deployment package to a centralized location can provide opportunities for easier management and control of configuration data, and sharing configuration data across applications and application instances. The External Configuration Store pattern explains how you can do this.

MORE INFORMATION

All links in this book are accessible from the book's online bibliography available at: *http://aka.ms/cdpbibliography*.

- The articles *RoleEnvironment.Changing Event* and *Use the RoleEnvironment.Changing Event* on MSDN.

This pattern has a sample application associated with it. You can download the "Cloud Design Patterns – Sample Code" from the Microsoft Download Center at *http://aka.ms/cloud-design-patterns-sample*.

Scheduler Agent Supervisor Pattern

Coordinate a set of actions across a distributed set of services and other remote resources, attempt to transparently handle faults if any of these actions fail, or undo the effects of the work performed if the system cannot recover from a fault. This pattern can add resiliency to a distributed system by enabling it to recover and retry actions that fail due to transient exceptions, long-lasting faults, and process failures.

CONTEXT AND PROBLEM

An application performs tasks that comprise a number of steps, some of which may invoke remote services or access remote resources. The individual steps may be independent of each other, but they are orchestrated by the application logic that implements the task.

Whenever possible, the application should ensure that the task runs to completion and resolve any failures that might occur when accessing remote services or resources. These failures could occur for a variety of reasons. For example, the network might be down, communications could be interrupted, a remote service may be unresponsive or in an unstable state, or a remote resource might be temporarily inaccessible—perhaps due to resource constraints. In many cases these failures may be transient and can be handled by using the Retry Pattern.

If the application detects a more permanent fault from which it cannot easily recover, it must be able to restore the system to a consistent state and ensure integrity of the entire end-to-end operation.

SOLUTION

The Scheduler Agent Supervisor pattern defines the following actors. These actors orchestrate the *steps* (individual items of work) to be performed as part of the *task* (the overall process):

- The **Scheduler** arranges for the individual steps that comprise the overall task to be executed and orchestrates their operation. These steps can be combined into a pipeline or workflow, and the Scheduler is responsible for ensuring that the steps in this workflow are performed in the appropriate order. The Scheduler maintains information about the state of the workflow as each step is performed (such as "step not yet started," "step running," or "step completed") and records information about this state. This state information should also include an upper limit of the time allowed for the step to finish (referred to as the *Complete By* time). If a step requires access to a remote service or resource, the Scheduler invokes the appropriate Agent, passing it the details of the work to be performed. The Scheduler typically communicates with an Agent by using asynchronous request/response messaging. This can be implemented by using queues, although other distributed messaging technologies could be used instead.

> The Scheduler performs a similar function to the Process Manager in the *Process Manager* pattern. The actual workflow is typically defined and implemented by a workflow engine that is controlled by the Scheduler. This approach decouples the business logic in the workflow from the Scheduler.

- The **Agent** contains logic that encapsulates a call to a remote service, or access to a remote resource referenced by a step in a task. Each Agent typically wraps calls to a single service or resource, implementing the appropriate error handling and retry logic (subject to a timeout constraint, described later). If the steps in the workflow being run by the Scheduler utilize several services and resources across different steps, each step might reference a different Agent (this is an implementation detail of the pattern).

- The **Supervisor** monitors the status of the steps in the task being performed by the Scheduler. It runs periodically (the frequency will be system-specific), examines the status of steps as maintained by the Scheduler. If it detects any that have timed out or failed, it arranges for the appropriate Agent to recover the step or execute the appropriate remedial action (this may involve modifying the status of a step). Note that the recovery or remedial actions are typically implemented by the Scheduler and Agents. The Supervisor should simply request that these actions be performed.

The Scheduler, Agent, and Supervisor are logical components and their physical implementation depends on the technology being used. For example, several logical agents may be implemented as part of a single web service.

The Scheduler maintains information about the progress of the task and the state of each step in a durable data store, referred to as the *State Store*. The Supervisor can use this information to help determine whether a step has failed. Figure 1 illustrates the relationship between the Scheduler, the Agents, the Supervisor, and the State Store.

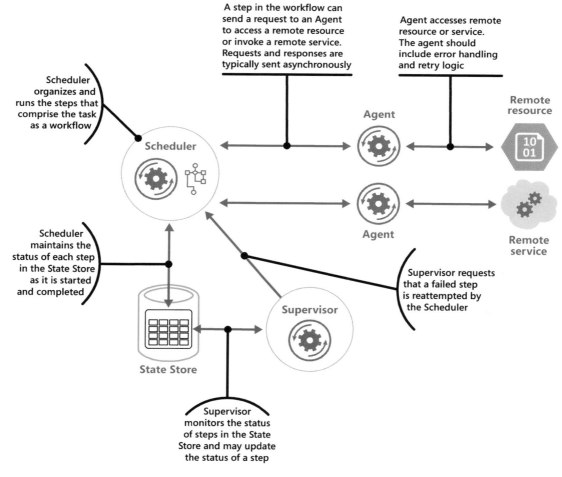

FIGURE 1
The actors in the Scheduler Agent Supervisor pattern

This diagram shows a simplified illustration of the pattern. In a real implementation, there may be many instances of the Scheduler running concurrently, each a subset of tasks. Similarly, the system could run multiple instances of each Agent, or even multiple Supervisors. In this case, Supervisors must coordinate their work with each other carefully to ensure that they don't compete to recover the same failed steps and tasks. The Leader Election Pattern provides one possible solution to this problem.

When an application wishes to run a task, it submits a request to the Scheduler. The Scheduler records initial state information about the task and its steps (for example, "step not yet started") in the State Store and then commences performing the operations defined by the workflow. As the Scheduler starts each step, it updates the information about the state of that step in the State Store (for example, "step running").

If a step references a remote service or resource, the Scheduler sends a message to the appropriate Agent. The message may contain the information that the Agent needs to pass to the service or access the resource, in addition to the *Complete By* time for the operation. If the Agent completes its operation successfully, it returns a response to the Scheduler. The Scheduler can then update the state information in the State Store (for example, "step completed") and perform the next step. This process continues until the entire task is complete.

An Agent can implement any retry logic that is necessary to perform its work. However, if the Agent does not complete its work before the *Complete By* period expires the Scheduler will assume that the operation has failed. In this case, the Agent should stop its work and not attempt to return anything to the Scheduler (not even an error message), or attempt any form of recovery. The reason for this restriction is that, after a step has timed out or failed, another instance of the Agent may be scheduled to run the failing step (this process is described later).

If the Agent itself fails, the Scheduler will not receive a response. The pattern may not make a distinction between a step that has timed out and one that has genuinely failed.

If a step times out or fails, the State Store will contain a record that indicates that the step is running ("step running"), but the *Complete By* time will have passed. The Supervisor looks for steps such as this and attempts to recover them. One possible strategy is for the Supervisor to update the *Complete By* value to extend the time available to complete the step, and then send a message to the Scheduler identifying the step that has timed out . The Scheduler can then attempt to repeat this step. However, such a design requires the tasks to be idempotent.

It may be necessary for the Supervisor to prevent the same step from being retried if it continually fails or times out. To achieve this, the Supervisor could maintain a retry count for each step, along with the state information, in the State Store. If this count exceeds a predefined threshold the Supervisor can adopt a strategy such as waiting for an extended period before notifying the Scheduler that it should retry the step, in the expectation that the fault will be resolved during this period. Alternatively, the Supervisor can send a message to the Scheduler to request the entire task be undone by implementing a Compensating Transaction (this approach will depend on the Scheduler and Agents providing the information necessary to implement the compensating operations for each step that completed successfully).

It is not the purpose of the Supervisor to monitor the Scheduler and Agents, and restart them if they fail. This aspect of the system should be handled by the infrastructure in which these components are running. Similarly, the Supervisor should not have knowledge of the actual business operations that the tasks being performed by the Scheduler are running (including how to compensate should these tasks fail). This is the purpose of the workflow logic implemented by the Scheduler. The sole responsibility of the Supervisor is to determine whether a step has failed and arrange either for it to be repeated or for the entire task containing the failed step to be undone.

If the Scheduler is restarted after a failure, or the workflow being performed by the Scheduler terminates unexpectedly, the Scheduler should be able to determine the status of any in-flight task that it was handling when it failed, and be prepared to resume this task from the point at which it failed. The implementation details of this process are likely to be system specific. If the task cannot be recovered, it may be necessary to undo the work already performed by the task. This may also require implementing a Compensating Transaction.

The key advantage of this pattern is that the system is resilient in the event of unexpected temporary or unrecoverable failures. The system can be constructed to be self-healing. For example, if an Agent or the Scheduler crashes, a new one can be started and the Supervisor can arrange for a task to be resumed. If the Supervisor fails, another instance can be started and can take over from where the failure occurred. If the Supervisor is scheduled to run periodically, a new instance may be automatically started after a predefined interval. The State Store may be replicated to achieve an even greater degree of resiliency.

ISSUES AND CONSIDERATIONS

You should consider the following points when deciding how to implement this pattern:

- This pattern may be nontrivial to implement and requires thorough testing of each possible failure mode of the system.
- The recovery/retry logic implemented by the Scheduler may be complex and dependent on state information held in the State Store. It may also be necessary to record the information required to implement a Compensating Transaction in a durable data store.
- The frequency with which the Supervisor runs will be important. It should run frequently enough to prevent any failed steps from blocking an application for an extended period, but it should not run so frequently that it becomes an overhead.
- The steps performed by an Agent could be run more than once. The logic that implements these steps should be idempotent.

WHEN TO USE THIS PATTERN

Use this pattern when a process that runs in a distributed environment such as the cloud must be resilient to communications failure and/or operational failure.

This pattern might not be suitable for tasks that do not invoke remote services or access remote resources.

EXAMPLE

A web application that implements an ecommerce system has been deployed on Windows Azure. Users can run this application to browse the products available from an organization, and place orders for these products. The user interface runs as a web role, and the order processing elements of the application are implemented as a set of worker roles. Part of the order processing logic involves accessing a remote service, and this aspect of the system could be prone to transient or more long-lasting faults. For this reason, the designers used the Scheduler Agent Supervisor pattern to implement the order processing elements of the system.

When a customer places an order, the application constructs a message that describes the order and posts this message to a queue. A separate Submission process, running in a worker role, retrieves this message, inserts the details of the order into the Orders database, and creates a record for the order process in the State Store. Note that the inserts into the Orders database and the State Store are performed as part of the same operation. The Submission process is designed to ensure that both inserts complete together.

The state information that the Submission process creates for the order includes:

- **OrderID**: The ID of the order in the Orders database.
- **LockedBy**: The instance ID of the worker role handling the order. There may be multiple current instances of the worker role running the Scheduler, but each order should only be handled by a single instance.
- **CompleteBy**: The time by which the order should be processed.
- **ProcessState**: The current state of the task handling the order. The possible states are:
    - **Pending**. The order has been created but processing has not yet been initiated.
    - **Processing**. The order is currently being processed.
    - **Processed**. The order has been processed successfully.
    - **Error**. The order processing has failed.
- **FailureCount**: The number of times that processing has been attempted for the order.

In this state information, the **OrderID** field is copied from the order ID of the new order. The **LockedBy** and **CompleteBy** fields are set to null, the **ProcessState** field is set to **Pending**, and the **FailureCount** field is set to 0.

> In this example, the order handling logic is relatively simple and only comprises a single step that invokes a remote service. In a more complex multi-step scenario, the Submission process would likely involve several steps, and so several records would be created in the State Store—each one describing the state of an individual step.

The Scheduler also runs as part of a worker role and implements the business logic that handles the order. An instance of the Scheduler polling for new orders examines the State Store for records where the **LockedBy** field is null and the **ProcessState** field is **Pending**. When the Scheduler finds a new order, it immediately populates the **LockedBy** field with its own instance ID, sets the **CompleteBy** field to an appropriate time, and sets the **ProcessState** field to **Processing**. The code that does this is designed to be exclusive and atomic to ensure that two concurrent instances of the Scheduler cannot attempt to handle the same order simultaneously.

The Scheduler then runs the business workflow to process the order asynchronously, passing it the value in the **OrderID** field from the State Store. The workflow handling the order retrieves the details of the order from the Orders database and performs its work. When a step in the order processing workflow needs to invoke the remote service, it uses an Agent. The workflow step communicates with the Agent by using a pair of Windows Azure Service Bus message queues acting as a request/response channel. Figure 2 shows a high-level view of the solution.

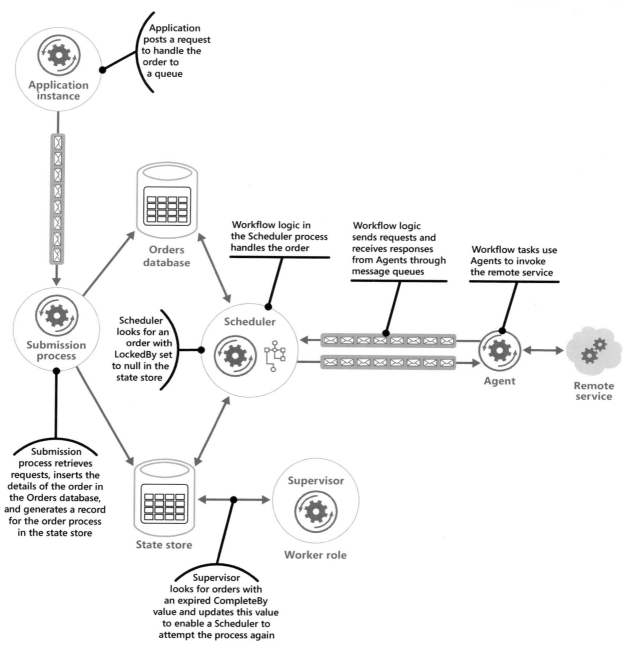

FIGURE 2
Using the Scheduler Agent Supervisor pattern to handle orders in a Windows Azure solution

The message sent to the Agent from a workflow step describes the order and includes the **CompleteBy** time. If the Agent receives a response from the remote service before the **CompleteBy** time expires, it constructs a reply message that it posts on the Service Bus queue on which the workflow is listening. When the workflow step receives the valid reply message, it completes its processing and the Scheduler sets the **ProcessState** field of the order state to **Processed**. At this point, the order processing has completed successfully.

If the **CompleteBy** time expires before the Agent receives a response from the remote service, the Agent simply halts its processing and terminates handling the order. Similarly, if the workflow handling the order exceeds the **CompleteBy** time, it also terminates. In both of these cases, the state of the order in the State Store remains set to **Processing**, but the **CompleteBy** time indicates that the time for processing the order has passed and the process is deemed to have failed. Note that if the Agent that is accessing the remote service, or the workflow that is handling the order (or both) terminate unexpectedly, the information in the State Store will again remain set to **Processing** and eventually will have an expired **CompleteBy** value.

If the Agent detects an unrecoverable non-transient fault while it is attempting to contact the remote service, it can send an error response back to the workflow. The Scheduler can set the status of the order to **Error** and raise an event that alerts an operator. The operator can then attempt to resolve the reason for the failure manually and resubmit the failed processing step.

The Supervisor periodically examines the State Store looking for orders with an expired **CompleteBy** value. If the Supervisor finds such a record, it increments the **FailureCount** field. If the **FailureCount** value is below a specified threshold value, the Supervisor resets the **LockedBy** field to null, updates the **CompleteBy** field with a new expiration time, and sets the **ProcessState** field to **Pending**. An instance of the Scheduler can pick up this order and perform its processing as before. If the **FailureCount** value exceeds a specified threshold, the reason for the failure is assumed to be non-transient. The Supervisor sets the status of the order to **Error** and raises an event that alerts an operator, as previously described.

> In this example, the Supervisor is implemented in a separate worker role. You can utilize a variety of strategies to arrange for the Supervisor task to be run, including using the Windows Azure Scheduler service (not to be confused with the Scheduler component in this pattern). For more information about the Windows Azure Scheduler service, visit the _Scheduler_ page.

Although it is not shown in this example, the Scheduler may need to keep the application that submitted the order in the first place informed about the progress and status of the order. The application and the Scheduler are isolated from each other to eliminate any dependencies between them. The application has no knowledge of which instance of the Scheduler is handling the order, and the Scheduler is unaware of which specific application instance posted the order.

To enable the order status to be reported, the application could use its own private response queue. The details of this response queue would be included as part of the request sent to the Submission process, which would include this information in the State Store. The Scheduler would then post messages to this queue indicating the status of the order ("request received," "order completed," "order failed," and so on). It should include the Order ID in these messages so that they can be correlated with the original request by the application.

RELATED PATTERNS AND GUIDANCE

The following patterns and guidance may also be relevant when implementing this pattern:
- **Retry Pattern**. An Agent can use this pattern to transparently retry an operation that accesses a remote service or resource, and that has previously failed, in the expectation that the cause of the failure is transient and may be corrected.
- **Circuit Breaker Pattern**. An Agent can use this pattern to handle faults that may take a variable amount of time to rectify when connecting to a remote service or resource.
- **Compensating Transaction Pattern**. If the workflow being performed by a Scheduler cannot be completed successfully, it may be necessary to undo any work it has previously performed. The Compensating Transaction pattern describes how this can be achieved for operations that follow the eventual consistency model. These are the types of operations that are commonly implemented by a Scheduler that performs complex business processes and workflows.

- **Asynchronous Messaging Primer**. The components in the Scheduler Agent Supervisor pattern typically run decoupled from each other and communicate asynchronously. The Asynchronous Messaging primer describes some of the approaches that can be used to implement asynchronous communication based on message queues.
- **Leader Election Pattern**. It may be necessary to coordinate the actions of multiple instances of a Supervisor to prevent them from attempting to recover the same failed process. The Leader Election pattern describes how this coordination can be achieved.

MORE INFORMATION

All links in this book are accessible from the book's online bibliography available at:
http://aka.ms/cdpbibliography.

- The post _Cloud Architecture: The Scheduler-Agent-Supervisor Pattern on Clemens Vasters' blog_.
- The _Process Manager_ pattern on the Enterprise Integration Patterns website.
- An example showing how the CQRS pattern uses a process manager is available in _Reference 6: A Saga on Sagas_ (part of the CQRS Journey guidance) on the MSDN website.
- The _Scheduler_ page on the Windows Azure website.

Sharding Pattern

Divide a data store into a set of horizontal partitions or shards. This pattern can improve scalability when storing and accessing large volumes of data.

CONTEXT AND PROBLEM

A data store hosted by a single server may be subject to the following limitations:

- **Storage space**. A data store for a large-scale cloud application may be expected to contain a huge volume of data that could increase significantly over time. A server typically provides only a finite amount of disk storage, but it may be possible to replace existing disks with larger ones, or add further disks to a machine as data volumes grow. However, the system will eventually reach a hard limit whereby it is not possible to easily increase the storage capacity on a given server.

- **Computing resources**. A cloud application may be required to support a large number of concurrent users, each of which run queries that retrieve information from the data store. A single server hosting the data store may not be able to provide the necessary computing power to support this load, resulting in extended response times for users and frequent failures as applications attempting to store and retrieve data time out. It may be possible to add memory or upgrade processors, but the system will reach a limit when it is not possible to increase the compute resources any further.

- **Network bandwidth**. Ultimately, the performance of a data store running on a single server is governed by the rate at which the server can receive requests and send replies. It is possible that the volume of network traffic might exceed the capacity of the network used to connect to the server, resulting in failed requests.

- **Geography**. It may be necessary to store data generated by specific users in the same region as those users for legal, compliance, or performance reasons, or to reduce latency of data access. If the users are dispersed across different countries or regions, it may not be possible to store the entire data for the application in a single data store.

Scaling vertically by adding more disk capacity, processing power, memory, and network connections may postpone the effects of some of these limitations, but it is likely to be only a temporary solution. A commercial cloud application capable of supporting large numbers of users and high volumes of data must be able to scale almost indefinitely, so vertical scaling is not necessarily the best solution.

SOLUTION

Divide the data store into horizontal partitions or *shards*. Each shard has the same schema, but holds its own distinct subset of the data. A shard is a data store in its own right (it can contain the data for many entities of different types), running on a server acting as a storage node.

This pattern offers the following benefits:

- You can scale the system out by adding further shards running on additional storage nodes.
- A system can use off the shelf commodity hardware rather than specialized (and expensive) computers for each storage node.
- You can reduce contention and improved performance by balancing the workload across shards.
- In the cloud, shards can be located physically close to the users that will access the data.

When dividing a data store up into shards, decide which data should be placed in each shard. A shard typically contains items that fall within a specified range determined by one or more attributes of the data. These attributes form the *shard key* (sometimes referred to as the *partition key*). The shard key should be static. It should not be based on data that might change.

Sharding physically organizes the data. When an application stores and retrieves data, the sharding logic directs the application to the appropriate shard. This sharding logic may be implemented as part of the data access code in the application, or it could be implemented by the data storage system if it transparently supports sharding.

Abstracting the physical location of the data in the sharding logic provides a high level of control over which shards contain which data, and enables data to migrate between shards without reworking the business logic of an application should the data in the shards need to be redistributed later (for example, if the shards become unbalanced). The tradeoff is the additional data access overhead required in determining the location of each data item as it is retrieved.

To ensure optimal performance and scalability, it is important to split the data in a way that is appropriate for the types of queries the application performs. In many cases, it is unlikely that the sharding scheme will exactly match the requirements of every query. For example, in a multi-tenant system an application may need to retrieve tenant data by using the tenant ID, but it may also need to look up this data based on some other attribute such as the tenant's name or location. To handle these situations, implement a sharding strategy with a shard key that supports the most commonly performed queries.

If queries regularly retrieve data by using a combination of attribute values, it may be possible to define a composite shard key by concatenating attributes together. Alternatively, use a pattern such as Index Table to provide fast lookup to data based on attributes that are not covered by the shard key.

Sharding Strategies

Three strategies are commonly used when selecting the shard key and deciding how to distribute data across shards. Note that there does not have to be a one-to-one correspondence between shards and the servers that host them—a single server can host multiple shards. The strategies are:

- **The Lookup strategy**. In this strategy the sharding logic implements a map that routes a request for data to the shard that contains that data by using the shard key. In a multi-tenant application all the data for a tenant might be stored together in a shard by using the tenant ID as the shard key. Multiple tenants might share the same shard, but the data for a single tenant will not be spread across multiple shards. Figure 1 shows an example of this strategy.

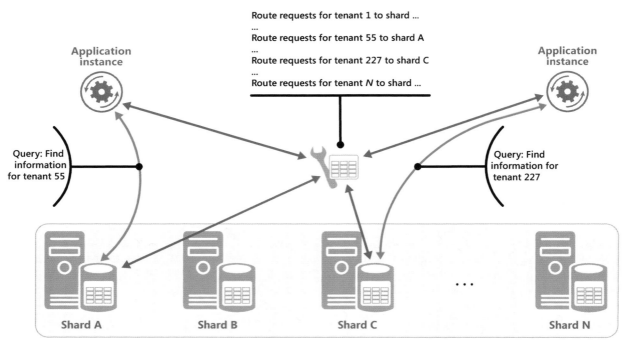

Sharding logic:

Route requests for tenant 1 to shard ...

...

Route requests for tenant 55 to shard A

...

Route requests for tenant 227 to shard C

...

Route requests for tenant *N* to shard ...

Application
instance

Application
instance

Query: Find
information
for tenant 55

Query: Find
information for
tenant 227

Shard A   Shard B   Shard C   Shard N

FIGURE 1
Sharding tenant data based on tenant IDs

The mapping between the shard key and the physical storage may be based on physical shards where each shard key maps to a physical partition. Alternatively, a technique that provides more flexibility when rebalancing shards is to use a virtual partitioning approach where shard keys map to the same number of virtual shards, which in turn map to fewer physical partitions. In this approach, an application locates data by using a shard key that refers to a virtual shard, and the system transparently maps virtual shards to physical partitions. The mapping between a virtual shard and a physical partition can change without requiring the application code to be modified to use a different set of shard keys.

- **The Range strategy**. This strategy groups related items together in the same shard, and orders them by shard key—the shard keys are sequential. It is useful for applications that frequently retrieve sets of items by using *range* queries (queries that return a set of data items for a shard key that falls within a given range). For example, if an application regularly needs to find all orders placed in a given month, this data can be retrieved more quickly if all orders for a month are stored in date and time order in the same shard. If each order was stored in a different shard, they would have to be fetched individually by performing a large number of *point* queries (queries that return a single data item). Figure 2 shows an example of this strategy.

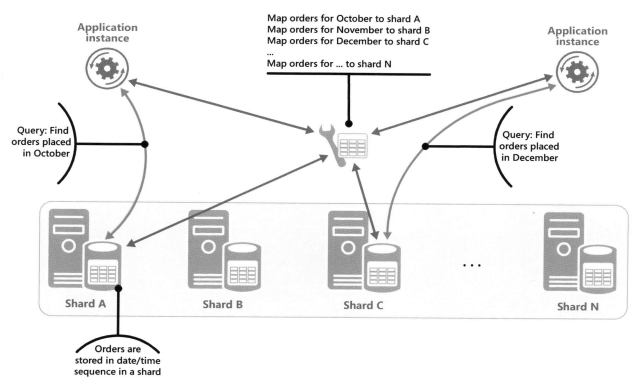

Sharding logic:

Map orders for October to shard A
Map orders for November to shard B
Map orders for December to shard C
...
Map orders for ... to shard N

Application instance

Application instance

Query: Find orders placed in October

Query: Find orders placed in December

Shard A   Shard B   Shard C   Shard N

Orders are stored in date/time sequence in a shard

FIGURE 2
Storing sequential sets (ranges) of data in shards

In this example, the shard key is a composite key comprising the order month as the most significant element, followed by the order day and the time. The data for orders is naturally sorted when new orders are created and appended to a shard. Some data stores support two-part shard keys comprising a *partition key* element that identifies the shard and a *row key* that uniquely identifies an item within the shard. Data is usually held in row key order within the shard. Items that are subject to range queries and need to be grouped together can use a shard key that has the same value for the *partition key* but a unique value for the *row key*.

- **The Hash strategy**. The purpose of this strategy is to reduce the chance of hotspots in the data. It aims to distribute the data across the shards in a way that achieves a balance between the size of each shard and the average load that each shard will encounter. The sharding logic computes the shard in which to store an item based on a hash of one or more attributes of the data. The chosen hashing function should distribute data evenly across the shards, possibly by introducing some random element into the computation. Figure 2 shows an example of this strategy.

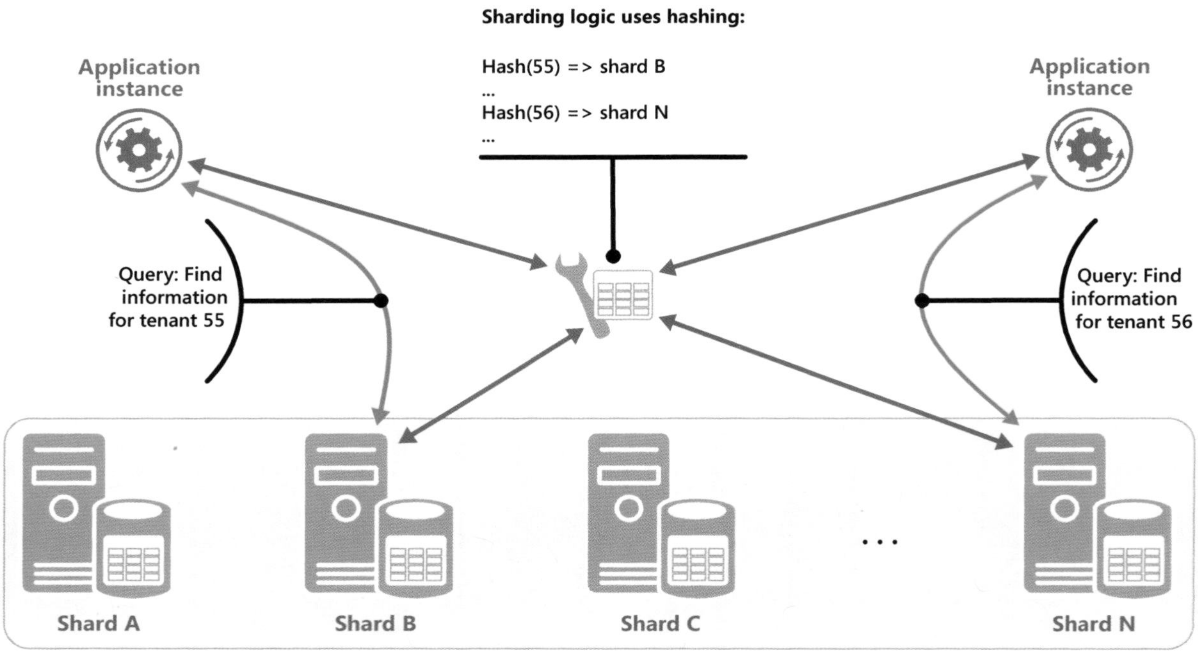

FIGURE 3
Sharding tenant data based on a hash of tenant IDs

To understand the advantage of the Hash strategy over other sharding strategies, consider how a multi-tenant application that enrolls new tenants sequentially might assign the tenants to shards in the data store. When using the Range strategy, the data for tenants 1 to *n* will all be stored in shard A, the data for tenants *n+1* to *m* will all be stored in shard B, and so on. If the most recently registered tenants are also the most active, most data activity will occur in a small number of shards—which could cause hotspots. In contrast, the Hash strategy allocates tenants to shards based on a hash of their tenant ID. This means that sequential tenants are most likely to be allocated to different shards, as shown in Figure 3 for tenants 55 and 56, which will distribute the load across these shards.

The following table lists the main advantages and considerations for these three sharding strategies.

Strategy	Advantages	Considerations
Lookup	More control over the way that shards are configured and used. Using virtual shards reduces the impact when rebalancing data because new physical partitions can be added to even out the workload. The mapping between a virtual shard and the physical partitions that implement the shard can be modified without affecting application code that uses a shard key to store and retrieve data.	Looking up shard locations can impose an additional overhead.
Range	Easy to implement and works well with range queries because they can often fetch multiple data items from a single shard in a single operation. Easier data management. For example, if users in the same region are in the same shard, updates can be scheduled in each time zone based on the local load and demand pattern.	May not provide optimal balancing between shards. Rebalancing shards is difficult and may not resolve the problem of uneven load if the majority of activity is for adjacent shard keys.
Hash	Better chance of a more even data and load distribution. Request routing can be accomplished directly by using the hash function. There is no need to maintain a map.	Computing the hash may impose an additional overhead. Rebalancing shards is difficult.

Most common sharding schemes implement one of the approaches described above, but you should also consider the business requirements of your applications and their patterns of data usage. For example, in a multi-tenant application:

- You can shard data based on workload. You could segregate the data for highly volatile tenants in separate shards. The speed of data access for other tenants may be improved as a result.

- You can shard data based on the location of tenants. It may be possible to take the data for tenants in a specific geographic region offline for backup and maintenance during off-peak hours in that region, while the data for tenants in other regions remains online and accessible during their business hours.

- High-value tenants could be assigned their own private high-performing, lightly loaded shards, whereas lower-value tenants might be expected to share more densely-packed, busy shards.

- The data for tenants that require a high degree of data isolation and privacy could be stored on a completely separate server.

Scaling and Data Movement Operations

Each of the sharding strategies implies different capabilities and levels of complexity for managing scale in, scale out, data movement, and maintaining state.

The **Lookup strategy** permits scaling and data movement operations to be carried out at the user level, either online or offline. The technique is to suspend some or all user activity (perhaps during off-peak periods), move the data to the new virtual partition or physical shard, change the mappings, invalidate or refresh any caches that hold this data, and then allow user activity to resume. Often this type of operation can be centrally managed. The Lookup strategy requires state to be highly cacheable and replica friendly.

The **Range strategy** imposes some limitations on scaling and data movement operations, which must typically be carried out when a part or all of the data store is offline because the data must be split and merged across the shards. Moving the data to rebalance shards may not resolve the problem of uneven load if the majority of activity is for adjacent shard keys or data identifiers that are within the same range. The Range strategy may also require some state to be maintained in order to map ranges to the physical partitions.

The **Hash strategy** makes scaling and data movement operations more complex because the partition keys are hashes of the shard keys or data identifiers. The new location of each shard must be determined from the hash function, or the function modified to provide the correct mappings. However, the Hash strategy does not require maintenance of state.

ISSUES AND CONSIDERATIONS

Consider the following points when deciding how to implement this pattern:

- Sharding is complementary to other forms of partitioning, such as vertical partitioning and functional partitioning. For example, a single shard may contain entities that have been partitioned vertically, and a functional partition may be implemented as multiple shards. For more information about partitioning, see the Data Partitioning Guidance.

- Keep shards balanced so that they all handle a similar volume of I/O. As data is inserted and deleted, it may be necessary to periodically rebalance the shards to guarantee an even distribution and to reduce the chance of hotspots. Rebalancing can be an expensive operation. To reduce the frequency with which rebalancing becomes necessary you should plan for growth by ensuring that each shard contains sufficient free space to handle the expected volume of changes. You should also develop strategies and scripts that you can use to quickly rebalance shards should this become necessary.

- Use stable data for the shard key. If the shard key changes, the corresponding data item may have to move between shards, increasing the amount of work performed by update operations. For this reason, avoid basing the shard key on potentially volatile information. Instead, look for attributes that are invariant or that naturally form a key.

- Ensure that shard keys are unique. For example, avoid using auto-incrementing fields as the shard key. Is some systems, auto-incremented fields may not be coordinated across shards, possibly resulting in items in different shards having the same shard key.

  > Auto-incremented values in fields that do not comprise the shard key can also cause problems. For example, if you use auto-incremented fields to generate unique IDs, then two different items located in different shards may be assigned the same ID.

- It may not be possible to design a shard key that matches the requirements of every possible query against the data. Shard the data to support the most frequently performed queries, and if necessary create secondary index tables to support queries that retrieve data by using criteria based on attributes that are not part of the shard key. For more information, see the Index Table Pattern.

- Queries that access only a single shard will be more efficient than those that retrieve data from multiple shards, so avoid implementing a sharding scheme that results in applications performing large numbers of queries that join data held in different shards. Remember that a single shard can contain the data for multiple types of entities. Consider denormalizing your data to keep related entities that are commonly queried together (such as the details of customers and the orders that they have placed) in the same shard to reduce the number of separate reads that an application performs.

  > If an entity in one shard references an entity stored in another shard, include the shard key for the second entity as part of the schema for the first entity. This can help to improve the performance of queries that reference related data across shards.

- If an application must perform queries that retrieve data from multiple shards, it may be possible to fetch this data by using parallel tasks. Examples include *fan-out* queries, where data from multiple shards is retrieved in parallel and then aggregated into a single result. However, this approach inevitably adds some complexity to the data access logic of a solution.

- For many applications, creating a larger number of small shards can be more efficient than having a small number of large shards because they can offer increased opportunities for load balancing. This approach can also be useful if you anticipate the need to migrate shards from one physical location to another. Moving a small shard is quicker than moving a large one.

- Make sure that the resources available to each shard storage node are sufficient to handle the scalability requirements in terms of data size and throughput. For more information, see the section "Designing Partitions for Scalability" in the Data Partitioning Guidance.

- Consider replicating reference data to all shards. If an operation that retrieves data from a shard also references static or slow-moving data as part of the same query, add this data to the shard. The application can then fetch all of the data for the query easily, without having to make an additional round trip to a separate data store.

  > If reference data held in multiple shards changes, the system must synchronize these changes across all shards. The system may experience a degree of inconsistency while this synchronization occurs. If you follow this approach, you should design your applications to be able to handle this inconsistency.

- It can be difficult to maintain referential integrity and consistency between shards, so you should minimize operations that affect data in multiple shards. If an application must modify data across shards, evaluate whether complete data consistency is actually a requirement. Instead, a common approach in the cloud is to implement eventual consistency. The data in each partition is updated separately, and the application logic must take responsibility for ensuring that the updates all complete successfully, as well as handling the inconsistencies that can arise from querying data while an eventually consistent operation is running. For more information about implementing eventual consistency, see the Data Consistency Primer.

- Configuring and managing a large number of shards can be a challenge. Tasks such as monitoring, backing up, checking for consistency, and logging or auditing must be accomplished on multiple shards and servers, possibly held in multiple locations. These tasks are likely to be implemented by using scripts or other automation solutions, but scripting and automation might not be able to completely eliminate the additional administrative requirements.

- Shards can be geo-located so that the data that they contain is close to the instances of an application that use it. This approach can considerably improve performance, but requires additional consideration for tasks that must access multiple shards in different locations.

WHEN TO USE THIS PATTERN

Use this pattern:

- When a data store is likely to need to scale beyond the limits of the resources available to a single storage node.

- To improve performance by reducing contention in a data store.

> The primary focus of sharding is to improve the performance and scalability of a system, but as a by-product it can also improve availability by virtue of the way in which the data is divided into separate partitions. A failure in one partition does not necessarily prevent an application from accessing data held in other partitions, and an operator can perform maintenance or recovery of one or more partitions without making the entire data for an application inaccessible. For more information, see the Data Partitioning Guidance.

EXAMPLE

The following example uses a set of SQL Server databases acting as shards. Each database holds a subset of the data used by an application. The application retrieves data that is distributed across the shards by using its own sharding logic (this is an example of a *fan-out* query). The details of the data that is located in each shard is returned by a method called **GetShards**. This method returns an enumerable list of **ShardInformation** objects, where the **ShardInformation** type contains an identifier for each shard and the SQL Server connection string that an application should use to connect to the shard (the connection strings are not shown in the code example).

```csharp
C#
private IEnumerable<ShardInformation> GetShards()
{
  // This retrieves the connection information from a shard store
  // (commonly a root database).
  return new[]
  {
    new ShardInformation
    {
      Id = 1,
      ConnectionString = ...
    },
    new ShardInformation
    {
      Id = 2,
      ConnectionString = ...
    }
  };
}
```

The code below shows how the application uses the list of **ShardInformation** objects to perform a query that fetches data from each shard in parallel. The details of the query are not shown, but in this example the data that is retrieved comprises a string which could hold information such as the name of a customer if the shards contain the details of customers. The results are aggregated into a **ConcurrentBag** collection for processing by the application.

```csharp
C#
// Retrieve the shards as a ShardInformation[] instance.
var shards = GetShards();

var results = new ConcurrentBag<string>();

// Execute the query against each shard in the shard list.
// This list would typically be retrieved from configuration
// or from a root/master shard store.
Parallel.ForEach(shards, shard =>
{
  // NOTE: Transient fault handling is not included,
  // but should be incorporated when used in a real world application.
  using (var con = new SqlConnection(shard.ConnectionString))
  {
    con.Open();
    var cmd = new SqlCommand("SELECT ... FROM ...", con);

    Trace.TraceInformation("Executing command against shard: {0}", shard.Id);

    var reader = cmd.ExecuteReader();
    // Read the results in to a thread-safe data structure.
    while (reader.Read())
```

```
      {
        results.Add(reader.GetString(0));
      }
    }
  }
});

Trace.TraceInformation("Fanout query complete - Record Count: {0}",
                       results.Count);
```

RELATED PATTERNS AND GUIDANCE

The following patterns and guidance may also be relevant when implementing this pattern:

- **Data Consistency Primer**. It may be necessary to maintain consistency for data distributed across different shards. The Data Consistency Primer summarizes the issues surrounding maintaining consistency over distributed data, and describes the benefits and tradeoffs of different consistency models.
- **Data Partitioning Guidance**. Sharding a data store can introduce a range of additional issues. The Data Partitioning Guidance describes these issues in relation to partitioning data stores in the cloud to improve scalability, reduce contention, and optimize performance.
- **Index Table Pattern**. Sometimes it is not possible to completely support queries just through the design of the shard key. The Index Table pattern enables an application to quickly retrieve data from a large data store by specifying a key other than the shard key.
- **Materialized View Pattern**. To maintain the performance of some query operations, it may be beneficial to create materialized views that aggregate and summarize data, especially if this summary data is based on information that is distributed across shards. The Materialized View pattern describes how to generate and populate these views.

MORE INFORMATION

All links in this book are accessible from the book's online bibliography available at:
http://aka.ms/cdpbibliography.

- The article *Shard Lessons* on the Adding Simplicity blog.
- The page *Database Sharding* on the CodeFutures web site.
- The article *Scalability Strategies Primer: Database Sharding* on Max Indelicato's blog.
- The article *Building Scalable Databases: Pros and Cons of Various Database Sharding Schemes* on Dare Obasanjo's blog.

Static Content Hosting Pattern

Deploy static content to a cloud-based storage service that can deliver these directly to the client. This pattern can reduce the requirement for potentially expensive compute instances.

Context and Problem

Web applications typically include some elements of static content. This static content may include HTML pages and other resources such as images and documents that are available to the client, either as part of an HTML page (such as inline images, style sheets, and client-side JavaScript files) or as separate downloads (such as PDF documents).

Although web servers are well tuned to optimize requests through efficient dynamic page code execution and output caching, they must still handle requests to download static content. This absorbs processing cycles that could often be put to better use.

Solution

In most cloud hosting environments it is possible to minimize the requirement for compute instances (for example, to use a smaller instance or fewer instances), by locating some of an application's resources and static pages in a storage service. The cost for cloud-hosted storage is typically much less than for compute instances.

When hosting some parts of an application in a storage service, the main considerations are related to deployment of the application and to securing resources that are not intended to be available to anonymous users.

Issues and Considerations

Consider the following points when deciding how to implement this pattern:

- The hosted storage service must expose an HTTP endpoint that users can access to download the static resources. Some storage services also support HTTPS, which means that it is possible to host resources in storage service that require the use of SSL.
- For maximum performance and availability, consider using a content delivery network (where available) to cache the contents of the storage container in multiple datacenters around the world. However, this will incur additional cost for the use of the content delivery network.
- Storage accounts are often geo-replicated by default to provide resiliency against events that might impact a datacenter. This means that the IP address may change, but the URL will remain the same.

- When some content is located in a storage account and other content is in a hosted compute instance it becomes more challenging to deploy an application and to update it. It may be necessary to perform separate deployments, and version the application and content in order to manage it more easily—especially when the static content includes script files or UI components. However, if only static resources are to be updated they can simply be uploaded to the storage account without needing to redeploy the application package.

- Storage services may not support the use of custom domain names. In this case it is necessary to specify the full URL of the resources in links because they will be in a different domain from the dynamically generated content containing the links.

- The storage containers must be configured for public read access, but it is vital to ensure that they are not configured for public write access to prevent users being able to upload content. Consider using a valet key or token to control access to resources that should not be available anonymously—see Valet Key Pattern for more information.

WHEN TO USE THIS PATTERN

This pattern is ideally suited for:

- Minimizing the hosting cost for websites and applications that contain some static resources.
- Minimizing the hosting cost for websites that consist of only static content and resources. Depending on the capabilities of the hosting provider's storage system, it might be possible to host a fully static website in its entirety within a storage account.
- Exposing static resources and content for applications running in other hosting environments or on-premises servers.
- Locating content in more than one geographical area by using a content delivery network that caches the contents of the storage account in multiple datacenters around the world.
- Monitoring costs and bandwidth usage. Using a separate storage account for some or all of the static content allows the costs to be more easily distinguished from hosting and runtime costs.

This pattern might not be suitable in the following situations:

- The application needs to perform some processing on the static content before delivering it to the client. For example, it may be necessary to add a timestamp to a document.
- The volume of static content is very small. The overhead of retrieving this content from separate storage may outweigh the cost benefit of separating it out from the compute resources.

> It is sometimes possible to store a complete website that contains only static content such as HTML pages, images, style sheets, client-side JavaScript files, and downloadable documents such as PDF files in a cloud-hosted storage. For more information see _An efficient way of deploying a static web site on Windows Azure_ on the Infosys blog.

EXAMPLE

Static content located in Windows Azure blob storage can be accessed directly by a web browser. Windows Azure provides an HTTP-based interface over storage that can be publicly exposed to clients. For example, content in a Windows Azure blob storage container is exposed using a URL of the form:

http://[_storage-account-name_]**.blob.core.windows.net/**[_container-name_]**/**[_file-name_]

When uploading the content for the application it is necessary to create one or more blob containers to hold the files and documents. Note that the default permission for a new container is Private, and you must change this to Public to allow clients to access the contents. If it is necessary to protect the content from anonymous access, you can implement the Valet Key Pattern so users must present a valid token in order to download the resources.

> The page *Blob Service Concepts* on the Windows Azure website contains information about blob storage, and the ways that you can access it and use it.

The links in each page will specify the URL of the resource and the client will access this resource directly from the storage service. Figure 1 shows this approach.

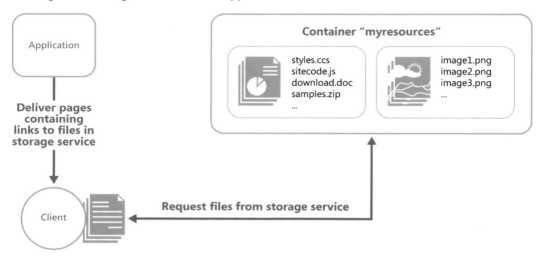

FIGURE 1
Delivering static parts of an application directly from a storage service

The links in the pages delivered to the client must specify the full URL of the blob container and resource. For example, a page that contains a link to an image in a public container might contain the following.

HTML
```
<img src="http://mystorageaccount.blob.core.windows.net/myresources/image1.png"
    alt="My image" />
```

> If the resources are protected by using a valet key, such as a Windows Azure Shared Access Signature (SAS), this signature must be included in the URLs in the links.

The examples available for this guide contain a solution named StaticContentHosting that demonstrates using external storage for static resources. The StaticContentHosting.Cloud project contains configuration files that specify the storage account and container that holds the static content.

XML
```
<Setting name="StaticContent.StorageConnectionString"
        value="UseDevelopmentStorage=true" />
<Setting name="StaticContent.Container" value="static-content" />
```

The **Settings** class in the file Settings.cs of the StaticContentHosting.Web project contains methods to extract these values and build a string value containing the cloud storage account container URL.

```csharp
// C#
public class Settings
{
  public static string StaticContentStorageConnectionString {
    get
    {
      return RoleEnvironment.GetConfigurationSettingValue(
                         "StaticContent.StorageConnectionString");
    }
  }

  public static string StaticContentContainer
  {
    get
    {
      return RoleEnvironment.GetConfigurationSettingValue("StaticContent.Container");
    }
  }

  public static string StaticContentBaseUrl
  {
    get
    {
      var account = CloudStorageAccount.Parse(StaticContentStorageConnectionString);

      return string.Format("{0}/{1}", account.BlobEndpoint.ToString().TrimEnd('/'),
                           StaticContentContainer.TrimStart('/'));
    }
  }
}
```

The **StaticContentUrlHtmlHelper** class in the file StaticContentUrlHtmlHelper.cs exposes a method named **StaticContentUrl** that generates a URL containing the path to the cloud storage account if the URL passed to it starts with the ASP.NET root path character (~).

```csharp
// C#
public static class StaticContentUrlHtmlHelper
{
  public static string StaticContentUrl(this HtmlHelper helper, string contentPath)
  {
    if (contentPath.StartsWith("~"))
    {
      contentPath = contentPath.Substring(1);
    }

    contentPath = string.Format("{0}/{1}", Settings.StaticContentBaseUrl.TrimEnd('/'),
                           contentPath.TrimStart('/'));

    var url = new UrlHelper(helper.ViewContext.RequestContext);

    return url.Content(contentPath);
  }
}
```

The file Index.cshtml in the Views\Home folder contains an image element that uses the **StaticContentUrl** method to create the URL for its **src** attribute.

HTML
```
<img src="@Html.StaticContentUrl("~/Images/orderedList1.png")" alt="Test Image" />
```

RELATED PATTERNS AND GUIDANCE

The following pattern may also be relevant when implementing this pattern:

- **Valet Key Pattern**. If the target resources are not supposed to be available to anonymous users it is necessary to implement security over the store that holds the static content. The Valet Key pattern describes how to use a token or key that provides clients with restricted direct access to a specific resource or service such as a cloud-hosted storage service.

More Information

All links in this book are accessible from the book's online bibliography available at:
http://aka.ms/cdpbibliography.

- The article _An efficient way of deploying a static web site on Windows Azure_ on the Infosys blog.
- The page _Blob Service Concepts_ on the Windows Azure website.

This pattern has a sample application associated with it. You can download the "Cloud Design Patterns – Sample Code" from the Microsoft Download Center at _http://aka.ms/cloud-design-patterns-sample_.

Throttling Pattern

Control the consumption of resources used by an instance of an application, an individual tenant, or an entire service. This pattern can allow the system to continue to function and meet service level agreements, even when an increase in demand places an extreme load on resources.

CONTEXT AND PROBLEM

The load on a cloud application typically varies over time based on the number of active users or the types of activities they are performing. For example, more users are likely to be active during business hours, or the system may be required to perform computationally expensive analytics at the end of each month. There may also be sudden and unanticipated bursts in activity. If the processing requirements of the system exceed the capacity of the resources that are available, it will suffer from poor performance and may even fail. The system may be obliged to meet an agreed level of service, and such failure could be unacceptable.

There are many strategies available for handling varying load in the cloud, depending on the business goals for the application. One strategy is to use autoscaling to match the provisioned resources to the user needs at any given time. This has the potential to consistently meet user demand, while optimizing running costs. However, while autoscaling may trigger the provisioning of additional resources, this provisioning is not instantaneous. If demand grows quickly, there may be a window of time where there is a resource deficit.

SOLUTION

An alternative strategy to autoscaling is to allow applications to use resources only up to some soft limit, and then throttle them when this limit is reached. The system should monitor how it is using resources so that, when usage exceeds some system-defined threshold, it can throttle requests from one or more users to enable the system to continue functioning and meet any service level agreements (SLAs) that are in place. For more information on monitoring resource usage, see the Instrumentation and Telemetry Guidance.

The system could implement several throttling strategies, including:

- Rejecting requests from an individual user who has already accessed system APIs more than n times per second over a given period of time. This requires that the system meters the use of resources for each tenant or user running an application. For more information, see the Service Metering Guidance.

- Disabling or degrading the functionality of selected nonessential services so that essential services can run unimpeded with sufficient resources. For example, if the application is streaming video output, it could switch to a lower resolution.

- Using load leveling to smooth the volume of activity (this approach is covered in more detail by the Queue-based Load Leveling Pattern). In a multitenant environment, this approach will reduce the performance for every tenant. If the system must support a mix of tenants with different SLAs, the work for high-value tenants might be performed immediately. Requests for other tenants can be held back, and handled when the backlog has eased. The Priority Queue Pattern could be used to help implement this approach.
- Deferring operations being performed on behalf of lower priority applications or tenants. These operations can be suspended or curtailed, with an exception generated to inform the tenant that the system is busy and that the operation should be retried later.

Figure 1 shows an area graph for resource utilization (a combination of memory, CPU, bandwidth, and other factors) against time for applications that are making use of three *features*. A *feature* is an area of functionality, such as a component that performs a specific set of tasks, a piece of code that performs a complex calculation, or an element that provides a service such as an in-memory cache. These features are labeled A, B, and C.

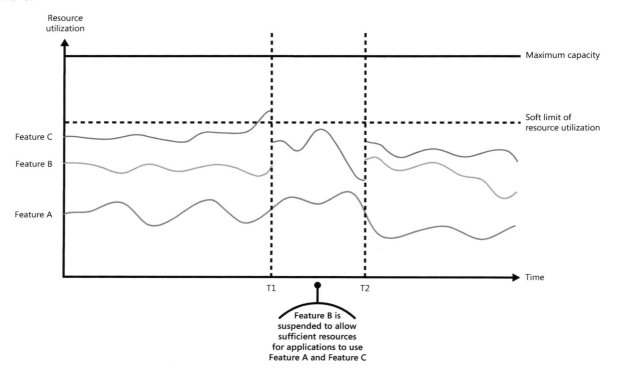

FIGURE 1
Graph showing resource utilization against time for applications running on behalf of three users

The area immediately below the line for a feature indicates the resources used by applications when they invoke this feature. For example, the area below the line for Feature A shows the resources used by applications that are making use of Feature A, and the area between the lines for Feature A and Feature B indicates the resources by used by applications invoking Feature B. Aggregating the areas for each feature shows the total resource utilization of the system.

The graph in Figure 1 illustrates the effects of deferring operations. Just prior to time T1, the total resources allocated to all applications using these features reach a threshold (the soft limit of resource utilization). At this point, the applications are in danger of exhausting the resources available. In this system, Feature B is less critical than Feature A or Feature C, so it is temporarily disabled and the resources that it was using are released. Between times T1 and T2, the applications using Feature A and Feature C continue running as normal. Eventually, the resource use of these two features diminishes to the point when, at time T2, there is sufficient capacity to enable Feature B again.

The autoscaling and throttling approaches can also be combined to help keep the applications responsive and within SLAs. If the demand is expected to remain high, throttling may provide a temporary solution while the system scales out. At this point, the full functionality of the system can be restored.

Figure 2 shows an area graph of the overall resource utilization by all applications running in a system against time, and illustrates how throttling can be combined with autoscaling.

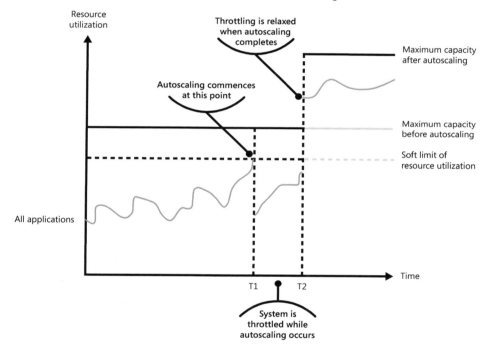

FIGURE 2
Graph showing the effects of combining throttling with autoscaling

At time T1, the threshold specifying the soft limit of resource utilization is reached. At this point, the system can start to scale out. However, if the new resources do not become available sufficiently quickly then the existing resources may be exhausted and the system could fail. To prevent this from occurring, the system is temporarily throttled, as described earlier. When autoscaling has completed and the additional resources are available, throttling can be relaxed.

ISSUES AND CONSIDERATIONS

You should consider the following points when deciding how to implement this pattern:

- Throttling an application, and the strategy to use, is an architectural decision that impacts the entire design of a system. Throttling should be considered early on in the application design because it is not easy to add it once a system has been implemented.

- Throttling must be performed quickly. The system must be capable of detecting an increase in activity and react accordingly. The system must also be able to revert back to its original state quickly after the load has eased. This requires that the appropriate performance data is continually captured and monitored.
- If a service needs to temporarily deny a user request, it should return a specific error code so that the client application understands that the reason for the refusal to perform an operation is due to throttling. The client application can wait for a period before retrying the request.
- Throttling can be used as an interim measure while a system autoscales. In some cases it may be better to simply throttle, rather than to scale, if a burst in activity is sudden and is not expected to be long lived because scaling can add considerably to running costs.
- If throttling is being used as a temporary measure while a system autoscales, and if resource demands grow very quickly, the system might not be able to continue functioning—even when operating in a throttled mode. If this is not acceptable, consider maintaining larger reserves of capacity and configuring more aggressive autoscaling.

WHEN TO USE THIS PATTERN

Use this pattern:

- To ensure that a system continues to meet service level agreements.
- To prevent a single tenant from monopolizing the resources provided by an application.
- To handle bursts in activity.
- To help cost-optimize a system by limiting the maximum resource levels needed to keep it functioning.

EXAMPLE

Figure 3 illustrates how throttling can be implemented in a multi-tenant system. Users from each of the tenant organizations access a cloud-hosted application where they fill out and submit surveys. The application contains instrumentation that monitors the rate at which these users are submitting requests to the application.

In order to prevent the users from one tenant affecting the responsiveness and availability of the application for all other users, a limit is applied to the number of requests per second that the users from any one tenant can submit. The application blocks requests that exceed this limit.

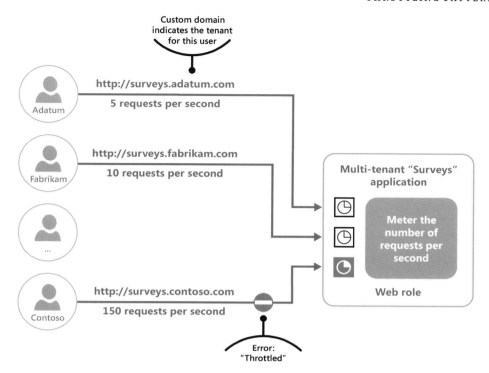

FIGURE 3
Implementing throttling in a multi-tenant application

RELATED PATTERNS AND GUIDANCE

The following patterns and guidance may also be relevant when implementing this pattern:

- **Instrumentation and Telemetry Guidance**. Throttling depends on gathering information on how heavily a service is being used. The Instrumentation and Telemetry Guidance describes how to generate and capture custom monitoring information.

- **Service Metering Guidance**. This guidance describes how to meter the use of services in order to gain an understanding of how they are used. This information can be useful in determining how to throttle a service.

- **Autoscaling Guidance**. Throttling can be used as an interim measure while a system autoscales, or to remove the need for a system to autoscale. The Autoscaling Guidance contains more information on autoscaling strategies.

- **Queue-based Load Leveling Pattern**. Queue-based load leveling is a commonly used mechanism for implementing throttling. A queue can act as a buffer that helps to even out the rate at which requests sent by an application are delivered to a service.

- **Priority Queue Pattern**. A system can use priority queuing as part of its throttling strategy to maintain performance for critical or higher value applications, while reducing the performance of less important applications.

Valet Key Pattern

Use a token or key that provides clients with restricted direct access to a specific resource or service in order to offload data transfer operations from the application code. This pattern is particularly useful in applications that use cloud-hosted storage systems or queues, and can minimize cost and maximize scalability and performance.

CONTEXT AND PROBLEM

Client programs and web browsers often need to read and write files or data streams to and from an application's storage. Typically, the application will handle the movement of the data—either by fetching it from storage and streaming it to the client, or by reading the uploaded stream from the client and storing it in the data store. However, this approach absorbs valuable resources such as compute, memory, and bandwidth.

Data stores have the capability to handle upload and download of data directly, without requiring the application to perform any processing to move this data, but this typically requires the client to have access to the security credentials for the store. While this can be a useful technique to minimize data transfer costs and the requirement to scale out the application, and to maximize performance, it means that the application is no longer able to manage the security of the data. Once the client has a connection to the data store for direct access, the application cannot act as the gatekeeper. It is no longer in control of the process and cannot prevent subsequent uploads or downloads from the data store.

This is not a realistic approach in modern distributed systems that may need to serve untrusted clients. Instead, applications must be able to securely control access to data in a granular way, but still reduce the load on the server by setting up this connection and then allowing the client to communicate directly with the data store to perform the required read or write operations.

SOLUTION

To resolve the problem of controlling access to a data store where the store itself cannot manage authentication and authorization of clients, one typical solution is to restrict access to the data store's public connection and provide the client with a key or token that the data store itself can validate.

This key or token is usually referred to as a *valet key*. It provides time-limited access to specific resources and allows only predefined operations such as reading and writing to storage or queues, or uploading and downloading in a web browser. Applications can create and issue valet keys to client devices and web browsers quickly and easily, allowing clients to perform the required operations without requiring the application to directly handle the data transfer. This removes the processing overhead, and the consequent impact on performance and scalability, from the application and the server.

The client uses this token to access a specific resource in the data store for only a specific period, and with specific restrictions on access permissions, as shown in Figure 1. After the specified period, the key becomes invalid and will not allow subsequent access to the resource.

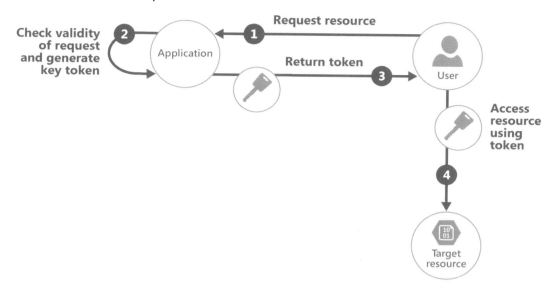

FIGURE 1
Overview of the pattern

It is also possible to configure a key that has other dependencies, such as the scope of the location of the data. For example, depending on the data store capabilities, the key may specify a complete table in a data store, or only specific rows in a table. In cloud storage systems the key may specify a container, or just a specific item within a container.

The key can also be invalidated by the application. This is a useful approach if the client notifies the server that the data transfer operation is complete. The server can then invalidate that key to prevent its use for any subsequent access to the data store.

Using this pattern can simplify managing access to resources because there is no requirement to create and authenticate a user, grant permissions, and then remove the user again. It also makes it easy to constrain the location, the permission, and the validity period—all by simply generating a suitable key at runtime. The important factors are to limit the validity period, and especially the location of the resource, as tightly as possible so that the recipient can use it for only the intended purpose.

ISSUES AND CONSIDERATIONS

Consider the following points when deciding how to implement this pattern:

- **Manage the validity status and period of the key**. The key is a bearer instrument that, if leaked or compromised, effectively unlocks the target item and makes it available for malicious use during the validity period. A key can usually be revoked or disabled, depending on how it was issued. Server-side policies can be changed or, in the ultimate case, the server key it was signed with can be invalidated. Specify a short validity period to minimize the risk of allowing subsequent unwarranted operations to take place against the data store. However, if the validity period is too short, the client may not be able to complete the operation before the key expires. Allow authorized users to renew the key before the validity period expires if multiple accesses to the protected resource are required.

- **Control the level of access the key will provide**. Typically, the key should allow the user to perform only the actions necessary to complete the operation, such as read-only access if the client should not be able to upload data to the data store. For file uploads, it is common to specify a key that provides write-only permission, as well as the location and the validity period. It is vital to accurately specify the resource or the set of resources to which the key applies.

- **Consider how to control users' behavior**. Implementing this pattern means some loss of control over the resources to which users are granted access. The level of control that can be exerted is limited by the capabilities of the policies and permissions available for the service or the target data store. For example, it is usually not possible to create a key that limits the size of the data to be written to storage, or the number of times the key can be used to access a file. This can result in huge unexpected costs for data transfer, even when used by the intended client, and might be caused by an error in the code that causes repeated upload or download. To limit the number of times a file can be uploaded or downloaded it may be necessary, where possible, to force the client to notify the application when one operation has completed. For example, some data stores raise events the application code can use to monitor operations and control user behavior. However, it may be hard to enforce quotas for individual users in a multi-tenant scenario where the same key is used by all the users from one tenant.

- **Validate, and optionally sanitize, all uploaded data**. A malicious user that gains access to the key could upload data aimed at further compromising the system. Alternatively, authorized users might upload data that is invalid and, when processed, could result in an error or system failure. To protect against this, ensure that all uploaded data is validated and checked for malicious content before use.

- **Audit all operations**. Many key-based mechanisms can log operations such as uploads, downloads, and failures. These logs can usually be incorporated into an audit process, and also used for billing if the user is charged based on file size or data volume. Use the logs to detect authentication failures that might be caused by issues with the key provider, or inadvertent removal of a stored access policy.

- **Deliver the key securely**. It may be embedded in a URL that the user activates in a web page, or it may be used in a server redirection operation so that the download occurs automatically. Always use HTTPS to deliver the key over a secure channel.

- **Protect sensitive data in transit**. Sensitive data delivered through the application will usually take place using SSL or TLS, and this should be enforced for clients accessing the data store directly.

Other issues to be aware of when implementing this pattern are:

- If the client does not, or cannot notify the server of completion of the operation, and the only limit is the expiry period of the key, the application will not be able to perform auditing operations such as counting the number of uploads or downloads, or preventing multiple uploads or downloads.

- The flexibility of key policies that can be generated may be limited. For example, some mechanisms may allow only the use of a timed expiry period. Others may not be able to specify a sufficient granularity of read/write permissions.

- If the start time for the key or token validity period is specified, ensure that it is a little earlier than the current server time to allow for client clocks that might be slightly out of synchronization. The default if not specified is usually the current server time.

- The URL containing the key will be recorded in server log files. While the key will typically have expired before the log files are used for analysis, ensure that you limit access to them. If log data is transmitted to a monitoring system or stored in another location, consider implementing a delay to prevent leakage of keys until after their validity period has expired.

- If the client code runs in a web browser, the browser may need to support cross-origin resource sharing (CORS) to enable code that executes within the web browser to access data in a different domain from the originating domain that served the page. Some older browsers and some data stores do not support CORS, and code that runs in these browsers may not be able to use a valet key to provide access to data in a different domain, such as a cloud storage account.

WHEN TO USE THIS PATTERN

This pattern is ideally suited for the following situations:

- To minimize resource loading and maximize performance and scalability. Using a valet key does not require the resource to be locked, no remote server call is required, there is no limit on the number of valet keys that can be issued, and it avoids a single point of failure that would arise from performing the data transfer through the application code. Creating a valet key is typically a simple cryptographic operation of signing a string with a key.
- To minimize operational cost. Enabling direct access to stores and queues is resource and cost efficient, can result in fewer network round trips, and may allow for a reduction in the number of compute resources required.
- When clients regularly upload or download data, particularly where there is a large volume or when each operation involves large files.
- When the application has limited compute resources available, either due to hosting limitations or cost considerations. In this scenario, the pattern is even more advantageous if there are many concurrent data uploads or downloads because it relieves the application from handling the data transfer.
- When the data is stored in a remote data store or a different datacenter. If the application was required to act as a gatekeeper, there may be a charge for the additional bandwidth of transferring the data between datacenters, or across public or private networks between the client and the application, and then between the application and the data store.

This pattern might not be suitable in the following situations:

- If the application must perform some task on the data before it is stored or before it is sent to the client. For example, the application may need to perform validation, log access success, or execute a transformation on the data. However, some data stores and clients are able to negotiate and carry out simple transformations such as compression and decompression (for example, a web browser can usually handle GZip formats).
- If the design and implementation of an existing application makes it difficult and costly to implement. Using this pattern typically requires a different architectural approach for delivering and receiving data.
- If it is necessary to maintain audit trails or control the number of times a data transfer operation is executed, and the valet key mechanism in use does not support notifications that the server can use to manage these operations.
- If it is necessary to limit the size of the data, especially during upload operations. The only solution to this is for the application to check the data size after the operation is complete, or check the size of uploads after a specified period or on a scheduled basis.

EXAMPLE

Windows Azure supports Shared Access Signatures (SAS) on Windows Azure storage for granular access control to data in blobs, tables, and queues, and for Service Bus queues and topics. An SAS token can be configured to provide specific access rights such as read, write, update, and delete to a specific table; a key range within a table; a queue; a blob; or a blob container. The validity can be a specified time period or with no time limit.

Windows Azure SAS also supports server-stored access policies that can be associated with a specific resource such as a table or blob. This feature provides additional control and flexibility compared to application-generated SAS tokens, and should be used whenever possible. Settings defined in a server-stored policy can be changed and are reflected in the token without requiring a new token to be issued, but settings defined in the token itself cannot be changed without issuing a new token. This approach also makes it possible to revoke a valid SAS token before it has expired.

> For more information see _Introducing Table SAS (Shared Access Signature), Queue SAS and update to Blob SAS_ in the Windows Azure Storage Team blog and _Shared Access Signatures, Part 1: Understanding the SAS Model_ on MSDN.

The following code demonstrates how to create a SAS that is valid for five minutes. The **GetSharedAccessReferenceForUpload** method returns a SAS that can be used to upload a file to Windows Azure Blob Storage.

```csharp
C#
public class ValuesController : ApiController
{
  private readonly CloudStorageAccount account;
  private readonly string blobContainer;
  ...
  /// <summary>
  /// Return a limited access key that allows the caller to upload a file
  /// to this specific destination for a defined period of time.
  /// </summary>
  private StorageEntitySas GetSharedAccessReferenceForUpload(string blobName)
  {
    var blobClient = this.account.CreateCloudBlobClient();
    var container = blobClient.GetContainerReference(this.blobContainer);

    var blob = container.GetBlockBlobReference(blobName);

    var policy = new SharedAccessBlobPolicy
    {
      Permissions = SharedAccessBlobPermissions.Write,

      // Specify a start time five minutes earlier to allow for client clock skew.
      SharedAccessStartTime = DateTime.UtcNow.AddMinutes(-5),

      // Specify a validity period of five minutes starting from now.
      SharedAccessExpiryTime = DateTime.UtcNow.AddMinutes(5)
    };

    // Create the signature.
    var sas = blob.GetSharedAccessSignature(policy);

    return new StorageEntitySas
    {
      BlobUri = blob.Uri,
      Credentials = sas,
      Name = blobName
    };
  }

  public struct StorageEntitySas
  {
    public string Credentials;
    public Uri BlobUri;
    public string Name;
  }
}
```

The complete sample containing this code is available in the ValetKey solution available for download with this guidance. The ValetKey.Web project in this solution contains a web application that includes the **ValuesController** class shown above. A sample client application that uses this web application to retrieve a SAS key and upload a file to blob storage is available in the ValetKey.Client project.

RELATED PATTERNS AND GUIDANCE

The following patterns and guidance may also be relevant when implementing this pattern:

- **Gatekeeper Pattern**. This pattern can be used in conjunction with the Valet Key pattern to protect applications and services by using a dedicated host instance that acts as a broker between clients and the application or service. The gatekeeper validates and sanitizes requests, and passes requests and data between the client and the application. This pattern can provide an additional layer of security, and reduce the attack surface of the system.
- **Static Content Hosting Pattern**. This pattern describes how to deploy static resources to a cloud-based storage service that can deliver these resources directly to the client in order to reduce the requirement for expensive compute instances. Where the resources are not intended to be publicly available, the Valet Key pattern can be used to secure them.

MORE INFORMATION

All links in this book are accessible from the book's online bibliography available at: http://aka.ms/cdpbibliography.

- The article *Introducing Table SAS (Shared Access Signature), Queue SAS and update to Blob SAS* on the Windows Azure Storage Team blog.
- *Shared Access Signatures, Part 1: Understanding the SAS Model* on MSDN.
- *Shared Access Signature Authentication with Service Bus* on MSDN.

You can download the "Cloud Design Patterns – Sample Code" from the Microsoft Download Center at http://aka.ms/cloud-design-patterns-sample.

Asynchronous Messaging Primer

Messaging is a key strategy employed in many distributed environments such as the cloud. It enables applications and services to communicate and cooperate, and can help to build scalable and resilient solutions. Messaging supports asynchronous operations, enabling you to decouple a process that consumes a service from the process that implements the service.

MESSAGE QUEUING ESSENTIALS

Asynchronous messaging in the cloud is usually implemented by using message queues. Regardless of the technology used to implement them, most message queues support three fundamental operations:

- A sender can post a message to the queue.
- A receiver can retrieve a message from the queue (the message is removed from the queue).
- A receiver can examine (or *peek*) the next available message in the queue (the message is not removed from the queue).

Sending and Receiving Messages by Using a Message Queue

Conceptually, you can think of a message queue as a buffer that supports send and receive operations. A sender constructs a message in an agreed format, and posts the message to a queue. A receiver retrieves the message from the queue and processes it. If a receiver attempts to retrieve a message from an empty queue, the receiver may be blocked until a new message arrives on that queue. Many message queues enable a receiver to query the current length of a queue, or peek to see whether one or messages are available, enabling the receiver to avoid being blocked if the queue is empty.

The infrastructure that implements a queue is responsible for ensuring that, once a message has been successfully posted, it will not be lost.

FIGURE 1
Sending and receiving messages by using a message queue

Some message queuing systems support transactions to ensure atomicity of queue operations, allow senders to define the lifespan of a message on the queue, attach proprietary properties to messages being enqueued and provide other advanced messaging functionality.

Message queuing is ideally suited to performing asynchronous operations. A sender can post a message to a queue, but it does not have to wait while the message is retrieved and processed. A sender and receiver do not even have to be running concurrently.

Message queues are often shared between many senders and receivers. Any number of senders can post messages to the same queue, and each message could be processed by any of the receivers that retrieve messages from this queue.

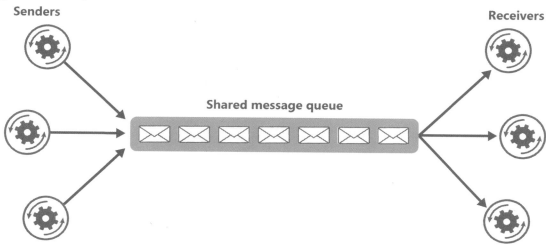

FIGURE 2
Sharing a message queue between many senders and receivers

> By default, senders compete for messages and no two senders should be able to retrieve the same message simultaneously.

Retrieving a message is normally a destructive operation. When a message is retrieved, it is removed from the queue. A message queue may also support message peeking. This is a nondestructive receive operation that retrieves a copy of a message from the queue but leaves the original message on the queue. This mechanism can be useful if several receivers are retrieving messages from the same queue, but each receiver only wishes to handle specific messages. The receiver can examine the message it has peeked, and decide whether to retrieve the message (which removes it from the queue) or leave it on the queue for another receiver to handle.

Message Queuing in Windows Azure

Windows Azure provides several technologies that enable you to build messaging solutions. These include Windows Azure storage queues, Service Bus queues, and Service Bus topics and subscriptions. At the highest level of abstraction, these technologies all offer very similar features. However, they are generally used in different situations.

For example, a Windows Azure storage queue is typically used to communicate between roles running as part of the same Windows Azure cloud service. A Service Bus queue is more suited to use in large-scale integration solutions, enabling disparate applications and services to connect and communicate. Service Bus topics and subscriptions extend the capabilities of message queuing to enable a system to broadcast messages to multiple receivers.

> The article _Windows Azure Queues and Windows Azure Service Bus Queues - Compared and Contrasted_ on MSDN contains detailed information about the different types of queues that Windows Azure provides.

BASIC MESSAGE QUEUING PATTERNS

Distributed applications typically use message queues to implement one or more of the following basic message exchange patterns:

- **One-way messaging**. This is the most basic pattern for communicating between a sender and a receiver. In this pattern, the sender simply posts a message to the queue in the expectation that a receiver will retrieve it and process it at some point.

- **Request/response messaging**. In this pattern a sender posts a message to a queue and expects a response from the receiver. You can use this pattern to implement a reliable system where you must confirm that a message has been received and processed. If the response is not delivered within a reasonable interval, the sender can either send the message again or handle the situation as a timeout or failure. This pattern usually requires a separate communications channel in the form of a dedicated message queue to which the receiver can post its response messages (the sender can provide the details of this queue as part of the message that it posts to the receiver). The sender listens for a response on this queue. This pattern typically requires some form of correlation to enable the sender to determine which response message corresponds to which request sent to the receiver.

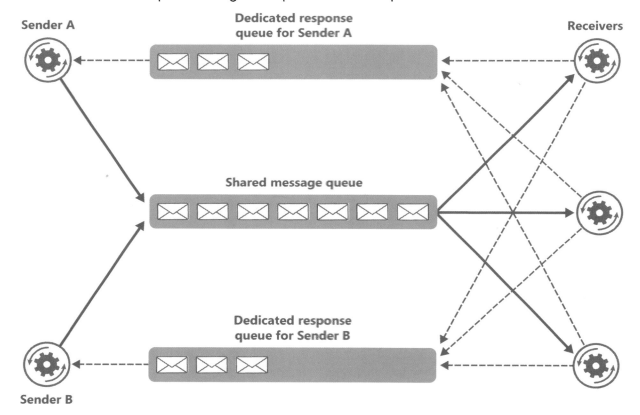

FIGURE 3
Request/response messaging with dedicated response queues for each sender

Messages posted to Windows Azure Service Bus Queues contain a **ReplyTo** property that can be populated by a sender to specify the queue to which any replies should be sent.

- **Broadcast messaging**. In this pattern a sender posts a message to a queue, and multiple receivers can read a copy of the message (receivers do not compete for messages in this scenario). This mechanism can be used to notify receivers that an event has occurred of which they should all be aware, and may be used to implement a publisher/subscriber model. This pattern depends on the message queue being able to disseminate the same message to multiple receivers. Windows Azure Service Bus topics and subscriptions provide a mechanism for broadcast messaging, as shown in Figure 4. A topic acts like a queue to which the senders can post messages that include metadata in the form of attributes. Each receiver can create a subscription for the topic, specifying a filter that examines the values of message attributes. Any messages posted to the topic with attribute values that match the filter are automatically forwarded to that subscription. A receiver retrieves messages from a subscription in a similar way to a queue.

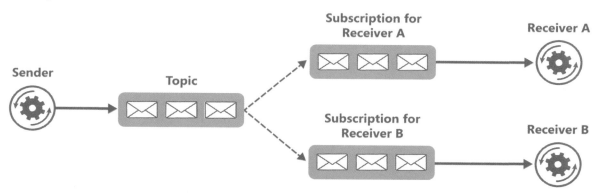

FIGURE 4
Broadcast messaging by using a topic and subscriptions

SCENARIOS FOR ASYNCHRONOUS MESSAGING

The basic message queuing patterns enable you to construct solutions that address most common asynchronous messaging scenarios. The following list contains some examples:

- **Decoupling workloads**. Using a message queue enables you to decouple the logic that generates work from that logic that performs the work. For example, components in the user interface of a web application could generate messages in response to user input and post these messages to a queue. Receivers can retrieve these messages and process them, performing whatever work is required. In this way the user interface can remain responsive. It is not blocked while the messages are handled asynchronously.

- **Temporal decoupling**. A sender and a receiver do not have to be running at the same time. A sender can post a message to the queue when the receiver is not available to process it, and a receiver can read messages from the queue even when the sender is not available.

- **Load balancing**. You can use message queues to distribute processing across servers and improve throughput. Senders may post a large number of requests to a queue that is serviced by many receivers. Receivers can run on different servers to spread the load. Receivers can be added dynamically to scale out the system if the queue length grows, and they can be removed when the queue has drained. You may be able to use autoscaling to scale the system automatically based on the queue length. This is described in more detail in the Autoscaling Guidance.

- **Load leveling**. This scenario covers sudden bursts of activity by senders. A large number of senders might suddenly generate a large volume of messages. Starting a large number of receivers to handle this work could overwhelm the system. Instead, the message queue acts as a buffer, and receivers gradually drain the queue at their own pace without stressing the system. The Queue-based Load Leveling Pattern provides more information. You can also use this approach to implement service throttling, and to prevent an application from exhausting the available resources.
- **Cross-platform integration**. Message queues can be beneficial for implementing solutions that need to integrate components running on different platforms, and that are built by using different programming languages and technologies. The decoupled nature of senders and receivers can help to remove any implementation dependencies between them. All that is required is that senders and receivers agree on a common format for messages and their contents.
- **Asynchronous workflow**. An application might implement a complex business process as a workflow. The individual steps in the workflow can be implemented by senders and receivers, coordinated by using messages posted to or read from a queue. If the work for each step is designed carefully, you may be able to eliminate any dependencies between steps. In this case, the messages can be processed in parallel by multiple receivers.
- **Deferred processing**. You can use a message queue to delay processing until off peak hours, or you can arrange for messages to be processed according to a specific schedule. Senders post messages to a queue. At the appointed time the receivers are started up and process the messages in the queue. When the queue has drained, or the timeslot for processing messages has elapsed, the receivers are shut down. Any unprocessed messages will be handled the next time the receivers are started.
- **Reliable messaging**. Using a message queue can help to ensure that messages are not lost, even if communication between a sender and a receiver fails. The sender can post messages to a queue and the receiver can retrieve these messages from the queue when communications are reestablished. The sender is not blocked unless it loses connectivity with the queue.

> How a sender or receiver handles loss of connectivity with the queue is an application design consideration. In many cases, such failures are transient and the application can simply repeat the operation that posts the message to the queue by following the Retry Pattern. If the failure is likely to be more long lived, you can implement the Circuit Breaker Pattern to prevent continual retries from blocking the sender.

- **Resilient message handling**: You can use a message queue to add resiliency to the receivers in your system. In some message queue implementations, a receiver can peek and lock the next available message in a queue. This action retrieves a copy of the message leaving the original on the queue, but also locks it to prevent the same message being read by another receiver. If the receiver fails, the lock will time out and be released. Another receiver can then process the message. Note that if the message processing performed by the receiver updates the system state, this processing should be idempotent to prevent a repeated update from causing multiple changes to the state.

> This scenario requires that the message queue can lock messages. Windows Azure Service Bus provides a peek-lock mode that can be used to lock a message in a queue without removing it. This lock can also be renewed if it is likely to timeout before the receiver has finished processing the message. Windows Azure Storage queues also provide the ability to peek at messages without dequeueing them, but an application must modify the message to lock it. For more information, see the section "How to: Change the Contents of a Message" of the topic *How to Use the Storage Queue Service* on MSDN.

- **Non-blocking receivers**. In many message queue implementations, by default a receiver blocks when it attempts to retrieve a message and no messages are available in the queue. If the message queue implementation supports message peeking it may be possible for a receiver to poll the queue for messages and attempt to retrieve a message only if there is one available.

CONSIDERATIONS FOR IMPLEMENTING ASYNCHRONOUS MESSAGING

Conceptually, implementing asynchronous messaging by using message queues is a simple idea, but a solution based on this model might need to address a number of concerns. The following list summarizes some of the items that you may need to consider:

- **Message ordering**. The order of messages may not be guaranteed. Some message queuing technologies specify that messages are received in the order in which they are posted, but in other cases the message ordering could depend on a variety of other factors. Some solutions may require that messages are processed in a specific order. The Priority Queue Pattern provides a mechanism for ensuring specific messages are delivered before others.
- **Message grouping.** When multiple receivers retrieve messages from a queue, there is usually no guarantee over which receiver handles any specific message. Messages should ideally be independent. However, there may be occasions when it is difficult to eliminate dependencies, and it may be necessary to group messages together so that they are all handled by the same receiver.

> Windows Azure Service Bus queues and subscriptions support message grouping by enabling a sender to place related messages in a session, specified by the SessionID property of a message. A receiver can lock the messages that are part of the same session to prevent them from being handled by a different receiver. Session state information, stored in the queue or subscription with the messages that comprise the session, records information about the session and which messages have been processed. If the receiver handling a session fails, the lock is released and another receiver can pick up the session. The new receiver can use the information in the session state to determine how to continue processing.

- **Idempotency**. Some message queuing systems guarantee *at least once* delivery of messages, but it is possible that the same message could be received and processed more than once. This can occur if a receiver fails after having completed much of its processing and the message is returned to the queue (as described in the Resilient Message Handling scenario in the previous section of this topic). Ideally the message processing logic in a receiver should be idempotent so that, if the work performed is repeated, this repetition does not change the state of the system. However, it can be very difficult to implement idempotency, and it requires very careful design of the message processing code. For more information about idempotency, see *Idempotency Patterns* on Jonathon Oliver's blog.
- **Repeated messages**. It is possible that the same message could be sent more than once if, for example, the sender fails after posting a message but before completing any other work it was performing. Another sender could be started and run in its place, and this new sender could repeat the message. Some message queuing systems implement duplicate message detection and removal (also known as *de-duping*) based on message IDs. Message queues with this capability provide *at most once delivery* of messages.

> Windows Azure Service Bus queues provide a built-in de-duping capability. Each message can be assigned a unique ID, and a message queue can record a list of the IDs for messages that have been posted (the period during which message IDs are retained is configurable). If a message posted to a queue has the same ID as a message found in this list, the new message is discarded by the queue. Detailed information about implementing de-duping with Windows Azure queues is available in the article *Configuring Duplicate Message Detection* on the CloudCasts.net website.

172

- **Poison messages**. A poison message is a message that cannot be handled, often because it is malformed or contains unexpected information. A receiver processing the message could throw an exception and fail, causing the message to be returned to the queue for another receiver to handle (see the Resilient Message Handling scenario above). The new receiver, performing the same logic as the first, could also throw an exception and cause the message to be returned to the queue again. This cycle could continue indefinitely. Poison messages can obstruct the processing of other valid messages in the queue. Therefore it is necessary to be able to detect and discard them.

  > Windows Azure storage queues and Service Bus queues provide support for detecting poison messages. If the number of times the same message is received exceeds a specified threshold defined by the **MaxDeliveryCount** property of the queue, the message can be removed from the queue and placed in an application-defined dead-letter queue.

- **Message expiration**. A message might have a limited lifetime, and if it is not processed within this period it might no longer be relevant and should be discarded. A sender can specify the date and time by which the message should be processed as part of the data in the message. A receiver can examine this information before deciding whether to perform the business logic associated with the message.

  > Windows Azure storage queues and Service Bus queues enable you to post messages with a *time-to-live* attribute. If this period expires before the message is received, the message is silently removed from the queue and placed in a dead-letter queue. Note that, for a Windows Azure storage queue, the maximum time-to-live value for a message is seven days, but there is no limit on the time-to-live value for messages posted to Windows Azure Service Bus queues and topics.

- **Message scheduling**. A message might be temporarily embargoed and should not be processed until a specific date and time. The message should not be available to a receiver until this time.

  > Windows Azure storage queues and Service Bus queues enable a sender to specify a time when the message should become available. The message remains invisible to receivers until this time occurs, whereupon it becomes accessible and a receiver can retrieve it. If the message expires before this time it will not be delivered.

RELATED PATTERNS AND GUIDANCE

The following patterns and guidance may also be relevant to your scenario when implementing asynchronous messaging:

- **Autoscaling Guidance**. You may be able to start and stop instances of receivers if the length of the queue on which they are receiving messages exceeds predefined thresholds. This approach can help to maintain performance in a system that implements asynchronous messaging. The Autoscaling Guidance provides more information about the benefits and tradeoffs of this approach.
- **Circuit Breaker Pattern**. If the reason that a sender or receiver cannot connect to a queue is more long lasting, it may be necessary to prevent them from repeatedly attempting to perform an operation that is likely to fail until the reason for the failure has been resolved. The Circuit Breaker Pattern describes how to handle this scenario.
- **Competing Consumers Pattern**. Multiple consumers may need to compete to read messages from a queue. The Competing Consumers Pattern explains how to process multiple messages concurrently to optimize throughput, to improve scalability and availability, and to balance the workload.
- **Priority Queue Pattern**. This pattern describes how messages posted by a sender that have a higher priority can be received and processed more quickly by a consumer than those of a lower priority.

- **Queue-based Load Leveling Pattern**. This pattern uses a queue to act as a buffer between a sender and a receiver to help to minimize the impact on availability and responsiveness of intermittent heavy loads for both the sender and the receiver.

- **Retry Pattern**. A sender or receiver might be unable connect to a queue, but the reasons for this failure may be temporary and quickly pass. The Retry Pattern describes how to handle this situation in order to add resiliency to an application.

- **Scheduler Agent Supervisor Pattern**. Messaging is often used as part of a workflow implementation. The Scheduler Agent Supervisor Pattern demonstrates how messaging can be used to coordinate a set of actions across a distributed set of services and other remote resources, and enable a system to recover and retry actions that fail.

MORE INFORMATION

All links in this book are accessible from the book's online bibliography available at: _http://aka.ms/cdpbibliography_.

- The article _Idempotency Patterns_ on Jonathan Oliver's blog.
- The article _Windows Azure Queues and Windows Azure Service Bus Queues - Compared and Contrasted_ on MSDN.
- The article _Best Practices for Maximizing Scalability and Cost Effectiveness of Queue-Based Messaging Solutions on Windows Azure_ on MSDN.
- The page _How to use the Queue Storage Service_ on MSDN.
- The article _Configuring Duplicate Message Detection_ on the CloudCasts.net website.

Autoscaling Guidance

Constantly monitoring performance and scaling a system to adapt to fluctuating workloads to meet capacity targets and optimize operational cost can be a labor-intensive process. It may not be feasible to perform these tasks manually. This is where autoscaling is useful.

WHAT IS AUTOSCALING?

Autoscaling is the process of dynamically allocating the resources required by an application to match performance requirements and satisfy service level agreements (SLAs). As the volume of work grows, an application may require additional resources to enable it to perform its tasks in a timely manner.

Autoscaling is often an automated process that can help to ease management overhead by reducing the need for an operator to continually monitor the performance of a system and make decisions about adding or removing resources.

Autoscaling should also be an elastic process; more resources can be provisioned as the load increases on the system, but as demand slackens resources can be de-allocated to minimize costs while still maintaining adequate performance and meeting SLAs.

> Autoscaling applies to all of the resources used by an application, not just the compute resources. For example, if your system uses message queues to send and receive information, it could create additional queues as it scales.

Types of Scaling

Scaling typically takes one of two forms—vertical and horizontal scaling:

- **Vertical Scaling** (often referred to as *scaling up*) requires that you redeploy the solution using different hardware. In a cloud environment the hardware platform is typically a virtualized environment, and vertical scaling involves provisioning more powerful resources for this environment and moving the system onto these new resources. Vertical scaling is often a disruptive process that requires making the system temporarily unavailable while it is being redeployed. It may be possible to keep the original system running while the new hardware is provisioned and brought online, but there will likely be some interruption while the processing transitions from the old environment to the new one. It is uncommon to use autoscaling to implement a vertical scaling strategy.

- **Horizontal Scaling** (often referred to as *scaling out*) requires deploying the system on additional resources. The system can continue running without interruption while these resources are provisioned. When the provisioning process is complete, copies of the elements that comprise the system can be deployed on these additional resources and made available. If demand drops, the additional resources can be reclaimed after the elements using them have been shut down cleanly. Many cloud-based systems, including Windows Azure, support this form of autoscaling.

IMPLEMENTING AN AUTOSCALING STRATEGY

Implementing an autoscaling strategy typically involves the following processes and components:

- Instrumentation at the application level to capture key performance and scaling factors such as response times, queue lengths, CPU utilization, and memory usage.
- Monitoring components that can observe these performance and scaling factors.
- Decision-making logic that can evaluate the monitored scaling factors against predefined system thresholds and make decisions regarding whether to scale or not. Time plays a critical factor in these evaluations. The decision making logic should avoid making scaling decisions too frequently as this can cause the system to oscillate. It may be possible to semi-automate the scaling decision with the final decision left to an operator.
- Execution components that are responsible for carrying out tasks associated with scaling the system. These components typically use tools and scripts to perform the following tasks:
  - Provision or de-provision resources.
  - Reconfigure the system.
- Testing and validation of the autoscaling strategy to ensure that it functions as expected.

Traditionally, many autoscaling solutions for the cloud depended on writing and configuring scripts that gathered the appropriate performance data, analyzed this data, and then added or removed resources as appropriate. It is now becoming increasingly common for cloud-based systems to provide built-in tooling to help reduce the time and effort required to implement autoscaling.

However, it is important to implement an autoscaling strategy based on the specific requirements of the application rather than being driven by the features provided by any specific toolset. Scripting is still an essential skill, and a good autoscaling solution combines the features provided by the selected toolset with customizations in the form of scripts.

> If you are using Windows Azure, you can access the Windows Azure Management API through Windows PowerShell to script many tasks associated with starting and stopping instances and provisioning services.

CONSIDERATIONS FOR IMPLEMENTING AUTOSCALING

Autoscaling is not an instant solution. Simply adding resources to a system or running more instances of a process does not guarantee that the performance of the system will improve. Consider the following points when designing an autoscaling strategy:

- The system must be designed to be horizontally scalable. Avoid making assumptions about instance affinity; do not design solutions that require that the code is always running in a specific instance of a process. When scaling a cloud service or web site horizontally, do not assume that a series of requests from the same source will always be routed to the same instance. For the same reason, design services to be stateless to avoid requiring that a series of requests from an application are always routed to the same instance of a service. When designing a service that reads messages from a queue and processes them, do not make any assumptions about which instance of the service handles a specific message because autoscaling could start additional instances of a service as the queue length grows. The Competing Consumers Pattern describes how to handle this scenario.

- If the solution implements a long-running task, design this task to support both scaling out and scaling in. Without due care, such a task could prevent an instance of a process from being shutdown cleanly when the system scales in, or it could lose data if the process is forcibly terminated. Ideally, refactor a long-running task and break up the processing that it performs into smaller, discrete chunks. The Pipes and Filters Pattern provides an example of how you can achieve this. Alternatively, you can implement a checkpoint mechanism that records state information about the task at regular intervals, and save this state in durable storage that can be accessed by any instance of the process running the task. In this way, if the process is shutdown, the work that it was performing can be resumed from the last checkpoint by using another instance.

- If the solution comprises multiple items, such as web roles, worker roles, and other resources, it might be necessary to scale all of these items as a unit. It is important to understand the relationships between the items that comprise a solution, and identify groupings that should be scaled together (as a *scale unit*) to achieve a given performance metric. For example, if you know that to handle 10,000 more active users you need to add two more instances of a given web role, three more instances of a particular worker role, and add an additional Service Bus queue, then this is your scalability unit. Obtaining this knowledge takes time and requires careful analysis of telemetry data.

- To prevent a system from attempting to scale out excessively (and to prevent the costs associated with running many thousands of instances), consider limiting the degree of autoscaling. Consider gracefully degrading the functionality that the system provides if the required resources are currently overloaded. Keep in mind that autoscaling might not be the most appropriate mechanism to handle a sudden burst in workload. It takes time to provision and start new instances of a service or add resources to a system, and the peak may have passed by the time these additional resources have been made available. In this scenario, it may be better to throttle the service. For more information, see the Throttling Pattern.

- The system should be configured to monitor the autoscaling process, and log the details of each autoscaling event (what triggered it, what resources were added or removed, and when). This information can be analyzed to help measure the effectiveness of the autoscaling strategy, and tune it if necessary. If the system hits the upper limit defined for autoscaling, it might also alert an operator. The operator could examine the system and may be able to manually start additional resources if the situation warrants them. Note that, under these circumstances, the operator may also be responsible for manually removing these resources after the workload eases.

Autoscaling in a Windows Azure Solution

Windows Azure provides several options for configuring autoscaling for your solutions:

- **Windows Azure Autoscaling**. This feature supports the most common scaling scenarios, and you can configure a solution by using the Windows Azure Management Portal.

- **Microsoft Enterprise Library Autoscaling Application Block**. This utility enables you to scale a solution based on custom rules and performance data. This approach is more flexible, but more complex, and requires you to write code to capture performance data that is specific to your solutions.

- **Microsoft Windows Azure Monitoring Services Management Library**. This library provides access to Windows Azure Monitoring Services operations, including a unified API for retrieving, and configuring metrics, alerts, and autoscale rules for Windows Azure services.

The following sections summarize these approaches.

Using Windows Azure Autoscaling

Windows Azure Autoscaling enables you to configure scale out and scale in options for a solution. Using this feature you can automatically add and remove instances of Windows Azure Cloud Services web and worker roles, Windows Azure Websites applications, and Windows Azure Virtual Machines. There are two approaches for configuring autoscaling in Windows Azure:

- Configure autoscaling based on metrics such as average CPU utilization over the last hour, or the backlog of items in a message queue that the solution is processing. You configure the parameters used by Windows Azure Autoscaling, monitor the performance of your system, and then adjust the way in which the system scales if necessary. However, keep in mind that autoscaling is not an instantaneous process—it takes time to react to a metric such as average CPU utilization exceeding (or dropping below) a specified threshold. Avoid setting finely balanced thresholds that could attempt to start and stop instances very frequently; Windows Azure enforces this rule by permitting only one scaling action to occur in a five minute period. You can increase this period if you find that the system is still overreacting.

- Configure time-based autoscaling to ensure that additional instances are available to coincide with an expected peak in usage, and scale in once the peak time has passed. This strategy enables you to ensure that you have sufficient instances already running without waiting for the system to react to the load.

You should also consider scaling other resources linked to a compute instances as part of the same scalability unit. For example, you could resize SQL databases or add storage accounts as the system scales. However, at the time of writing, you must either perform these operations manually or use the Microsoft Enterprise Library Autoscaling Application Block.

> For more information about configuring autoscaling by using the Windows Azure Management Portal, see *How to Scale an Application* on MSDN.

Implementing Custom Autoscaling by Using the Microsoft Enterprise Library Autoscaling Application Block

The Microsoft Enterprise Library Autoscaling Application Block provides a highly customizable approach to scalability, enabling you to make scaling decisions based on performance counters or other custom metrics.

You specify rules that determine how the Autoscaling Application Block reacts to the metrics. These rules can be complex, and may reference combinations of metrics. For example, you could specify that the Autoscaling Application Block should start an additional instance of a worker role if the length of a message queue is growing at a certain speed and the role has less than 10% of available memory.

As with Windows Azure Autoscaling, the Autoscaling Application Block also supports time-based scaling, and you can restrict the degree of autoscaling that can occur to help prevent excessive costs.

> The *Autoscaling Application Block* page on MSDN provides detailed information on configuring autoscaling, defining rules, and gathering performance data.

Implementing Custom Autoscaling by Using Windows Azure Monitoring Service Library

The Windows Azure Monitoring Service Library, which is in preview at the time of writing, can be used to monitor and automatically scale Windows Azure deployments. In addition to defining autoscaling rules, this library provides options for monitoring and alerting. You can download the library from the *NuGet gallery*.

RELATED PATTERNS AND GUIDANCE

The following patterns and guidance may also be relevant to your scenario when implementing autoscaling:

- **Throttling Pattern**. This pattern describes how an application can continue to function and meet service level agreements when an increase in demand places an extreme load on resources. Throttling can be used with autoscaling to prevent a system from being overwhelmed while the system scales out.

- **Competing Consumers Pattern**. This pattern describes how to implement a pool of service instances that can handle messages from any application instance. Autoscaling can be used to start and stop service instances to match the anticipated workload. This approach enables a system to process multiple messages concurrently to optimize throughput, improve scalability and availability, and balance the workload.

- **Instrumentation and Telemetry Guidance**. Instrumentation and telemetry are vital for gathering the information that can drive the autoscaling process.

MORE INFORMATION

All links in this book are accessible from the book's online bibliography available at: *http://aka.ms/cdpbibliography*.

- The page *How to Scale an Application* on MSDN.
- The *Microsoft Enterprise Library Autoscaling Application Block* documentation and key scenarios on MSDN.

Caching Guidance

Caching is a common technique that aims to improve the performance and scalability of a system by temporarily copying frequently accessed data to fast storage located close to the application. Caching is most effective when an application instance repeatedly reads the same data, especially if the original data store is slow relative to the speed of the cache, is subject to a high level of contention, or is far away when network latency can cause access to be slow.

Caching in Cloud Applications

There are two main types of cache commonly used by cloud applications:

- An in-memory cache, where data is held locally on the computer running an instance of an application.
- A shared cache, which can be accessed by several instances of an application running on different computers.

In-Memory Caching

The most basic type of cache is an in-memory store, held in the address space of a single process and accessed directly by the code that runs in that process. This type of cache is very quick to access, and it can provide an extremely effective strategy for storing modest amounts of static data (the size of a cache is typically constrained by the volume of memory available on the machine hosting the process). If you have multiple instances of an application that uses this model running concurrently, each application instance will have its own independent cache holding its own copy of data.

You should think of a cache as a snapshot of the original data at some point in the past. If this data is not static, it is likely that different application instances will hold different versions of the data in their caches. Therefore, the same query performed by these instances could return different results, as shown in Figure 1.

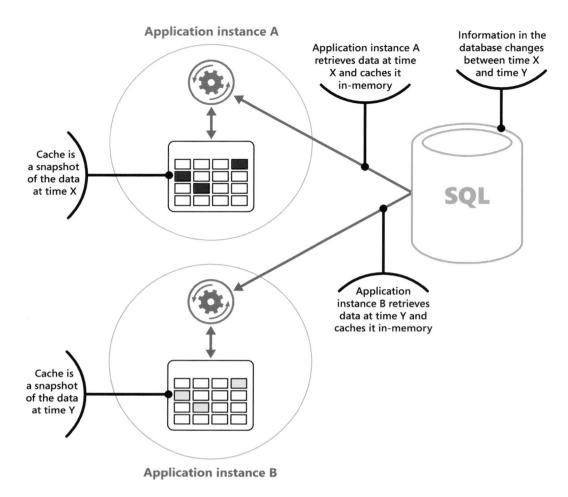

FIGURE 1
Using an in-memory cache in different instances of an application

Shared Caching

Using a shared cache can help to alleviate the concern that data may differ in each cache, as can occur with in-memory caching. Shared caching ensures that different application instances see the same view of cached data by locating the cache in a separate location, typically hosted as part of a separate service, as shown in Figure 2.

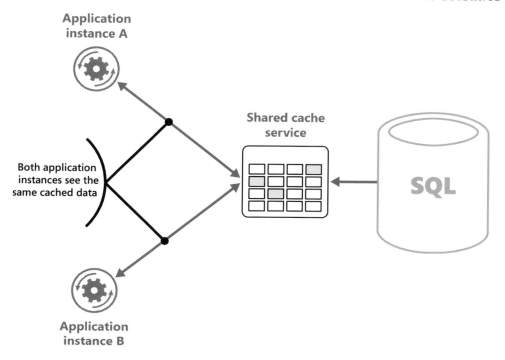

FIGURE 2
Using a shared cache

An important benefit of using the shared caching approach is the scalability it can provide. Many shared cache services are implemented by using a cluster of servers, and utilize software that distributes the data across the cluster in a transparent manner. An application instance simply sends a request to the cache service, and the underlying infrastructure is responsible for determining the location of the cached data in the cluster. You can easily scale the cache by adding more servers.

The disadvantages of the shared caching approach are that the cache is slower to access because it is no longer held in the memory of each application instance, and the requirement to implement a separate cache service may add complexity to the solution.

CONSIDERATIONS FOR USING CACHING

Caching is ideally suited to data that has a high proportion of reads compared to writes. The following sections describe in more detail the considerations for designing and using a cache.

Types of Data and Cache Population Strategies

The key to using a cache effectively lies in determining the most appropriate data to cache, and caching it at the appropriate time. The data may be added to the cache on demand the first time it is retrieved by an application, so that the application needs fetch the data only once from the data store and subsequent accesses can be satisfied by using the cache.

Alternatively, a cache may be partially or fully populated with data in advance, typically when the application starts (an approach known as *seeding*). However, it may not be advisable to implement seeding for a large cache as this approach can impose a sudden, high load on the original data store when the application starts running.

Often an analysis of usage patterns can help to decide whether to fully or partially prepopulate a cache, and to choose the data that should be cached. For example, it would probably be useful to seed the cache with the static user profile data for customers who use the application regularly (perhaps every day), but not for customers who use the application only once a week.

Caching typically works well with data that is immutable or that changes infrequently. Examples include reference information such as product and pricing information in an ecommerce application, or shared static resources that are costly to construct. Some or all of this data can be loaded into the cache at application startup to minimize demand on resources and to improve performance. It may also be appropriate to have a background process that periodically updates reference data in the cache to ensure it is up to date, or re-freshes the cache when reference data changes.

Caching may be less useful for dynamic data. When the original data regularly changes, either the cached information can become stale very quickly or the overhead of keeping the cache synchronized with the original data store reduces the effectiveness of caching.

Performance testing and usage analysis should be carried out to determine whether prepopulation or on-demand loading of the cache, or a combination of both, is appropriate. The decision should be based on a combination of the volatility and usage pattern of the data. Cache utilization and performance analysis is particularly important in applications that encounter heavy loads and must be highly scalable. For example, in highly scalable scenarios it may make sense to seed the cache to reduce the load on the data store at peak times.

Caching can also be used to avoid repeating computations as the application is running. If an operation transforms data or performs a complicated calculation, it can save the results of the operation in the cache. If the same calculation is required subsequently, the application can simply retrieve the results from the cache.

An application *can* modify data held in a cache, but you should consider the cache as a transient data store that could disappear at any time. Do not store valuable data only in the cache, but make sure that you maintain the information in the original data store as well. In this way, if the cache should become unavailable, you minimize the chance of losing data.

Using Read-Through and Write-Through Caching

Some commercial caching solutions implement read-through and write-through caching whereby an application always reads and writes data by using the cache. When an application fetches data, the underlying cache service determines whether the data is currently held in the cache, and if not the cache service retrieves the data from the original data store and adds it to the cache before returning the data to the application. Subsequent read requests should find the data in the cache.

Read-through caching effectively caches data on demand. Data that an application does not use will not be cached. When an application modifies data, it writes the changes to the cache. The cache service transparently makes the same change to the original data store.

Write-through caches typically write changes to the data store synchronously, at the same time as the cache is updated. Some caching solutions implement the write-behind strategy whereby the write to the data store is postponed until the data is about to be removed from cache. This strategy can reduce the number of write operations performed and improve performance at the risk of the increased inconsistency between the data store and the cache that may arise as a result.

For systems that do not provide read-through and write-through caching, it is the responsibility of the applications that use the cache to maintain the data in the cache. The most straightforward approach to implement read-through caching is to implement the Cache-Aside pattern. You can use this strategy to implement an abstraction layer in your application code that emulates a read-through and write-through cache.

In some scenarios, caching data that experiences high volatility without immediately persisting changes to the original data store can be advantageous. For example, an application can modify the data in cache, and if the application expects the data to be changed again very quickly it can refrain from updating the original data store until the system becomes inactive, and then save the data in the original data store only as it appears in this inactive state. In this way, the application can avoid performing a number of slow, expensive write operations to the data store and the data store experiences less contention. However, do not use this strategy if the application cannot safely reconstruct its state if the cache is lost, or if the system requires a full audit trail of every change made to the data.

Managing Data Expiration in a Cache

In most cases, data held in a cache is a copy of the data held in the original data store. It is possible that the data in the original data store might change after it was cached, causing the cached data to become stale. Many caching systems enable you to configure the cache to expire data and reduce the period for which data may be out of date.

When cached data expires it is removed from the cache, and the application must retrieve the data from the original data store (it can put the newly-fetched information back into cache). You can set a default expiration policy when you configure the cache. In many cache services you can also stipulate the expiration period for individual objects when you store them programmatically in the cache. This setting overrides any cache-wide expiration policy, but only for the specified objects.

> Consider the expiration period for the cache and the objects that it contains carefully. If you make it too short, objects will expire too quickly and you will reduce the benefits of using the cache. If you make the period too long, you risk the data becoming stale.

It is also possible that the cache might fill up if data is allowed to remain resident for a long time. In this case, any requests to add new items to the cache might cause some items to be forcibly removed, in a process known as eviction. Cache services typically evict data on a least-recently-used (LRU) basis, but you can usually override this policy and prevent items from being evicted. However, if you adopt this approach you risk your cache exceeding the memory that it has available, and an application that attempts to add an item to the cache will fail with an exception.

Some caching implementations may provide additional eviction policies. These typically include the most-recently-used policy (in the expectation that the data will not be required again) and first-in-first-out policy (oldest data is evicted first).

Managing Concurrency in a Cache

Caches are often designed to be shared by multiple instances of an application. Each application instance can read and modify data in the cache. Consequently, the same concurrency issues that arise with any shared data store are also applicable to a cache. In a situation where an application needs to modify data held in the cache, you may need to ensure that updates made by one instance of the application do not blindly overwrite the changes made by another instance. Depending on the nature of the data and the likelihood of collisions, you can adopt one of two approaches to concurrency:

- **Optimistic**. The application checks to see whether the data in the cache has changed since it was retrieved, immediately prior to updating it. If the data is still the same, the change can be made. Otherwise, the application has to decide whether to update it (the business logic that drives this decision will be application-specific). This approach is suitable for situations where updates are infrequent, or where collisions are unlikely to occur.

- **Pessimistic**. The application locks the data in the cache when it retrieves it to prevent another instance from changing the data. This process ensures that collisions cannot occur, but could block other instances that need to process the same data. Pessimistic concurrency can affect the scalability of the solution and should be used only for short-lived operations. This approach may be appropriate for situations where collisions are more likely, especially if an application updates multiple items in the cache and must ensure that these changes are applied consistently.

Implementing High Availability and Security

Some cache services provide a high-availability option that implements automatic failover if part of the cache becomes unavailable. Additionally, irrespective of the cache service you use, you should consider how to protect the data held in the cache from unauthorized access.

Determining whether to implement caching, deciding which data to cache, estimating the size of the cache, and planning the most appropriate caching topology to use, is a complex and application-specific task. The topic *Capacity Planning for Windows Azure Cache Service* on MSDN provides some detailed guidance and tools that you can use to determine a cost-effective strategy for caching data using Windows Azure Cache.

RELATED PATTERNS AND GUIDANCE

The following pattern may also be relevant to your scenario when implementing caching in your applications:

- **Cache-Aside Pattern**. This pattern describes how to load data on-demand into a cache from a data store. This pattern also helps to maintain consistency between data held in the cache and the data in the original data store.

MORE INFORMATION

All links in this book are accessible from the book's online bibliography available at: *http://aka.ms/cdpbibliography*.

- The page *MemoryCache Class* on MSDN.
- The page *Windows Azure Cache* on MSDN.
- The page *ASP.NET 4 Cache Providers for Windows Azure Cache* on MSDN.
- The page *Capacity Planning for Windows Azure Cache Service* on MSDN.

Compute Partitioning Guidance

When deploying an application to the cloud it may be desirable to allocate the services and components it uses in a way that helps to minimize running costs while maintaining the scalability, performance, availability, and security of the application.

Overview of Windows Azure Compute Options

Windows Azure provides three distinct solutions for hosting applications in the cloud. Windows Azure Web Sites is simple website hosting technology designed to help you quickly build a website or migrate an existing website to the cloud. Windows Azure Cloud Services is a comprehensive hosting technology aimed at more complex web applications, and applications that must be highly scalable or globally available. Windows Azure Virtual Machines allows you to deploy virtual web servers and other services in the cloud.

The key differences between the hosting solutions are the level of control, the methods used to deploy applications, the options for scaling and elasticity, and the use of durable storage. For information about choosing a hosting technology, see _Web Sites_, _Cloud Services_, and _Virtual Machines (VMs)_ on MSDN and the section "Evaluating Cloud Hosting Opportunities" in Chapter 1, _The Adatum Scenario_, of the patterns & practices guide _Moving Applications to the Cloud_.

Each technology offers a range of sizes for the hosting server, including the number of CPU cores, amount of memory, and bandwidth usage limits. For information about choosing the appropriate size, see _Real World: Considerations When Choosing a Web Role Instance Size: How small should I go?_ on MSDN.

Guidelines for Designing the Compute Boundary

The following sections describe the steps for designing the compute boundary for an application, and the primary factors that require consideration at each stage.

Decompose Applications into Logical Components

Applications you deploy in Windows Azure can be decomposed into multiple components. For example, you might choose to decompose a complex application into separate logical compute instances that implement the website UI, API, administration site, background processing, caches, and more.

When considering decomposing applications, the primary design decision is to define the boundary between the separate parts of the application. Many applications have natural boundaries. For example, it is common to separate the UI from the background processing tasks and offload work to these tasks to maintain performance and responsiveness of the UI. Where an application contains distinct and separate UI sections, such as public and restricted areas, these may also be candidates for decomposition. Even a simple website UI can be decomposed into multiple components, for example by separating the pages that require high throughput from the remainder of the site.

If an application uses services that expose an API, these services are likely to be implemented as separate components or roles in order to manage their scale independently from the website UI. It may be appropriate to separate the tasks in these components or roles as part of the decomposition process.

You should also take into account the workload of each separate part of the application. Workload decomposition refers to decomposing an application into parts based on functional workloads that may have different scale, security and management requirements. This may help you define the decomposition boundaries of the application.

Figure 1 shows an example where an application that evolves to contain a range of different types of component can be decomposed into multiple separate compute host instances, depending on the requirements of each component.

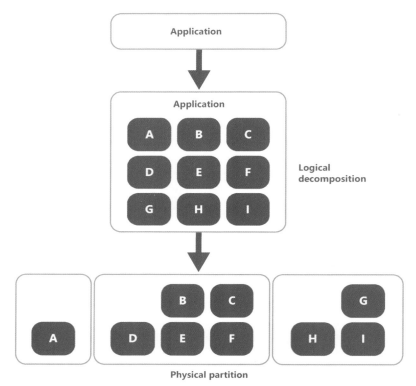

FIGURE 1
Decomposing an application into multiple separate compute host instances

In Figure 1, the components of the application fall into three partitions. The actual types of component in each partition have similar requirements in terms of scalability, availability, and security. Components of the same type can be hosted together. Where the requirements differ, hosting in different compute instances allows the parameters of that instance to be fine-tuned to match the requirements.

The physical deployment of each component also depends on the hosting technology you choose. For example, when using Windows Azure Virtual Machines you can separate the components by installing them on separate virtual machines. When using Windows Azure Cloud Services, you can separate the components by using web and worker roles.

Identify Requirements

To identify the groups and plan the physical deployment, you must determine the non-functional requirements for each logical component. The following requirements must be identified for each component:

- **Performance and scalability.** Often the main considerations when assembling the required compute instances, components, and services for an application are performance and throughput and, to achieve this, the application may make use of multiple instances. Decomposing applications will allow you to more closely control the number of instances of each one you deploy to ensure that your application can meet peaks in demand. You can scale out as demand increases, and scale in when the application is not busy. You can configure automatic scaling for Windows Azure hosted applications. For more information, see Autoscaling Guidance in this guide.

- **Availability.** Business and commercial applications typically need to meet strict service level agreements (SLAs) and other organizational requirements in terms of availability, responsiveness, and minimum downtime. Decomposing compute instances, components, and services that have differing requirements can improve availability because you can host additional instances of the vital ones and fewer of those that have lower availability requirements.

- **Deployment and updating.** Applications will need to be deployed to the hosting environment, and updated as new features are added or bugs are fixed. However, each component may have a different update and deployment cycle. Grouping components that have the same update cycle will simplify management.

- **Security.** It is vital to consider how partitioning affects the security boundaries within the application. Decomposing applications may be necessary to maximize security. For example, you may want to implement the Gatekeeper Pattern that helps to protect applications from intrusive attacks, or isolate components and services for the tenants in a multi-tenant application by deploying some tasks in separate components or compute instances.

- **Resource utilization.** Different component parts of an application may have differing requirements for memory, bandwidth, CPU, and more. Decomposing parts of an application allows you to match the requirements for each part with the size of the hosting instance. For example, a small instance may be sufficient for background processing tasks that run occasionally and have low demand for memory and CPU power, whereas other more intensive tasks may require large or even extra-large compute hosts to manage the demand. However, if the demand fluctuates to a large degree, consider using a smaller host size and deploying multiple instances through autoscaling.

- **Hosting environment.** Components may have specific demands or limitations that affect the choice of hosting environment. For example, third-party components that require special configuration of the operating system will probably need to be hosted in a virtual machine.

- **Background tasks.** If the application performs background processing, these tasks are often good candidates for decomposition. The types of processing that usually work well as background tasks are those that perform a large amount of I/O or network activity, and those that run asynchronously. For example, a long-running workflow that includes external service calls or batch operations that periodically process large volumes of data could be decomposed into worker roles as background tasks.

Allocate Components to Compute Instances

Decisions about how the components of an application are grouped into a single or multiple compute hosts must be based on the requirements of the individual logical components. Components that have similar requirements can be grouped into the same partition. However, the requirements of the application as a whole must be considered. When allocating components to compute resources, consider:

- **Management and Maintenance**. The cost and effort of managing, monitoring, and maintaining applications (and the services, components, and tasks each one requires) depend to some extent on the range of different items that are deployed. Decomposing applications will increase management, monitoring, and maintenance overhead; although this is not a linear relationship because you will typically be able to extend existing tools and systems to include the additional deployments.
- **Runtime cost**. You are billed for every hosted compute instance you deploy to the cloud environment, and so decomposing applications is likely to increase runtime costs. However, implementing autoscaling can minimize the runtime cost for items that are subject to variable demand or load, while maintaining availability. For more information see the Autoscaling Guidance.
- **Dependencies**. Some components may have dependencies that prevent them from being separated. It may also be advantageous to minimize the requirements for inter-process communication between components by hosting them in the same compute instance, for example, to minimize latency or reduce deployment complexity.
- **Inter-process Communication**. Tasks may need to communicate with components in other compute instances, perhaps by using shared memory, private HTTP or TCP endpoints, asynchronous messaging, named pipes, data stores, or a global cache. When this is the case, consider how it will affect the design. Extremely chatty components, or components that are heavily dependent upon each other, could be hosted in the same instance to reduce the communication overhead. For more information about implementing communication between the component parts using queues, see the Asynchronous Messaging Guidance, Queue-based Load Leveling pattern, and Priority Queue Pattern.

Related Patterns and Guidance

The following patterns and guidance may also be relevant to your scenario when consolidating or decomposing application and service instances:

- **Autoscaling Guidance**. Autoscaling can be used to maintain availability of solutions automatically instead of the labor-intensive process of constantly monitoring performance and scaling individual components and services in a partitioned application to meet capacity and to optimize cost targets.
- **Competing Consumers Pattern**. Components in a partitioned application may need to retrieve messages from the same source and process multiple messages concurrently in order to optimize throughput, to improve scalability and availability, and to balance the workload. The Competing Consumers pattern demonstrates how this can be achieved.
- **Compute Resource Consolidation Pattern**. In some cases, it may be appropriate to consolidate multiple tasks or operations into a single computational unit to increase compute resource utilization, and reduce the costs and management overhead associated with performing compute processing in cloud-hosted applications. The Compute Resource Consolidation Pattern describes this approach.
- **Gatekeeper Pattern**. This pattern can help to add additional protection to a partitioned application by using a dedicated host instance that acts as a broker between clients and the application, validates and sanitizes requests, and passes requests and data between them.
- **Leader Election Pattern**. Components in a partitioned application may execute a collection of collaborating task instances, with one task coordinating the actions being performed by the others. The Leader Election Pattern shows how one task can be elected as the leader, and can assume responsibility for managing the other instances.

MORE INFORMATION

All links in this book are accessible from the book's online bibliography available at:
http://aka.ms/cdpbibliography.

- The pages *Web Sites*, *Cloud Services*, and *Virtual Machines (VMs)* on MSDN.
- The article *Real World: Considerations When Choosing a Web Role Instance Size: How small should I go?* on MSDN.
- For information about designing applications for scalability see the following sections of the patterns & practices guide *Developing Multi-tenant Applications for the Cloud* on MSDN:
    - The section "Making the Application Scalable" in Chapter 2, *Hosting a Multi-Tenant Application on Windows Azure*.
    - The section "Partitioning a Windows Azure Application" in Chapter 4, *Partitioning Multi-Tenant Applications*.
    - The section "Scaling Windows Azure Applications with Worker Roles" in Chapter 5, *Maximizing Availability, Scalability, and Elasticity*.

Data Consistency Primer

Cloud applications typically use data that is dispersed across data stores. Managing and maintaining data consistency in this environment can become a critical aspect of the system, particularly in terms of the concurrency and availability issues that can arise. You frequently need to trade strong consistency for availability. This means that you may need to design some aspects of your solutions around the notion of eventual consistency and accept that the data that your applications use might not be completely consistent all of the time.

MANAGING DATA CONSISTENCY

Every web application and service uses data. This data is frequently required to help users and organizations make business decisions, and therefore it may be important that this data accurately represents the most current information available and that it is consistent. Data consistency implies that all instances of an application are presented with the same set of data values all of the time. This approach is sometimes referred to as *strong* data consistency.

In the world of relational databases, consistency is often enforced by transactional models that use locks to prevent concurrent application instances from modifying the same data at the same time. In a strongly consistent system, the locks also block concurrent requests to query data, but many relational databases enable an application to relax this rule and provide access to a copy of the data that reflects the state it was in before the update started. Many applications that store data in non-relational databases, flat files, or other structures follow a similar strategy, known as pessimistic locking. An application instance locks data while it is being modified, and then releases the lock when the update is complete.

In a modern cloud application, the data is likely to be partitioned across data stores hosted at different sites, some of which could be dispersed over a wide geography. This can occur for a variety of reasons: to improve scalability by balancing the load across multiple computers, to improve response time by co-locating data close to the users and services that access it, or to improve availability by replicating data across different sites.

Maintaining data consistency across distributed data stores can be a significant challenge. The issue is that strategies such as serialization and locking only work well if all application instances share the same data store, and the application is designed to ensure that the locks are very short-lived. However, if data is partitioned or replicated across different data stores, locking and serializing data access to maintain consistency can become an expensive overhead that impacts the throughput, response time, and scalability of a system. Therefore, most modern distributed applications do not lock the data that they modify, and they take a rather more relaxed approach to consistency, known as *eventual* consistency.

> For information about distributing data across remote locations, co-locating data, and replicating and synchronizing data, see Data Partitioning Guidance and Data Replication and Synchronization Guidance.

The following sections provide more information on strong consistency and eventual consistency, and the issues that surround these different approaches to maintaining data consistency in a distributed environment such as the cloud.

Strong Consistency

In the strong consistency model, all changes are atomic. If a transaction updates multiple data items, the transaction is not allowed to complete until either all of the changes have been made successfully, or (in the event of a failure) they have all been undone. In the time between a transaction starting and completing, other concurrent transactions may not be able access any of the data that has been modified; they will be blocked. If data is being replicated, a transaction that implements strong consistency may not be allowed to complete until every copy of each item that has changed has been successfully updated.

The aim of the strong consistency model is to minimize the chance that an application instance might be presented with an inconsistent view of the data. The cost of implementing this model is the impact it has on the availability, performance, and scalability of the resulting solution. In a distributed environment, if the data stores holding the data affected by a transaction are geographically remote from each other, network latency could adversely impact the performance of such transactions and result in concurrent access to data being blocked for an extended period. If a network failure renders one or more of the data stores inaccessible during a transaction, an application updating data in a system that implements strong consistency may be blocked until every data store becomes accessible again.

Additionally, in a distributed environment such as the cloud, implementing strong consistency is not tolerant of the types of failure that may occur. For example, it may not be possible to roll back a transaction and release the resources that it holds if a component participating in the transaction has stopped responding due to a long-lasting network outage. In this case, it will be necessary to resolve the situation through other means, such as manually reconciling the data.

> Many forms of data storage used by cloud-based applications do not support strong consistency across different data stores. For example, when using Windows Azure Storage it is not possible to implement transactions that span multiple blob or table stores.

In a cloud application, you should implement strong consistency only where it is absolutely necessary. For example, if an application updates multiple items that are located within the same data store, the benefits of strong consistency may outweigh the disadvantages because data is likely to be locked only for a very short period. However, if the items to be updated are dispersed across a network, it may be more appropriate to relax the requirement for strong consistency.

In a system that implements strong consistency but also replicates data to remote locations, it may be appropriate to propagate changes to replicas outside the scope of a strongly consistent transaction. Some level of transient inconsistency is almost inevitable while replicas are updated—but the data will eventually become consistent after the synchronization between replicas has completed. For more information, see the Data Replication and Synchronization Guidance.

An alternative approach for maintaining strong consistency across replicated data that is frequently implemented by highly scalable NoSQL databases is to use read and write quorums and versioning. This approach avoids locking data, at the expense of some additional complexity in the processes that read and write data. For more information see the section "Improving Consistency" in Chapter 1, "Data Storage for Modern High-Performance Business Applications" of the guide _Data Access for Highly-Scalable Solutions: Using SQL, NoSQL, and Polyglot Persistence_ on MSDN.

> Not all data in an application has to be treated in the same way with respect to consistency. An application may implement different strategies for handling consistency across different data sets. The decision over which strategy and consistency model to use for any given dataset should be based on the business requirements of the application.

Eventual Consistency

Eventual consistency is a rather more pragmatic approach to data consistency. In many cases, strong consistency is not actually required as long all the work performed by a transaction is completed or rolled back at some point, and no updates are lost. In the eventual consistency model, data update operations that span multiple sites can ripple through the various data stores in their own time, without blocking concurrent application instances that access the same data.

One of the drives for eventual consistency is that distributed data stores are subject to the CAP Theorem. This theorem states that a distributed system can implement only two of the three features (Consistency, Availability, and Partition Tolerance) at any one time. In practice, this means that you can either:

- Provide a consistent view of distributed (*partitioned*) data at the cost of blocking access to that data while any inconsistencies are resolved. This may take an indeterminate time, especially in systems that exhibit a high degree of latency or if a network failure causes loss of connectivity to one or more partitions.

- Provide immediate access to the data at the risk of it being inconsistent across sites. Traditional database management systems focus on providing strong consistency, whereas cloud-based solutions that utilize partitioned data stores are typically motivated by ensuring higher availability, and are therefore more oriented towards eventual consistency.

> Eventual consistency is unlikely to be specified as an explicit requirement of a distributed system. Instead it is often a result of implementing a system that must exhibit scalability and high availability, which precludes most common strategies for providing strong consistency.

An application instance may see a view of a data item affected by an operation in the state it is in while the operation is in flight, and this view may be temporarily inconsistent. Depending on the requirements of the system, the developer might need to design applications to detect and handle such inconsistencies, and then take steps to resolve them if necessary.

Eventual consistency also impacts data consistency when using caching. If the data in the remote data store changes, all copies cached by applications will be most likely be out of date. Configuring a cache expiration policy that prevents cached data from becoming too stale, and implementing techniques such as the Cache Aside Pattern, can help to reduce the chances of inconsistencies occurring. However, these approaches are unlikely to completely eliminate inconsistencies in cached data, and it is important that applications that use caching as an optimization strategy can handle these inconsistencies.

It is worth bearing in mind that an application may not actually require data to be consistent all of the time. For example, in a typical ecommerce web application that enables a user to browse and purchase goods, any stock levels presented to a user are likely to be static values determined when the details for a stock item are queried. If another concurrent user purchases the same item, the stock level in the system will decrease but this change will probably not need to be reflected in the data displayed to the first user. If the stock level drops to zero and the first user attempts to purchase the item, the system could either alert the user that the item is now out of stock, or place the item on back order and inform the user that the delivery time may be extended.

Considerations for Implementing Eventual Consistency

Eventual consistency is often the preferred model for managing distributed data in a cloud environment, but there are many issues that you must consider if you follow this model. These issues are best summarized by using an example. Figure 1 shows a simple ecommerce application that could benefit from following the eventual consistency approach.

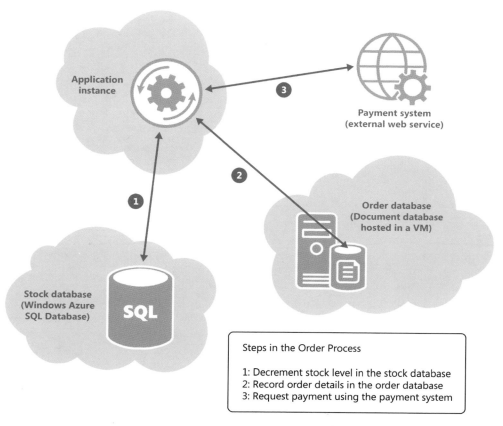

Steps in the Order Process

1: Decrement stock level in the stock database
2: Record order details in the order database
3: Request payment using the payment system

FIGURE 1
A distributed transaction spanning three heterogeneous data sources

When a customer places an order, the application instance performs the following operations across a collection of heterogeneous data stores held in various locations:

1. Update the stock level of the item ordered.
2. Record the details of the order.
3. Verify payment details for the order.

In some cases a data store can be an external service, such as the payment system shown in Figure 1.

Although these operations comprise a logical transaction, attempting to implement strong transactional consistency in this scenario is likely to be impractical. Instead, implementing the order process as an eventually consistent series of steps, where each step in the process is essentially an autonomous operation, is a much more scalable solution. While these steps are progressing, the state of the overall system is inconsistent. For example, after the stock level has been updated but before the details of the order have been recorded the system has temporarily *lost* some stock. However, when all the steps have been completed, the system returns to a consistent state and all stock items can be accounted for.

Despite the fact that implementing eventual consistency in this example appears to be conceptually quite simple, the developer must ensure that the system does eventually become consistent. In other words, the application is responsible for guaranteeing either that all three steps in the order process complete, or determining the actions to take if any of the steps fail. How you resolve this situation in any given system is inevitably application specific.

For an example showing how you can implement an eventually consistent system spanning different data stores, see Chapter 8, "*Building a Polyglot Solution*," in the guide "Data Access for Highly-Scalable Solutions: Using SQL, NoSQL, and Polyglot Persistence" on MSDN. The following sections of this guidance also provide some suggestions.

Retrying Failing Steps

In a distributed environment, the inability to complete an operation is often due to some type of temporary error (communication failure is always a possibility.) If such a failure occurs, an application might assume that the situation is transient and simply attempt to repeat the step that failed. Less transient exceptions, such as database or virtual machine failure, may also occur and the remedy might be similar—wait for the system to be recovered and then try the failing operation again. This approach could result in the same step actually being run twice, possibly resulting in multiple updates. It is very difficult to design a solution to prevent this repetition from occurring, but the application should attempt to render such repetition harmless.

One strategy is to design each step in an operation to be idempotent. This means that a step that had previously succeeded can be repeated without actually changing the state of the system. The steps that comprise a business operation are naturally heavily dependent on the business logic of your system, and the way in which you implement them will be heavily influenced by the structure of the data. Defining idempotent steps requires a deep, domain-specific understanding of your system.

Some steps might be naturally idempotent. For example, a step that sets a particular item to a specific value (such as "ZipCode = 11111") can be repeated many times and the result will always be the same. However, natural idempotency is not always possible. In a system that incorporates services, such as the payment system shown in the ecommerce example, it may be possible to implement some form of artificial idempotency. A common technique is to associate the message sent to the service with a unique identifier. The service can store the identifier for each message it receives locally, and only process a message if the identifier does not match that of a message it received earlier. This technique is known as *de-duping* (the removal of duplicate messages). This strategy, exemplified by the *Idempotent Receiver* pattern, depends on the service being able to store message identifiers successfully.

> For more information about idempotency, see *Idempotency Patterns* on Jonathan Oliver's blog.

Partitioning Data and Using Idempotent Commands

Multiple instances of an application competing to modify the same data at the same time are another common cause of failure to achieve eventual consistency. If possible, you should design your system to minimize these situations. You should try and partition your system to ensure that concurrent instances of an application attempting to perform the same operations simultaneously do not conflict with each other.

Rather than thinking in terms of simple CRUD (create, retrieve, update, and delete) operations, you can structure your system around atomic commands that perform business tasks in an idempotent style. For more information, see the Command and Query Responsibility Segregation Pattern. The commands in a CQRS solution are frequently implemented by following the Event Sourcing Pattern. Event sourcing performs operations on data by driving tasks from a sequence of events, each of which is recorded in an append-only store.

> For detailed information on using CQRS and Event Sourcing to implement eventual consistency, see *Reference 4: A CQRS and ES Deep Dive* on MSDN.

Implementing Compensating Logic

There may ultimately be situations where the logic in the application determines that an operation cannot or should not be allowed to complete (this could be for a variety of business-specific reasons). In these cases you can implement compensating logic that undoes the work performed by the operation, as described by the Compensating Transaction Pattern.

In the ecommerce example shown in Figure 1, as the application performs each step of the order process it can record the tasks necessary to undo this step. If the order process fails, the application can apply the "undo" steps for each step that had previously completed to restore the system to a consistent state. This technique may be complicated by the fact that undoing a step may not be as simple as performing the exact opposite of the original step, and there may be additional business rules that the application must apply. For example, undoing the step that records the details of an order in the document database may not be as straightforward as removing the document. For auditing purposes, it may be necessary to leave the original order document in place but change the status of the order in this document to "cancelled."

Compensating transactions can be complicated to implement and expensive to perform. You should only use them where they are absolutely necessary.

RELATED PATTERNS AND GUIDANCE

The following patterns and guidance may also be relevant when managing consistency in a cloud application:

- **Compensating Transaction Pattern**. This pattern describes how to undo the work performed by a series of steps, which together define an eventually consistent operation, if one or more of the operations fail.

- **Command and Query Responsibility Segregation Pattern**. This pattern describes how you can segregate the operations that read data from the operations that update data. This pattern can use different models of the same data, and it is necessary to ensure that the information in these models can become consistent.

- **Event Sourcing Pattern**. This pattern is frequently used with the Command and Query Responsibility Segregation Pattern. It can simplify tasks in complex domains; improve performance, scalability, and responsiveness; provide consistency for transactional data; and maintain full audit trails and history that may enable compensating actions.

- **Data Partitioning Guidance**. In many large-scale applications, data is divided into separate partitions that can be managed and accessed separately. It may be necessary to ensure that the data is consistent across partitions.

- **Data Replication and Synchronization Guidance**. Data replication and synchronization can help to maximize availability and performance, ensure consistency, and minimize data transfer costs between locations.

- **Caching Guidance**. Data in application caches can become inconsistent across instances and with the data store that acts as the original source of the data. This guidance describes how caches may support expiration policies that can help to reduce the period during which cached data is inconsistent.

- **Cache-Aside Pattern**. This pattern describes how to fetch data into a cache on demand, as the data is required by an application. It can be used to good effect to reduce the overhead associated with repeatedly accessing the same data.

MORE INFORMATION

All links in this book are accessible from the book's online bibliography available at: *http://aka.ms/cdpbibliography*.

- The guide *Data Access for Highly-Scalable Solutions: Using SQL, NoSQL, and Polyglot Persistence* on MSDN.
- The *Idempotent Receiver* pattern by Gregor Hohpe and Bobby Woolf on the Enterprise Integration Patterns website.
- The article *Idempotency Patterns* on Jonathan Oliver's blog.
- *Reference 4: A CQRS and ES Deep Dive* on MSDN.
- The article *Eventually Consistent* on the ACM website.
- *CAP Theorem* on Wikipedia.

Data Partitioning Guidance

In many large-scale solutions, data is divided into separate partitions that can be managed and accessed separately. The partitioning strategy must be chosen carefully to maximize the benefits while minimizing adverse effects. Partitioning can help to improve scalability, reduce contention, and optimize performance.

WHY PARTITION DATA?

Most cloud applications and services store and retrieve data as part of their operations. The design of the data stores that an application uses can have a significant bearing on the performance, throughput, and scalability of a system. One technique that is commonly applied in large-scale systems is to divide the data into separate partitions.

> The term *partitioning* used in this guidance refers to the process of physically dividing data into separate data stores. This is not the same as SQL Server Table Partitioning, which is a different concept.

Partitioning data can offer a number of benefits. For example, it can be applied in order to:

- **Improve scalability**. Scaling up a single database system will eventually reach a physical hardware limit. Dividing data across multiple partitions, each of which is hosted on a separate server, allows the system to scale out almost indefinitely.

- **Improve performance**. Data access operations on each partition take place over a smaller volume of data. Provided that the data is partitioned in a suitable way, this is much more efficient. Operations that affect more than one partition can execute in parallel. Each partition can be located near the application that uses it to minimize network latency.

- **Improve availability**. Separating data across multiple servers avoids a single point of failure. If a server fails, or is undergoing planned maintenance, only the data in that partition is unavailable. Operations on other partitions can continue. Increasing the number of partitions reduces the relative impact of a single server failure by reducing the percentage of the data that will be unavailable. Replicating each partition can further reduce the chance of a single partition failure affecting operations. It also enables the separation of critical data that must be continually and highly available from low value data (such as log files) that has lower availability requirements.

- **Improve security**. Depending on the nature of the data and how it is partitioned, it may be possible to separate sensitive and non-sensitive data into different partitions, and therefore different servers or data stores. Security can then be specifically optimized for the sensitive data.

- **Provide operational flexibility**. Partitioning offers many opportunities for fine tuning operations, maximizing administrative efficiency, and minimizing cost. Some examples are defining different strategies for management, monitoring, backup and restore, and other administrative tasks based on the importance of the data in each partition.

- **Match the data store to the pattern of use**. Partitioning allows each partition to be deployed on a different type of data store, based on cost and the built-in features that data store offers. For example, large binary data could be stored in a blob data store, while more structured data could be held in a document database. For more information see *Building a Polyglot Solution* in the patterns & practices guide *Data Access for Highly-Scalable Solutions: Using SQL, NoSQL, and Polyglot Persistence* on MSDN.

DESIGNING PARTITIONS

Data can be partitioned in different ways: horizontally, vertically, or functionally. The strategy you choose depends on the reason for partitioning the data, and the requirements of the applications and services that will use the data.

> The partitioning schemes described in this guidance are explained in a way that is independent of the underlying data storage technology. They can be applied to many types of data stores, including relational and NoSQL databases.

Partitioning Strategies

The three typical strategies for partitioning data are:

- **Horizontal partitioning** (often called *sharding*). In this strategy each partition is a data store in its own right, but all partitions have the same schema. Each partition is known as a *shard* and holds a specific subset of the data, such as all the orders for a specific set of customers in an ecommerce application.
- **Vertical partitioning**. In this strategy each partition holds a subset of the fields for items in the data store. The fields are divided according to their pattern of use, such as placing the frequently accessed fields in one vertical partition and the less frequently accessed fields in another.
- **Functional partitioning**. In this strategy data is aggregated according to how it is used by each bounded context in the system. For example, an ecommerce system that implements separate business functions for invoicing and managing product inventory might store invoice data in one partition and product inventory data in another.

It's important to note that the three strategies described here can be combined. They are not mutually exclusive and you should consider them all when you design a partitioning scheme. For example, you might divide data into shards and then use vertical partitioning to further subdivide the data in each shard. Similarly, the data in a functional partition may be split into shards (which may also be vertically partitioned).

However, the differing requirements of each strategy can raise a number of conflicting issues that you must evaluate and balance when designing a partitioning scheme that meets the overall data processing performance targets for your system. The following sections explore each of the strategies in more detail.

Horizontal Partitioning (Sharding)

Figure 1 shows an overview of horizontal partitioning or sharding. In this example, product inventory data is divided into shards based on the product key (each shard holds the data for a contiguous range of shard keys, organized alphabetically).

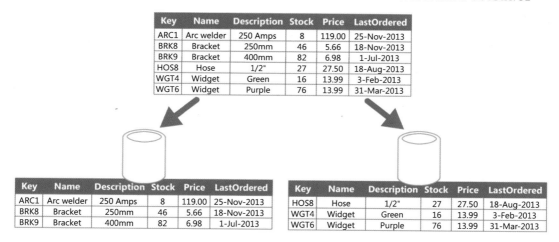

FIGURE 1
Horizontal partitioning (sharding) divides the data based on a partition key

Sharding enables you to spread the load over more computers; reducing contention, and improving performance. You can scale the system out by adding further shards running on additional servers.

The most important factor when implementing this partitioning strategy is the choice of sharding key. It can be difficult to change the key after the system is in operation. The key must ensure that data is partitioned so that the workload is as even as possible across the shards—some shards may be very large but each item is the subject of a low number of access operations, while other shards may be smaller but each item is accessed much more frequently. It is also important to ensure that a single shard does not exceed the scale limits of the data store being used to host that shard.

The sharding scheme should also avoid creating hotspots (or hot partitions) that may affect performance and availability. For example, using a hash of a customer identifier instead of the first letter of a customer's name will prevent the unbalanced distribution that would result from common and less common initial letters. This is a typical technique that helps to distribute the data more evenly across partitions.

The sharding key you choose should minimize any future requirements to split large shards into smaller pieces, coalesce small shards into larger partitions, or change the schema that describes the data stored in a set of partitions. These operations can be very time consuming, and may require taking one or more shards offline while they are performed. If shards are replicated, it may be possible to keep some of the replicas online while others are split, merged, or reconfigured, but the system may need to limit the operations that can be performed on the data in these shards while the reconfiguration is taking place. For example, the data in the replicas could be marked as read-only to limit the scope of any inconsistences that could otherwise occur while shards are being restructured.

For more detailed information and guidance about many of these considerations, and good practice techniques for designing data stores that implement horizontal partitioning, see the Sharding Pattern.

Vertical Partitioning

The most common use for vertical partitioning is to reduce the size of the items that are accessed most frequently in the queries performed by the application. Figure 2 shows an overview of an example of vertical partitioning, where different properties for each data item are held in different partitions.

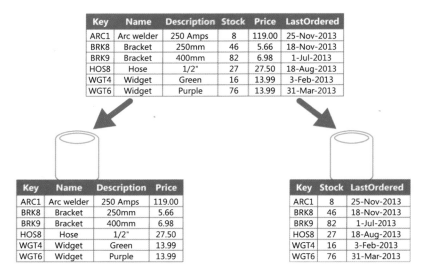

Key	Name	Description	Stock	Price	LastOrdered
ARC1	Arc welder	250 Amps	8	119.00	25-Nov-2013
BRK8	Bracket	250mm	46	5.66	18-Nov-2013
BRK9	Bracket	400mm	82	6.98	1-Jul-2013
HOS8	Hose	1/2"	27	27.50	18-Aug-2013
WGT4	Widget	Green	16	13.99	3-Feb-2013
WGT6	Widget	Purple	76	13.99	31-Mar-2013

Key	Name	Description	Price
ARC1	Arc welder	250 Amps	119.00
BRK8	Bracket	250mm	5.66
BRK9	Bracket	400mm	6.98
HOS8	Hose	1/2"	27.50
WGT4	Widget	Green	13.99
WGT6	Widget	Purple	13.99

Key	Stock	LastOrdered
ARC1	8	25-Nov-2013
BRK8	46	18-Nov-2013
BRK9	82	1-Jul-2013
HOS8	27	18-Aug-2013
WGT4	16	3-Feb-2013
WGT6	76	31-Mar-2013

FIGURE 2
Vertical partitioning organizes data by its pattern of use

In this example, the application regularly queries the product name, description, and price together when displaying the details of products to customers. The stock level and date when the product was last ordered from the manufacturer are held in a separate partition because these two items are commonly used together. This partitioning scheme has the added advantage that the relatively slow-moving data (product name, description, and price) is separated from the more dynamic data (stock level and last ordered date). An application may find it beneficial to cache the slow-moving data in memory.

Another typical scenario for this partitioning strategy is to maximize the security of sensitive data. For example, by storing credit card numbers and the corresponding card security verification numbers in separate partitions.

Vertical partitioning can also reduce the amount of concurrent access required to the data.

> Vertical partitioning operates at the entity level within a data store, partially normalizing an entity that comprises multiple fields into multiple entities with fewer fields.

Functional Partitioning

For systems where it is possible to identify a bounded context for each distinct business area or service in the application, functional partitioning provides a technique for improving isolation and data access performance. Figure 3 shows an overview of functional partitioning where inventory data is separated from customer data.

Corporate data domain

Key	Name	Description	Price	...
ARC1	Arc welder	250 Amps	119.00	...
BRK8	Bracket	250mm	5.66	...
BRK9	Bracket	400mm	6.98	...
HOS8	Hose	1/2"	27.50	...
WGT4	Widget	Green	13.99	...
WGT6	Widget	Purple	13.99	...

Key	Customer	Address	Phone	...
1630	[name]	[address]	12345	...
1631	[name]	[address]	12345	...
1648	[name]	[address]	12345	...
1842	[name]	[address]	12345	...
2055	[name]	[address]	12345	...
2139	[name]	[address]	12345	...

Key	Name	Description	Price	...
ARC1	Arc welder	250 Amps	119.00	...
BRK8	Bracket	250mm	5.66	...
BRK9	Bracket	400mm	6.98	...
HOS8	Hose	1/2"	27.50	...
WGT4	Widget	Green	13.99	...
WGT6	Widget	Purple	13.99	...

Key	Customer	Address	Phone	...
1630	[name]	[address]	12345	...
1631	[name]	[address]	12345	...
1648	[name]	[address]	12345	...
1842	[name]	[address]	12345	...
2055	[name]	[address]	12345	...
2139	[name]	[address]	12345	...

FIGURE 3
Functional partitioning separates data by bounded context or subdomain

This partitioning strategy can help to reduce data access contention across different parts of the system.

Designing Partitions for Scalability

It is vital to consider size and workload for each partition and balance them so that data is distributed to achieve maximum scalability. However, you must also partition the data so that it does not exceed the vertical scaling limits of a single partition store.

Follow these steps when designing the partitions for scalability:

1. Analyze the application to understand the data access patterns, such as size of each query, the frequency of access, the inherent latency, and the compute processing requirements such as stored procedures. In many cases, a few major entities will demand most of the processing resources.

2. Based on the analysis, determine the current and future scalability targets such as data size and workload, and distribute the data across the partitions to meet the scalability target. In the horizontal partitioning strategy, choosing the appropriate shard key is important to make sure distribution is even. For more information see the Sharding Pattern.

3. Make sure that the resources available to each partition are sufficient to handle the scalability requirements in terms of data size and throughput. For example, the node hosting a partition might impose a hard limit on the amount of storage space, processing power, or network bandwidth that it provides. If the data storage and processing requirements are likely to exceed these limits it may be necessary to refine your partitioning strategy or split data out further. For example, one scalability approach might be to separate logging data from the core application features by using separate data stores to prevent the total data storage requirements exceeding the scaling limit of the node. If the total number of data stores exceeds the node limit, it may be necessary to use separate storage nodes.

4. Monitor the system under use to verify that the data is distributed as expected and that the partitions can handle the load imposed on them. It could be possible that the usage does not match that anticipated by the analysis, and it may be necessary to redesign some parts of the system to gain the balance that is required.

Note that some cloud environments allocate resources in terms of infrastructure boundaries, and you should ensure that the limits of your selected boundary provide enough room for any anticipated growth in the volume of data, in terms of data storage, processing power, and bandwidth. For example, if you use Windows Azure table storage, a busy shard might require more resources than are available to a single table to handle requests (there is a limit to the volume of requests that can be handled by a single table in a given period of time). In this case, the shard may need to be split across multiple tables to spread the load. If the total size of these tables exceeds capacity of a storage account, it may be necessary to create additional storage accounts and spread the tables across these accounts. If the number of storage accounts exceeds the number of accounts that are available to a subscription, then it may be necessary to use multiple subscriptions.

Designing Partitions for Query Performance

Query performance can typically be boosted by using smaller data sets and parallel query execution. Each partition should contain a small proportion of the entire data set, and this reduction in volume can improve the performance of queries. However, partitioning is not an alternative for designing and configuring a database appropriately. For example, make sure that you have the necessary indexes in place if you are using a relational database.

Follow these steps when designing the partitions for query performance:

1. Analyze the application to identify:
   - Queries that perform slowly.
   - Critical queries that must always perform quickly.
2. Partition the data that is causing slow performance. Ensure that you:
   - Limit the size of each partition so that the query response time is within target.
   - Design the shard key in a way that the application can easily find the partition if you are implementing horizontal partitioning. This prevents the query needing to scan through every partition.
   - Consider the location of a partition on the performance of queries. If possible, try to keep data in partitions that are geographically close to the applications and users that access it.
3. If an entity has throughput and query performance requirements, use functional partitioning based on that entity. If this is still not able to satisfy the requirements, apply horizontal partitioning as well. In most cases a single partitioning strategy will suffice, but in some cases it is more efficient to combine both strategies.
4. Consider using parallel queries across partitions to improve the performance.

Designing Partitions for Availability

Partitioning data can improve the availability of applications by ensuring that the entire dataset does not constitute a single point of failure and that individual subsets of the dataset can be managed independently. When designing and implementing partitions, consider the following factors that affect availability:

- How individual partitions can be managed. Designing partitions to support independent management and maintenance provides several advantages. For example:
  - If a partition fails, it can be recovered independently without affecting instances of applications that access data in other partitions.
  - Partitioning data by geographical area may allow scheduled maintenance tasks to occur at off-peak hours for each location. Ensure that partitions are not too big to prevent any planned maintenance from being completed during this period.

- How critical the data is to business operations. Some data may comprise critical business information such as invoice details or bank transactions. Other data might simply be less critical operational data, such as log files, performance traces, and so on. After identifying each type of data, consider:
  - Storing critical data in highly-available partitions with an appropriate back up plan.
  - Establishing separate management and monitoring mechanisms or procedures for the different criticalities of each dataset. Place data that has the same level of criticality in the same partition so that it can backed up together at an appropriate frequency. For example, partitions holding data for bank transactions may need to be backed up more frequently than partitions holding logging or trace information.
- Whether to replicate critical data across partitions. This strategy can improve availability and performance, although it can also introduce consistency issues. It takes time for changes made to data in a partition to be synchronized with every replica, and during this period different partitions will contain different data values.

Issues and Considerations

The considerations for designing data partitioning are:

- Where possible, keep data for the most common database operations together in each partition to minimize cross-partition data access operations. Querying across partitions can be more time-consuming than querying only within a single partition, but optimizing partitions for one set of queries might adversely affect other sets of queries. To minimize the query time across partitions where this cannot be avoided, execute parallel queries over the partitions and aggregate the results within the application. However, this approach may not be possible in some cases, such as when it is necessary to obtain a result from one query and use this in the next query.
- If queries make use of relatively static reference data, such as postal code tables or product lists, consider replicating this data in all of the partitions to reduce the requirement for a separate lookup operation in a different partition.
- Where possible, minimize requirements for referential integrity across vertical and functional partitions. In these schemes, the application itself is responsible for maintaining referential integrity across partitions when data is updated and consumed. Queries that must join data across multiple partitions run more slowly than queries that join data only within the same partition because the application will typically need to perform consecutive queries based on a key and then on a foreign key. Instead, consider replicating or de-normalizing the relevant data. To minimize the query time where cross-partition joins are necessary, execute parallel queries over the partitions and join the data within the application.
- Consider the effect that the partitioning scheme might have on the data consistency across partitions. You should evaluate whether strong consistency is actually a requirement. Instead, a common approach in the cloud is to implement eventual consistency. The data in each partition is updated separately, and the application logic can take responsibility for ensuring that the updates all complete successfully—as well as handling the inconsistencies that can arise from querying data while an eventually consistent operation is running. For more information about implementing eventual consistency, see the Data Consistency Primer.
- Consider how queries will locate the correct partition. If a query must scan all partitions to locate the required data there will be a significant impact on performance, even when using multiple parallel queries. Queries used with the vertical and functional partitioning strategies can naturally specify the partitions. However, when using horizontal partitioning (sharding), locating an item can be difficult because every shard has the same schema. A typical solution for sharding is to maintain a map that can be used to look up the shard location for specific items of data. This map may be implemented in the sharding logic of the application, or maintained by the data store if it supports transparent sharding.

- When using a horizontal partitioning strategy, consider periodically rebalancing the shards to distribute the data evenly by size and by workload to minimize hotspots, maximize query performance, and work around physical storage limitations. However, this is a complex task that often requires the use of a custom tool or process.

- Replicating each partition provides additional protection against failure. If a single replica fails, queries can be directed towards a working copy.

- If you reach the physical limits of a partitioning strategy, you may need to extend the scalability to a different level. For example, if partitioning is at the database level it may mean locating or replicating partitions in multiple databases. If partitioning is already at the database level, and physical limitations are an issue, it may mean locating or replicating partitions in multiple hosting accounts.

- Avoid transactions that access data in multiple partitions. Some data stores implement transactional consistency and integrity for operations that modify data, but only when it is located in a single partition. If you need transactional support across multiple partitions, you will probably need to implement this as part of your application logic because most partitioning systems do not provide native support.

All data stores require some operational management and monitoring activity. The tasks can range from loading data, backing up and restoring data, reorganizing data, and ensuring that the system is performing correctly and efficiently.

Consider the following factors that affect operational management:

- Consider executing a periodic process to locate any data integrity issues and either attempt to fix these issues automatically or raise an alert.

- Consider how you will implement appropriate management and operational tasks when the data is partitioned, such as backup and restore, archiving data, monitoring the system, and other administrative tasks. For example, maintaining logical consistency during backup and restore operations can be a challenge.

- How the data can be loaded into multiple partitions, and how new data arriving from other sources might be added. Some tools and utilities may not support sharded data operations such as loading data into the correct partition, and so this may require creating or obtaining new tools and utilities.

- How the data will be archived and deleted on a regular basis (perhaps monthly) to prevent excessive growth of partitions. It may be necessary to transform the data to match a different archive schema.

RELATED PATTERNS AND GUIDANCE

The following patterns and guidance may also be relevant to your scenario when implementing data partitioning in your applications and data stores:

- **Sharding Pattern**. Sharding enables a data store to scale more easily by distributing partitions across storage nodes. This pattern describes how to divide a data store into horizontal partitions.

- **Data Consistency Primer**. Managing and maintaining data consistency across partitions is an important concern, particularly in terms of the concurrency and availability issues that can arise. You frequently need to trade strong consistency for performance by adopting an eventual consistency model. This primer discusses the advantages and limitations of the two consistency models.

- **Data Replication and Synchronization Guidance**. Data can be replicated across partitions in different locations, and it may be necessary to ensure that the replicas are synchronized periodically to ensure that they remain consistent. This guidance summarizes the issues related to replicating data that is distributed across multiple locations, and describes solutions for resolving these issues.

- **Index Table Pattern**. This pattern describes how to create indexes that enable data to be retrieved quickly in a partitioned data store.

- **Materialized View Pattern**. This pattern describes how to generate pre-populated views that summarize data to support fast query operations. This approach can be useful in a partitioned data store if the partitions containing the data being summarized are distributed across multiple sites.

MORE INFORMATION

All links in this book are accessible from the book's online bibliography available at:
http://aka.ms/cdpbibliography.

- The section _Building a Polyglot Solution_ in the patterns & practices guide _Data Access for Highly-Scalable Solutions: Using SQL, NoSQL, and Polyglot Persistence_ on MSDN.
- The page _Real World: Designing a Scalable Partitioning Strategy for Windows Azure Table Storage_ on MSDN.

Data Replication and Synchronization Guidance

When you deploy an application to more than one datacenter, such as cloud and on-premises locations, you must consider how you will replicate and synchronize the data each instance of the application uses in order to maximize availability and performance, ensure consistency, and minimize data transfer costs between locations.

WHY REPLICATE AND SYNCHRONIZE DATA?

Cloud-hosted applications and services are often deployed to multiple datacenters. This approach can reduce network latency for globally located users, as well as providing a complete failover capability should one deployment or one datacenter become unavailable for any reason. For best performance, the data that an application uses should be located close to where the application is deployed, so it may be necessary to replicate this data in each datacenter. If the data changes, these modifications must be applied to every copy of the data. This process is called synchronization.

Alternatively, you might choose to build a hybrid application or service solution that stores and retrieves data from an on-premises data store hosted by your own organization. For example, an organization may hold the main data repository on-premises and then replicate only the necessary data to a data store in the cloud. This can help to protect sensitive data that is not required in all applications. It is also a useful approach if updates to the data occur mainly on-premises, such as when maintaining the catalog of an e-commerce retailer or the account details of suppliers and customers.

The key decisions in any distributed system that uses data replication concern where you will store the replicas, and how you will synchronize these replicas.

REPLICATING AND SYNCHRONIZING DATA

There are several topologies that you can use to implement data replication. The two most common approaches are:

- **Master-Master Replication**, in which the data in each replica is dynamic and can be updated. This topology requires a two-way synchronization mechanism to keep the replicas up to date and to resolve any conflicts that might occur. In a cloud application, to ensure that response times are kept to a minimum and to reduce the impact of network latency, synchronization typically happens periodically. The changes made to a replica are batched up and synchronized with other replicas according to a defined schedule. While this approach reduces the overheads associated with synchronization, it can introduce some inconsistency between replicas before they are synchronized.

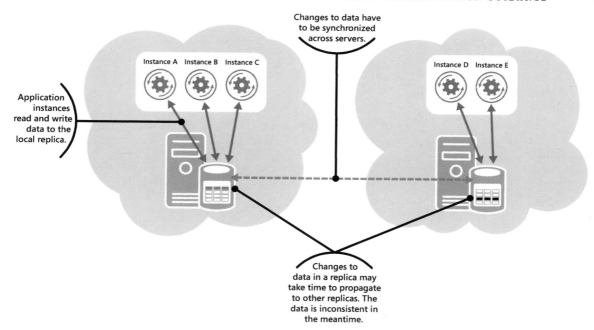

FIGURE 1
Master-Master replication

- **Master-Subordinate Replication**, in which the data in only one of the replicas is dynamic (the master), and the remaining replicas are read-only. The synchronization requirements for this topology are simpler than that of the Master-Master Replication topology because conflicts are unlikely to occur. However, the same issues of data consistency apply.

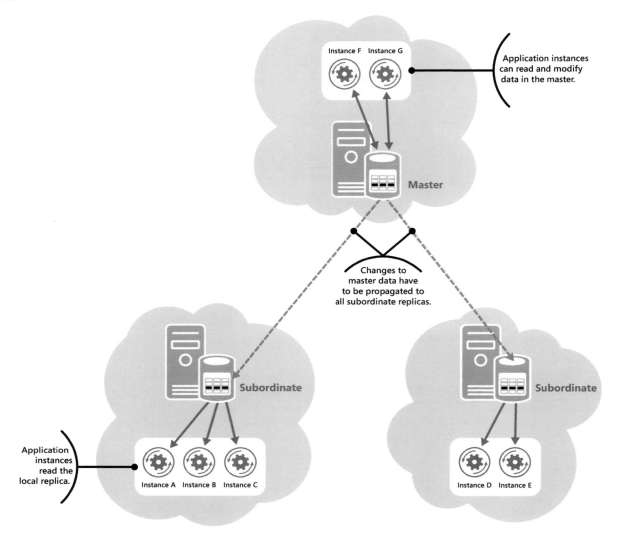

Figure 2
Master-Subordinate replication

Benefits of Replication

The following list provides suggestions for achieving the benefits of replicating data:

- **To improve performance and scalability:**
  - Use Master-Subordinate replication with read-only replicas to improve performance of queries. Locate the replicas close to the applications that access them and use simple one-way synchronization to push updates to them from a master database.
  - Use Master-Master replication to improve the scalability of write operations. Applications can write more quickly to a local copy of the data, but there is additional complexity because two-way synchronization (and possible conflict resolution) with other data stores is required.

- Include in each replica any reference data that is relatively static, and is required for queries executed against that replica to avoid the requirement to cross the network to another datacenter. For example, you could include postal code lookup tables (for customer addresses) or product catalog information (for an ecommerce application) in each replica.

- **To improve reliability:**

  - Deploy replicas close to the applications and inside the network boundaries of the applications that use them to avoid delays caused by accessing data across the Internet. Typically, the latency of the Internet and the correspondingly higher chance of connection failure are the major factors in poor reliability. If replicas are read-only to an application, they can be updated by pushing changes from the master database when connectivity is restored. If the local data is updateable, a more complex two-way synchronization will be required to update all data stores that hold this data.

- **To improve security:**

  - In a hybrid application, deploy only non-sensitive data to the cloud and keep the rest on-premises. This approach may also be a regulatory requirement, specified in a service level agreement (SLA), or as a business requirement. Replication and synchronization can take place over the non-sensitive data only.

- **To improve availability:**

  - In a global reach scenario, use Master-Master replication in datacenters in each country or region where the application runs. Each deployment of the application can use data located in the same datacenter as that deployment in order to maximize performance and minimize any data transfer costs. Partitioning the data may make it possible to minimize synchronization requirements.

  - Use replication from the master database to replicas in order to provide failover and backup capabilities. By keeping additional copies of the data up to date, perhaps according to a schedule or on demand when any changes are made to the data, it may be possible to switch the application to use the backup data in case of a failure of the original data store.

Simplifying Synchronization Requirements

Some of the ways that you can minimize or avoid the complexity of two-way synchronization include:

- Use a Master-Subordinate Replication topology wherever possible. This topology requires only one-way synchronization from the master to the subordinates. You may be able to send updates from a cloud-hosted application to the master database using a messaging service, or by exposing the master database across the Internet in a secure way.

- Segregate the data into several stores or partitions according to the replication requirements of the data that they hold. Partitions containing data that could be modified anywhere can be replicated by using the Master-Master topology, while data that can be updated only at a single location and is static everywhere else can be replicated by using the Master-Subordinate topology.

- Partition the data so that updates, and the resulting risk of conflicts, can occur only in the minimum number of places. For example, store the data for different retail locations in different databases so that synchronization must occur only between the retail location and the master database, and not across all databases. For more information see the Data Partitioning Guidance.

- Version the data so that no overwriting is required. Instead, when data is changed, a new version is added to the data store alongside the existing versions. Applications can access all the versions of the data and the update history, and can use the appropriate version. Many Command and Query Responsibility Segregation (CQRS) implementations use this approach, often referred to as Event Sourcing, to retain historical information and to accrue changes at specific points in time.

- Use a quorum-based approach where a conflicting update is applied only if the majority of data stores vote to commit the update. If the majority votes to abort the update then all the data stores must abort the update. Quorum-based mechanisms are not easy to implement but may provide a workable solution if the final value of conflicting data items should be based on a consensus rather than being based on the more usual conflict resolution techniques such as "last update wins" or "master database wins." For more information see _Quorum_ on TechNet.

Considerations for Data Replication and Synchronization

Even if you can simplify your data synchronization requirements, you must still consider how you implement the synchronization mechanism. Consider the following points:

- Decide which type of synchronization you need:
    - Master-Master replication involves a two-way synchronization process that is complex because the same data might be updated in more than one location. This can cause conflicts, and the synchronization must be able to resolve or handle this situation. It may be appropriate for one data store to have precedence and overwrite a conflicting change in other data stores. Other approaches are to implement a mechanism that can automatically resolve the conflict based on timings, or just record the changes and notify an administrator to resolve the conflict.
    - Master-Subordinate replication is simpler because changes are made in the master database and are copied to all subordinates.
    - Custom or programmatic synchronization can be used where the rules for handling conflicts are complex, where transformations are required on the data during synchronization, or where the standard Master-Master and Master-Subordinate approaches are not suitable. Changes are synchronized by reacting to events that indicate a data update, and applying this update to each data store while managing any update conflicts that might occur.
- Decide the frequency of synchronization. Most synchronization frameworks and services perform the synchronization operation on a fixed schedule. If the period between synchronizations is too long, you increase the risk of update conflicts and data in each replica may become stale. If the period is too short you may incur heavy network load, increased data transfer costs, and risk a new synchronization starting before the previous one has finished when there are a lot of updates. It may be possible to propagate changes across replicas as they occur by using background tasks that synchronize the data.
- Decide which data store will hold the master copy of the data where this is relevant, and the order in which updates are synchronized when there are more than two replicas of the data. Also consider how you will handle the situation where the master database is unavailable. It may be necessary to promote one replica to the master role in this case. For more information see the Leader Election Pattern.
- Decide what data in each store you will synchronize. The replicas may contain only a subset of the data. This could be a subset of columns to hide sensitive or non-required data, a subset of the rows where the data is partitioned so that only appropriate rows are replicated, or it could be a combination of both of these approaches.
- Beware of creating a synchronization loop in a system that implements the Master-Master replication topology. Synchronization loops can arise if one synchronization action updates a data store and this update prompts another synchronization that tries to apply the update back to the original data store. Synchronization loops can also occur when there are more than two data stores, where a synchronization update travels from one data store to another and then back to the original one.
- Consider if using a cache is worthwhile to protect against transient or short-lived connectivity issues.

- Ensure that the transport mechanism used by the synchronization process protects the data as it travels over the network. Typically this means using encrypted connections, SSL, or TLS. In extreme cases you may need to encrypt the data itself, but this is likely to require implementation of a custom synchronization solution.

- Consider how you will deal with failures during replication. This may require rerouting requests for data to another replica if the first cannot be accessed, or even rerouting requests to another deployment of the application.

- Make sure applications that use replicas of the data can handle situations that may arise when a replica is not fully consistent with the master copy of the data. For example, if a website accepts an order for goods marked as available but a subsequent update shows that no stock is available, the application must manage this—perhaps by sending an email to the customer and/or by placing the item on back order.

- Consider the cost and time implications of the chosen approach. For example, updating all or part of a data store though replication is likely to take longer and involve more bandwidth than updating a single entity.

> For more information about patterns for synchronizing data see _Appendix A - Replicating, Distributing, and Synchronizing Data_ in the p&p guide _Building Hybrid Applications in the Cloud on Windows Azure_. The topic _Data Movement Patterns_ on MSDN contains definitions of the common patterns for replicating and synchronizing data.

IMPLEMENTING SYNCHRONIZATION

Determining how to implement data synchronization is dependent to a great extent on the nature of the data and the type of the data stores. Some examples are:

- Use a ready-built synchronization service or framework. In Windows Azure hosted and hybrid applications you might choose to use:

  - **The Windows Azure SQL Data Sync service**. This service can be used to synchronize on-premises and cloud-hosted SQL Server instances, and Windows Azure SQL Database instances. Although there are a few minor limitations, it is a powerful service that provides options to select subsets of the data and specify the synchronization intervals. It can also perform one-way replication if required.

> For more information about using SQL Data Sync see _SQL Data Sync_ on MSDN and _Deploying the Orders Application and Data in the Cloud_ in the p&p guide _Building Hybrid Applications in the Cloud on Windows Azure_. Note that, at the time this guide was written, the SQL Data Sync service was a preview release and provided no SLA.

  - **The Microsoft Sync Framework**. This is a more flexible mechanism that enables you to implement custom synchronization plans, and capture events so that you can specify the actions to take when, for example, an update conflict occurs. It provides a solution that enables collaboration and offline access for applications, services, and devices with support for any data type, any data store, any transfer protocol, and any network topology.

> For more information see _Microsoft Sync Framework Developer Center_ on MSDN.

- Use a synchronization technology built into the data store itself. Some examples are:

     Windows Azure storage geo-replication. By default in Windows Azure data is automatically replicated in three datacenters (unless you turn it off) to protect against failures in one datacenter. This service can provide a read-only replica of the data.

     SQL Server database replication. Synchronization using the built-in features of SQL Server Replication Service can be achieved between on-premises installations of SQL Server and deployments of SQL Server in Windows Azure Virtual Machines in the cloud, and between multiple deployments of SQL Server in Windows Azure Virtual Machines.

- Implement a custom synchronization mechanism. For example, use a messaging technology to pass updates between deployments of the application, and include code in each application to apply these updates intelligently to the local data store and handle any update conflicts. Consider the following when building a custom mechanism:

    - Ready-built synchronization services may have a minimum interval for synchronization, whereas a custom implementation could offer near-immediate synchronization.

    - Ready-built synchronization services may not allow you to specify the order in which data stores are synchronized. A custom implementation may allow you to perform updates in a specific order between several data stores, or perform complex transformation or other operations on the data that are not supported in ready-built frameworks and services.

    - When you design a custom implementation you should consider two separate aspects: how to communicate updates between separate locations, and how to apply updates to the data stores. Typically, you will need to create an application or component that runs in each location where updates will be applied to local data stores. This application or component will accept instructions that it uses to update the local data store, and then pass the updates to other data stores that contain copies of the data. Within the application or component you can implement logic to manage conflicting updates. However, by passing updates between data store immediately, rather than on a fixed schedule as is the case with most ready-built synchronization services, you minimize the chances of conflicts arising.

RELATED PATTERNS AND GUIDANCE

The following patterns and guidance may also be relevant to your scenario when distributing and synchronizing data across different locations:

- **Caching Guidance**. This guidance describes how caching can be used to improve the performance and scalability of a distributed application running in the cloud.
- **Data Consistency Primer**. This primer summarizes the issues surrounding consistency over distributed data, and provides guidance for handling these concerns.
- **Data Partitioning Guidance**. This guidance describes how to partition data in the cloud to improve scalability, reduce contention, and optimize performance.

MORE INFORMATION

All links in this book are accessible from the book's online bibliography available at:
http://aka.ms/cdpbibliography.

- The guide *Data Access for Highly-Scalable Solutions: Using SQL, NoSQL, and Polyglot Persistence* on MSDN.
- *Appendix A - Replicating, Distributing, and Synchronizing Data* from the guide *Building Hybrid Applications in the Cloud on Windows Azure* on MSDN.
- The topic *Data Movement Patterns* on MSDN.
- The topic *SQL Data Sync* on MSDN.
- *Deploying the Orders Application and Data in the Cloud* from the guide *Building Hybrid Applications in the Cloud on Windows Azure*.
- The *Microsoft Sync Framework Developer Center* on MSDN.

Instrumentation and Telemetry Guidance

Most applications will include diagnostics features that generate custom monitoring and debugging information, especially when an error occurs. This is referred to as *instrumentation*, and is usually implemented by adding event and error handling code to the application. The process of gathering remote information that is collected by instrumentation is usually referred to as *telemetry*.

WHY IS INSTRUMENTATION AND TELEMETRY IMPORTANT?

While the logs of information generated by the built-in infrastructure and system diagnostics mechanism can provide useful information about operations and errors, most applications will include additional instrumentation that generates custom monitoring and debugging information. This instrumentation typically generates log entries in Windows Event Log, separate trace log files, custom log files, or entries in a data store such as a relational database. These logs provide the information required to monitor and debug the application.

However, in complex applications, and especially applications that must scale to extremely high capacity, the huge volume of data collected can overwhelm simple monitoring systems and techniques. For example, the amount of information generated by hundreds of web and worker roles, database shards, and additional services—much of which may be of relatively low statistical significance, uncorrelated, and delayed in delivery—can become almost impossible to handle in a meaningful way. Instead, you can implement a telemetry solution that collects and highlights operational events and reduces management costs, while at the same time giving useful insights into the application behavior in terms of meeting service level agreements (SLAs) and for guiding future decisions on resource planning.

> This topic does not discuss the details of writing code to instrument applications; in most cases the principles and practices for detecting and handling system and application events in cloud-hosted applications, and for defining metrics and key performance indicators (KPIs), is the same as for any other application.

INSTRUMENTATION

Instrumentation allows you to capture vital information about the operation of your application. This information will generally include:

- Details of operational events that occur as part of the normal operation of the application, together with useful information about that event. For example, in an ecommerce site it would be useful to record the order number and value of each order that is placed. These are typically informational events that are used to collect data about the way the application is used.

- Details of runtime events that occur, and useful information about that event such as the location or data store used and the response time for access to the data store. These are also informational events that can provide additional insight into the normal operation of the application. The event should not include any sensitive information such as credentials, or any other data that might enable an attacker obtaining the logs to compromise the system.

- Specific data about errors that occur at runtime, such as the customer ID and other values associated with an order update operation that failed. Typically these are warning or error events and will contain one or more system-generated error messages.

- Data from performance counters that measure specific values related to the operation of the application. These might be built-in system counters, such as those that measure processor load and network usage, or they might be custom performance counters that measure the number of orders placed or the average response time of a specific component.

A common implementation of instrumentation is an ability to change the level of detail that is collected on demand, usually by editing the configuration of the application. Under normal conditions the data from some informational events may not be required, thus reducing the cost of storage and the transactions required to collect it. When there is an issue with the application, you update the application configuration so that the diagnostics and instrumentation systems collect informational event data, as well as error and warning messages, to assist in isolating and fixing faults. It may be necessary to run the application in this extended reporting mode for some time if the problem appears only intermittently.

The fundamental approach to designing the instrumentation for any application can be defined by considering the requirements in terms of the basic stages for isolating and fixing errors:

1. **Detect performance issues and errors quickly**. Performance counters and event handlers can indicate problems in specific areas of the application due to component and service failures, overloading, and other issues; sometimes before end users are affected. This requires a constant or scheduled mechanism that monitors key thresholds and triggers the appropriate alerts. Detailed information from the instrumentation allows you to drill down into the execution and trace faults.

2. **Classify the issue to understand its nature**. In cloud-hosted applications that run in a shared multitenant environment such as Windows Azure, some issues such as connecting to a database may be transient and will resolve themselves. Other issues may be systemic, such as a coding error or an incorrect configuration setting, and will require intervention to resolve the problem.

3. **Recover from an incident and return the application to full operation**. Use the information you collect, perhaps after turning on additional logging settings, to fix the problem and return the application to full service. This is especially important if it is a commercially valuable application for the organization, such as an ecommerce site, or has SLAs that you must meet to avoid financial penalties and customer dissatisfaction.

4. **Diagnose the root cause of the problem and prevent it reoccurring**. Carry out root cause analysis to determine the original cause and the underlying nature of the problem, and make changes to prevent reoccurrence where this is possible. The instrumentation data collected over time will help you identify recurring patterns and trends that led up to the incident, such as overloading of a specific component or invalid data being accepted by the application.

To be able to perform these steps you will need to collect information from all levels of the application and infrastructure. For example, you should consider collecting data about the infrastructure such as CPU load, I/O load, and memory usage; data about the application such as database response times, exceptions, and custom performance counters; and data about business activities and KPIs such as the number of each type of business transaction per hour and the response time of each service the application uses.

For a comprehensive guide to topics related to monitoring, instrumentation, and telemetry in Windows Azure applications see *Cloud Service Fundamentals* on the TechNet Wiki. The topic *Telemetry – Application Instrumentation* provides information about designing and implementing instrumentation that will support telemetry.

You can use frameworks and third party products to help you implement the instrumentation in your applications. For example, Enterprise Library from the Microsoft patterns & practices team includes application blocks that can help you to simplify and standardize exception handling and logging in Windows Azure applications. For more information see *Enterprise Library 6* on MSDN.

Semantic Logging

Most logging mechanisms, including Windows Event Log, store log entries that contain a string value that is the description or message for the entry. With the advent of Event Tracing for Windows (ETW) it became possible to store a structured payload with the event entry. This payload is generated by the listener or sink that captures the event, and it can include typed information that makes it much easier for automated systems to discover useful information about the event. This approach to logging is often referred to a *structured logging*, *typed logging*, or *semantic logging*.

As an example, an event that indicates an order was placed can generate a log entry that contains the number of items as an Integer value, the total value as a decimal number, the customer identifier as a Long value, and the city for delivery as a String value. An order monitoring system can read the payload and easily extract the individual values. With traditional logging mechanisms the monitoring application would need to parse the message string to extract these values, increasing the chance that an error could occur if the message string was not formatted exactly as expected.

For more information about ETW see *Event Tracing* and *Windows Event Log* on MSDN.

ETW is a feature of all current versions of the Windows operating system, and can be leveraged in Windows Azure applications when you collect Event Log data as part of your diagnostics configuration.

It is possible to create events entries for ETW by using the **EventSource** class in the .NET framework directly, but it's not a simple task. Instead, consider using a logging framework that provides a simple and consistent interface to minimize errors and simplify the code required in the application. Most logging frameworks can write event data to different types of logging destinations, such as disk files, as well as to Windows Event Log.

The Semantic Logging Application Block developed by the Microsoft patterns & practices team is an example of a framework that makes comprehensive logging easier. You create a custom event source by inheriting and extending the **EventSource** class in the **System.Diagnostics.Tracing** namespace. When you write events to the custom event source the Semantic Logging Application Block detects this and allows you to write the event to other logging destinations such as a disk file, database, email message, and more.

You can use the Semantic Logging Application Block in Windows Azure applications that are written in .NET and run in Windows Azure Web Sites, Cloud Services, and Virtual Machines. However, the choice of logging destination varies depending on the hosting method you choose. Consider writing to Windows Azure storage or Windows Azure SQL Database if you need to log events outside of the Windows Event Log.

For more information see the blog post *Embracing Semantic Logging*.

TELEMETRY

Telemetry, in its most basic form, is the process of gathering information generated by instrumentation and logging systems. Typically, it is performed using asynchronous mechanisms that support massive scaling and wide distribution of application services. In large and complex applications, information is usually captured in a data pipeline and stored in a form that makes it easier to analyze, and capable of presenting information at different levels of granularity. This information is used to discover trends, gain insights into usage and performance, and to detect and isolate faults.

Windows Azure has no built-in system that directly provides a telemetry and reporting system of this type, but a combination of the features exposed by all of the Windows Azure services allows you to create telemetry mechanisms that span the range from simple monitoring to comprehensive dashboards. The complexity of the telemetry mechanism you require usually depends on the size of the application. This is based on several factors such as the number of role or virtual machine instances, the number of ancillary services it uses, the distribution of the application across different datacenters, and other related factors.

A common approach is to collect all of the data from instrumentation and monitoring functions into a central repository such as a database located close to the application. This minimizes the write time, though it is still good practice to use asynchronous techniques based on queues and listeners to collect this information in a way that minimizes the impact on the application. Patterns such as Queue-based Load Leveling and Priority Queue are useful here.

The combination of all of the data in the data store can then be used to update live displays of activity and errors, generate reports and charts, and can be analyzed using database queries or even a big data solution such as HDInsight.

CONSIDERATIONS FOR INSTRUMENTATION AND TELEMETRY

Consider the following points when designing an instrumentation and telemetry system:

- Identify the combination of information you need to collect from the built-in system monitoring features and instrumentation (such as logs and performance counters), and what additional instrumentation is required in order to comprehensively measure application performance, monitor availability, and isolate faults. There is no point in collecting information that you will never use. However, failing to collect something that might be useful, especially for debugging purposes, could make maintenance and troubleshooting more difficult. Also ensure that the logging configuration can be modified at runtime without requiring the application to be restarted; the Runtime Reconfiguration Pattern is useful in this scenario.

- Use the telemetry data not only to monitor performance and to obtain early warning of problems, but also to isolate issues that arise, detect the nature of faults, perform root cause analysis, and for metering. Telemetry should be applied to both test and staged versions of the application during development to measure and validate performance, and to ensure that instrumentation and telemetry systems are operating correctly. Consider making data such as real-time, summary, and trend views available to development teams as well as administrators in order that issues can be more quickly resolved, and the code can be improved where necessary.

- Consider implementing two (or more) separate channels for telemetry data, one of which is used for vital operational information such as failure of the application, services, or components. It is important that this channel receives a higher level of monitoring and alerting than channels that simply record day-to-day operational data. The Priority Queue Pattern is useful in this scenario. Fine tune the alerting mechanism over time to ensure that false alarms and noise are kept to a minimum.

- Ensure you collect all information from the exceptions you handle, not just the current exception message. Many exceptions wrap inner exceptions, which may provide additional useful information.

- Log all calls to external services. Include information about the context, destination, method, timing information (such as latency), and the result (such as success or failure, and the number of retries). This information may also be useful if you need to support reports of SLA violations, either from users of your application or when challenging your hosting provider regarding failures of their services.

- Log details of transient faults and failovers in order to detect emerging or ongoing problems. For example, record the number of times that a retry action occurs, the state of a circuit breaker changes, or the applications fails over to a different instance or configuration.

- Careful categorization of the data when it is written to the data store can simplify analysis and real-time monitoring, and can also assist in debugging and isolating faults. For example, it may be useful in the monitoring tools to be able to extract just data that arises from instrumentation of the application business functions, or from performance counters that measure certain infrastructure resources such as CPU and memory usage. Consider partitioning telemetry data by date, or even by hour, so that aggregators and database grooming tasks are not acting on tables that are actively being written to.

- The mechanisms for collecting and storing the data must themselves be scalable in order to match the number of items generated as the application and its services are scaled to an increasing number of instances. Ideally you should use a separate storage account for monitoring and logging data to minimize the impact of storage transactions for this data on the storage performance of the application itself, and to isolate the logging data from the application data for security purposes (for example, so that administrators and users of the monitoring system cannot access application data). Ensure the telemetry system itself is monitored so that a failure does not go undetected.

- If the application is located in different datacenters, you must decide whether to collect the data in each datacenter and combine the results in the monitoring system (such as an on-premises telemetry dashboard), or whether to centralize the data storage in one datacenter. Passing data between datacenters will incur additional costs, though this may be balanced by the savings in downloading only one dataset.

- Where possible, minimize the load on the application by using asynchronous code or queues to write events to the data store, and to move telemetry data between service instances. Avoid communicating telemetry information through a logging channel using a chatty approach, which might otherwise overwhelm the diagnostics system, or use separate channels for chunky (high-volume, high-latency, granular data) and chatty (low-volume, low-latency, high-value data) telemetry. One option for reducing the volume of telemetry data is to collect and store only data for events that are outside the normal operating limits.

- To prevent loss of data, include code to retry connections that may encounter transient errors. Design retry logic to be intelligent so that repeated failures are detected and the process abandoned after a preset number of attempts, and log the number of retries to help detect inherent or developing issues. Use variable retry intervals to minimize the chance that retry logic could overload a target system that is just recovering from a transient error when there are many queued retry attempts in the pipeline. See the Retry Pattern for more information.

- You may need to implement a scheduler that collects some data items, such as performance counter values, at regular intervals if your hosting environment does not provide this feature (in Windows Azure you can configure automatic collection in the diagnostics mechanism). Consider how often this data collection should occur, and the effect of the collection overhead on the performance of the application. Data such as performance counters, event logs, and trace events written into Windows Azure table service is written in a 60 seconds wide temporal partition. Attempting to write too much data, such as an excessive number of point sources or with too narrow a collection interval, can overwhelm the table partition. Also ensure that error spikes do not trigger a high volume of insert attempts into table storage because this might trigger a throttling event.

- Consider how you will remove old or stale telemetry data that is no longer relevant. This may be a scheduled task, or initiated manually when versions change.

> For more information see *Cloud Service Fundamentals: Telemetry basics and troubleshooting* on the Windows Azure blog and *Windows Azure: Telemetry Basics and Troubleshooting* on the TechNet Wiki.

RELATED PATTERNS AND GUIDANCE

The following patterns and guidance may also be relevant to your scenario when implementing instrumentation and telemetry for your applications:

- **Health Endpoint Monitoring Pattern**. It is typically necessary to supplement instrumentation and telemetry by monitoring applications and services to ensure that they are available, and are performing correctly. The Health Endpoint Monitoring pattern describes how to do this by submitting a request to a configurable set of endpoints and evaluating the results against a set of configurable rules.

- **Service Metering Guidance**. Instrumentation can be used to provide information for metering the use of applications and services. The Service Metering guidance explores how to meter the use of applications or services in order to plan future requirements; to gain an understanding of how they are used; or to bill users, organization departments, or customers.

- **Queue-based Load Leveling Pattern**. Telemetry systems should be designed in such a way that they exert minimum load on the monitored applications and services. Using queues to transmit telemetry data can help to achieve this. The Queue-based Load Leveling pattern explains how a queue can act as a buffer between a task and a service that it invokes to minimize the impact of peaks in demand on availability and responsiveness for both the task and the service.

- **Priority Queue Pattern**. Telemetry systems often need to transmit data over more than one channel to ensure that important information is delivered quickly. The Priority Queue pattern shows how you can prioritize requests sent to services so that requests with a higher priority are received and processed more quickly than those of a lower priority.

- **Retry Pattern**. Telemetry systems must be resilient to transient failures and able to recover gracefully. The Retry pattern explains how to handle temporary failures when connecting to a service or network resource by transparently retrying the operation in the expectation that the failure is transient.

- **Runtime Reconfiguration Pattern**. Instrumentation is typically designed in such a way as the level of detail it generates can be adjusted at runtime to assist with debugging and root cause analysis. The Runtime Reconfiguration pattern explores how components of monitoring mechanisms can be reconfigured without requiring redeployment or restarting the application.

MORE INFORMATION

All links in this book are accessible from the book's online bibliography available at: *http://aka.ms/cdpbibliography*.

- The article *Cloud Service Fundamentals* on the TechNet Wiki.
- The article *Telemetry – Application Instrumentation* on the TechNet Wiki.
- The *Enterprise Library 6* information on MSDN.
- The article *Windows Azure: Telemetry Basics and Troubleshooting* on the TechNet Wiki.
- The article *Event Tracing* on MSDN.
- The article *Windows Event Log* on MSDN.
- The article *Embracing Semantic Logging* on Grigori Melnik's blog.

Multiple Datacenter Deployment Guidance

Deploying an application to more than one datacenter can provide benefits such as increased availability and a better user experience across wider geographical areas. However, there are challenges that must be resolved, such as data synchronization and regulatory limitations.

WHY DEPLOY TO MULTIPLE DATACENTERS?

Organizations typically begin by deploying their applications to a single datacenter. This may be the local on-premises datacenter, or a remote environment such as a traditional hosting provider or a cloud provider. In addition to advantages such as easier scaling, improved reach, and cost effectiveness, cloud hosting typically offers service level guarantees of availability and throughput that can help to make applications more robust and available. However, a single deployment of an application is still at risk of becoming unavailable due to failure.

Deploying an application to more than one datacenter, and even to more than one hosting provider, can reduce the chance that events outside of your control (such as a failure of a datacenter, or global Internet connectivity issues between countries or regions) will cause it to become unavailable. For vital commercial applications such as ecommerce sites, where even short periods of downtime or reduced availability can have a huge impact on profitability, deployment to multiple datacenters is a solution you might consider.

Therefore, you might choose to deploy to multiple datacenters for one or more reasons, including:

- **Growing capacity over time**. Applications often start out as a single deployment, either on-premises or in the cloud, and grow over time as demand increases. This growth may be provided for by expanding deployment to a sub-region or availability set, to multiple sub-regions or availability sets, and then to full multi-region deployment. In some cases, parts of the application may be split between on-premises and the cloud, following a hybrid approach, move to the cloud, and then expand to multiple regions.

- **Providing global reach with minimum latency for users**. You can maintain multiple running versions of the application in datacenters located near the majority of users, and route users to the one that provides the best performance and lowest connection latency.

- **Maintaining performance and availability**. Deployment to more than one datacenter, and perhaps to more than one hosting provider, is a useful technique for reducing the risk that an application will become unavailable. Common scenarios are:

  - **Providing additional instances for resiliency**. Deploying to multiple datacenters, and choosing the number of instances based on demand at each datacenter, can improve resiliency and availability because there are additional alternative instances to which users can be re-routed if performance of one instance or datacenter is degraded, or if one instance should fail altogether.

> Deploying an application to multiple locations will not protect it from failure due to factors that are your fault, such as poor design or errors in the code.

220

- **Providing a facility for disaster recovery**. If the primary deployment fails, or becomes unavailable for any reason, you can start up the alternative offline deployment that is located in a different datacenter and switch requests to it while you resolve issues with the primary deployment. The backup deployment might be located in your own on-premises datacenter, and might even be designed to provide only minimal services while the primary deployment is brought back into use. Ideally, the process of recovering from backup and recreating the production environment should require the minimum number of tasks, be fully automated to minimize startup time, and must be tested regularly.

- **Providing a hot-swap standby capability**. You can maintain a second running deployment of the application (or more than one additional deployment), and instantly switch requests to the standby deployment if the primary one fails or an event occurs in the datacenter where the primary deployment is located. To minimize cost the standby application could be scaled down, perhaps with a fewer number of instances, and then rapidly ramped up through scripting or autoscaling when required. This is sometimes referred to as a "warm standby" approach.

ROUTING REQUESTS TO MULTIPLE APPLICATION DEPLOYMENTS

Deploying an application in more than one datacenter, and choosing datacenters that are local to the majority of users, can provide advantages in availability and user experience, but it does not provide a complete solution. For example, users that are accessing a US-hosted application will not be automatically redirected to an alternative deployment if the US deployment fails.

To resolve this issue you might decide to distribute requests using a round-robin approach, or by using a manual, custom, or third party mechanism to detect application failures and redirect traffic.

Round-robin routing is a traditional way to distribute requests to multiple deployments of an application or website, with each request being routed to the next deployment in a list and then starting again with the first item in the list. It can be implemented by using multiple entries for a domain name in a DNS server, each with an IP address that points to one deployment of the application. The DNS service will automatically hand out a different IP address to each DNS lookup request from users, working repeatedly though the list.

However, round robin routing is not an ideal solution in most cases because it will continue to hand out the IP address of failed deployments, and so some users will find the application is unavailable. Instead, you should consider a solution that routes requests only to deployments that are available, such as the solutions described in the following sections:

- Manual re-routing on application failure.
- Automated re-routing on application failure.
- Re-routing with Windows Azure Traffic Manager.

Manual Re-Routing On Application Failure

When using multiple deployments that act as disaster recovery or hot-swap services, you may choose the simplest approach of manually routing users to the appropriate deployment of the application. You can do this by changing the DNS entry for the application, or by using a redirection page. However, both of these approaches suffer from several issues:

- You must be able to quickly detect a failure (indicated by your application monitoring system) and perform the manual changeover. This might involve starting up a backup deployment in another datacenter and validating that it is operating correctly if you do not have a hot-swap deployment already running. If the failure occurs out of business hours, when nobody is on site, there may be additional delays in the changeover.

- If you reroute requests by changing the DNS entry it may take several hours, and even one or two days, before all of the global DNS servers pick up the change and start routing to the backup deployment. You can mitigate this to some extent by specifying a short expiration interval in the DNS records, though some global DNS caches may ignore this and apply their own expiration period. In addition, most client devices such as web browsers will cache the result of the DNS lookup for a specific period (typically 30 minutes) to reduce the number of DNS lookups required, and so users will be routed to the same deployment during that period.

- If you use a redirection page or mechanism to reroute requests to the backup copy, this becomes a single point of failure. If users cannot access the redirection mechanism they will not be able to access the backup application. For example, using a page in a separate website to redirect to the required deployment will not work if this website is unavailable for any reason.

- You must be prepared to manually change the routing back to the failed deployment after it has been recovered. This may take some time to propagate when using DNS routing, which will extend the period that it is unavailable.

Automated Re-Routing On Application Failure

To avoid delays when an application deployment becomes unavailable you might choose to use an automated mechanism that monitors each deployment and routes requests to the most suitable one that is operating. All requests for the application are initially routed to the automated mechanism, which then redirects the request to the appropriate deployment.

The way that you design or configure the mechanism depends on the reason you are using multiple datacenter deployments:

- For a disaster recovery scenario the automated mechanism must be able to start up the backup deployment and verify that it is operating, and then route users to it instead of the primary deployment.

- For a hot-swap scenario the automated mechanism needs only to verify that the backup deployment is working, and then route users to it.

- For a global reach scenario the automated mechanism may examine the request and route to the appropriate deployment. Requests from web browsers and many other client devices will include a language code that broadly indicates the country or region of the user, and so the mechanism can route to the datacenter nearest to the user. See *Accept-Language used for locale setting* on the W3C website for more information about browser language codes.

An advantage of a custom implementation is that you have complete flexibility in how you design the probe that checks for availability. For example, you can perform a range of tests on the application to ensure that it is performing correctly, perhaps by measuring the response and execution times of individual components and services.

> For more information about checking the operation of an application see the Heath Endpoint Monitoring Pattern.

However, there are some issues to be aware of if you design a custom automated routing implementation:

- You risk the effects of a single point of failure. This can be partly mitigated by deploying multiple instances of the mechanism in different datacenters and using DNS round robin to distribute requests between them. However, managing these multiple deployments means considering how you will replicate configuration and communicate changes to the routing tables they use.

- You should include a delay in the rerouting mechanism to prevent transient connectivity issues from causing intermittent flipping between deployments. Good practice is to wait until more than one probe to the applications fails before initiating a changeover to an alternative deployment.

- If you are using the alternative deployment as a disaster recovery solution it will probably not be running, and so the mechanism will need to start the application and verify it is operating correctly before switching requests to it.
- You should consider how you will route requests back to the failed application after it has been recovered. Typically, you will need to incorporate a mechanism that detects availability and updates the routing as necessary.

The alternative is to hand off the problem to a commercial organization that offers a global IP routing solution. These services usually include detection of availability, optimization based on user location, and other features. They are typically distributed services designed to be highly resilient and available, and are usually a better choice than attempting to implement your own solution. Some examples of providers of these services are _Akamai_, _SoftLayer_, and _Windows Azure Traffic Manager_ (which is described in the following section).

Re-Routing with Windows Azure Traffic Manager

Windows Azure Traffic Manager is an intelligent DNS service built into Windows Azure that combines application failure detection with dynamic DNS routing. However, because it acts as a DNS server and has very short expiration times for its DNS records, it does not suffer the delays inherent in a custom solution.

Traffic Manager maintains a list of the typical response times of the network paths to each of the Windows Azure global datacenters. You configure the service by specifying the location of your application deployments, and an endpoint in each one that will respond within ten seconds when Traffic Manager pings that endpoint. You also choose a policy that defines how Traffic Manager will behave.

The **Round-Robin** policy routes requests to the application deployment in each datacenter in turn. It detects failed application deployments and does not route to these in order to maintain availability, but this may not provide users with the best response times due to network latency. The main advantage of this policy is that it distributes load across all working deployments of the application.

The **Failover** policy allows you to configure a prioritized list of application deployments, and Traffic Manager will route requests to the first one in the list that it detects is responding to requests. If that application fails, Traffic Manager will route requests to the next application deployment in the list, and so on. Again this may not provide users with the best response times due to network latency, but it works well if you want all requests to go to a single deployment as long as it is responding. It is typically used for hot-swap scenarios, where the backup application is only accessed when the primary deployment is unavailable.

However, for the best combination of availability and performance you should use the aptly named **Performance** policy. This policy routes requests from users to the application deployment in the datacenter that provides the lowest network latency (it may not be the closest in purely geographical terms). It also detects failed applications and does not route to these, instead choosing the next closest working application deployment.

When a failed deployment comes back online, Traffic Manager will automatically detect this and include it in the routing table.

For more information see _Reducing Network Latency for Accessing Cloud Applications with Windows Azure Traffic Manager_ in the p&p guide _Building Hybrid Applications in the Cloud on Windows Azure_ and _Traffic Manager_ on the Windows Azure website.

CONSIDERATIONS FOR MULTIPLE DATACENTER DEPLOYMENT

If you do decide to deploy your application to more than one datacenter, you must be aware of some additional issues that this raises. For example, you should consider the following:

- **Datacenter location and domain names**. Consider how you can specify the location where you will host the application and services it uses, and how this relates to domain names you choose.
  - Cloud hosting providers usually allow you to specify a region for each deployment. In addition, you may be able to select a sub-region or an availability set, though the actual meaning of these terms varies. Typically, an availability set allows you to specify that deployments and services should be close together with low latency, but physically separated to enhance availability in case of issues that affect a datacenter. To enable efficient allocation of resources, providers often do not allow you to specify the actual datacenter—and in these cases using an availability set or a sub-region is the only way to specify the location for deployment.
  - Each region or geographical deployment must have a unique domain name. A common approach is to use country-specific top level domain (TLD) names such as **.co.us** or **.au**. However, this requires multiple registrations of TLDs with domain registries around the world. It may be more cost effective to use subdomain names based on a single root domain names such as **us.myapp.com**, **emea.my.com**, **asia.myapp.com** and point each one to the appropriate deployment of the application. For multi-tenant applications you can extend this with a tenant identifier if required; for example, **adatum.us.myapp.com** and **adatum.emea.my.com**
- **Regulatory or SLA restrictions**. You must take into account service availability obligations and any legal restrictions that may apply. These might include:
  - Local or international restrictions on the location of the application and the data it uses, or movement of this data. For example, in some countries or regions it is illegal to export data outside of a specific area, even just for processing. The location for storage of some types of data is also strictly mandated by law in some countries or regions, or may be specified in an SLA.
  - Availability requirements may be defined in an SLA or guaranteed in service documentation. There may be mandatory requirements for the recovery point objective (RPO–the amount of data that may be lost during a failure) or the recovery time objective (RTO–the time taken to recover after a failure). Depending on the routing technology used it may take several minutes, or even hours, for the routing mechanism to discover a service has failed, perhaps retry after a period to confirm it was not a transient error, set up a new routing, and for the changes to reach the user (for example, the time taken for a DNS change to propagate). Take these factors into account before agreeing recovery objectives with clients.
- **Data synchronization**. Different deployments of your application are likely to use different local data stores, and users may be routed to a datacenter where data is not available. Examples include:
  - Separate databases or data stores, where the data in each one may not be fully consistent with that in another datacenter if synchronization has not completed. In disaster recovery scenarios where the backup application is not running, it may be necessary to import or synchronize all of the data before the backup deployment can be used. If the application cannot function until all of the data is synchronized, this must be accounted for when agreeing the RTO. If some data may not have been replicated, and has been lost, this must be accounted for when agreeing the RPO. See the Data Replication and Synchronization Guidance for more information about data synchronization across application deployments.
  - Separate caching services, such as local caches on each server and distributed cache services located in each datacenter. Your application must be able to refresh the cache if data it expects to find there is not available. For more information see the Cache-Aside Pattern.

- **Data and service availability**. Depending on how you design and configure your application, some data and services may not be available in all of the datacenters. In some cases you may be able to design the application to downgrade its behavior or functionality automatically or through configuration. Examples of lack of availability include:
  - If you partition your data in different locations, which can minimize data transfer costs and reduce the chances of conflicting updates, the data required by the application for a user rerouted from another datacenter may not be available.
  - Some services you rely on require an absolute path, domain, or URL to be specified; examples are queues, authentication mechanisms, and external services. If there is only a single instance of these services, and the datacenter where they are located is unavailable, the application is likely to fail. You may need to configure multiple instances of these services in different datacenters and specify separate instances for each deployment of the application. This can make configuration and deployment more complex.

- **Application versions and functionality**. You may choose to deploy different versions of your application in each datacenter. Examples of this include:
  - In the global reach scenario, you may decide to deploy localized versions in each datacenter. However, this may be an issue when users are rerouted to a more distant datacenter when one deployment fails. A better approach is to use a single version that has built-in locale and accept-language detection, and so is suitable for all users.
  - You may decide to deploy a different number of instances of the application in each datacenter based on the average load under normal conditions. However, consider using an autoscaling solution so that each datacenter can cope with the extra load from rerouted users when one datacenter or deployment becomes unavailable. Alternatively, include the capability for the application to degrade functionality to manage the additional load for short periods; perhaps by temporarily disabling certain services or providing a simplified UI.
  - For hot swap and disaster recovery scenarios it may be possible to deploy a reduced functionality version of the application in backup locations to minimize cost and complexity. However, you must consider the impact of this on both the organization and customers should the primary deployment be unavailable for long periods.
  - Consider if you should partition the functionality of your application so that some non-essential services are available only in one or a few datacenters. This can simplify configuration and deployment. For example, the chapter *Maximizing Availability, Scalability, and Elasticity* in the p&p guide *Developing Multi-tenant Applications for the Cloud* demonstrates how an organization maximizes availability by using multiple deployments of the public website where users complete surveys, but only a single instance of the subscriber website where customers configure surveys. A short interruption to the availability of the subscriber website is less crucial than non-availability of the public website.

- **Testing and deployment**. When an application runs in multiple datacenters it is vital to perform thorough testing to ensure that the application will perform correctly in every location, and to plan how and when you will manage deployments, updates, and failures. For example:
  - Consider how you will upgrade to new versions of the application across all datacenters. Updating the deployment in one datacenter at a time reduces the chance of a global failure through incorrect configuration or an error in the application, and allows each deployment to be validated and the performance checked in a live environment.
  - It may be an advantage to schedule the update in datacenters in different time zones to coincide with the period when the application running there is less heavily loaded.

- Consider using automated mechanisms such as scripts or utilities that can be configured for deployment to multiple datacenters, and can ensure that the appropriate configuration is applied to each datacenter deployment.
- It may be necessary to roll back individual failed or underperforming updates after deployment, and restore the previous version. Consider how you can use the features of the hosting environment, and other tools and utilities, to achieve this.
- Be prepared to test resilience, autoscaling, rerouting, and failover features of the application by terminating services. Measure the impact on customer experience, the immediate and ongoing effects, and the time taken to recover. Fine tune the policies and deployments to minimize the impact on users.

- **Customer experience**. The routing solution you adopt should prevent regular or random flipping between datacenters, and only switch over when it can be definitely determined that the current deployment of the application is unavailable. However, the effects of routing to different deployments of your application may have side-effects you should plan to accommodate. These include:
  - Session management. For example, a user rerouted from another datacenter may need to sign on again, and may lose information that was cached locally such as a shopping cart.
  - Increased latency or reduced performance. For example, if users are rerouted to a very distant datacenter the additional delays might make the application less responsive and usable.
  - Application instability or errors. If the applications in each datacenter use different instances of features such as queues or third party services, messages and state held by these services will not be available. This may cause the application to behave in unpredictable ways.

You may consider displaying a message indicating to the user that they have been rerouted to another version of the application when this occurs to help mitigate complaints, and to explain the reason for any errors or unexplained behavior of the application. You might achieve this by using a cookie to identify the datacenter that delivered the most recent output to the client, and checking this with each request to see if it is different from the current datacenter.

RELATED PATTERNS AND GUIDANCE

The following patterns and guidance may also be relevant to your scenario when deploying your application in more than one datacenter:

- **Compute Partitioning Guidance**. It is often useful to partition applications into smaller segments, or separate functional areas such as public and administrative websites, when deploying them to more than one datacenter. The Compute Partitioning guidance describes how to allocate the services and components in a cloud-hosted application in a way that helps to minimize running costs while maintaining the scalability, performance, availability, and security of the service.
- **Data Replication and Synchronization Guidance**. When applications are deployed to more than one datacenter, it is common to deploy multiple copies of the data that they use to maintain performance and availability. The Data Replication and Synchronization guidance summarizes issues related to replicating the data each instance of the application uses, and how you will synchronize changes to the data.
- **Federated Identity Pattern**. Applications often need to authenticate users, and this may be more complicated when applications are deployed to more than one datacenter. The Federated Identity pattern describes how an application can delegate authentication to an external identity provider in order to simplify development, minimize the requirement for user administration, and reduce the management overheads for the application.

MORE INFORMATION

All links in this book are accessible from the book's online bibliography available at: _http://aka.ms/cdpbibliography._

- _Accept-Language used for locale setting_ on the W3C website.
- Global IP routing service providers: _Akamai_, _SoftLayer_, and _Windows Azure Traffic Manager._
- For more information about using Windows Azure Traffic Manager, see:
    - _Reducing Network Latency for Accessing Cloud Applications with Windows Azure Traffic Manager_ in the guide _Building Hybrid Applications in the Cloud on Windows Azure._
    - _Traffic Manager_ on the Windows Azure website.
- _Recovery Point Objective_ (RPO) on Wikipedia.
- _Recovery Time Objective_ (RTO) on Wikipedia.
- The chapter _Maximizing Availability, Scalability, and Elasticity_ in the guide _Developing Multi-tenant Applications for the Cloud._

Service Metering Guidance

You may need to meter the use of applications or services in order to plan future requirements; to gain an understanding of how they are used; or to bill users, organization departments, or customers. This is a common requirement, particularly in large corporations and for independent software vendors and service providers.

WHY IS METERING IMPORTANT?

Metering is the process of measuring and recording the usage of an entire application, individual parts of an application, or specific services and resources. For example, you may want to record the time a user or customer spends using an application or service, the number of queries against a database, the number of times a specific service is accessed, the processing time for requests, and more. You might also want to measure the amount of storage used by each user or customer, or the total size of data transfers.

It is also useful to meter specific scenarios or use cases, such as selecting a product and placing an order or performing a complex business operation. This requires end-to-end mapping of the operation so that all metered components of it can be combined to give an overall metric that provides useful business information.

Many cloud hosting environments, including Windows Azure, do not expose metering information other than the standard billing details accessible to the account owner. It may seem easy to use this billing information to gauge the usage of features, but the details are not broken down in a way that allows you to identify individual applications (or users).

If you need to implement metering for your applications and services, you must create custom mechanisms to achieve this. Typically the instrumentation you add to your applications can provide much of the base data you require. For example, you can use performance counters to measure the average and peak values for the number of a specific operation performed, the volume of data moved in or out of the application, or the average time a specific processes takes to execute. See the Instrumentation and Telemetry Guidance in this guide for more information.

SCENARIOS FOR METERING

When designing metering systems you must consider not only why you want to implement metering, but also the scenario in which it will operate. The appropriate choices for the metering methods, and the items that are metered, differ based on factors such as business requirements, application type, and the customer or user base. The following sections include some examples.

Metering for Forward Planning

Metering can provide valuable information about the way that an application is used, and can identify trends that indicate future requirements such as storage and compute resources. This information is also useful for deciding which features of an application are the most popular, as well as identifying relationships between features and resource usage. For example, metering may indicate that only a very small percentage of users take advantage of one feature of an application, but another feature is very popular and the load at peak periods is affecting response times.

Metering can also provide trend data, such as the average rate of growth of storage used by the application and the cost of this storage per user. This may be useful in directing development effort towards improving storage methods, or moving to a different type of store that can provide additional capacity or reduce storage costs.

Metering for Internal Business Use

When planning for metering business use in a large organization, the primary requirement is to be able to identify each item at the required level of granularity. The data you log for each function can include the current user ID or name or a department name, depending on the purpose of the metering. For example, in an organization that needs to bill individual departments for the use of an application, the metering granularity needs only be at department level. However, if at some point you need to identify which user in a department is using specific features, the logs must also include the user ID or name.

Consider using a structured or semantic logging approach so that the data from the log entry can be easily extracted (see the Instrumentation and Telemetry Guidance for more information). It may also be possible to use data from the built-in infrastructure logs. For example, the IIS request log entries may contain a user ID in the query string.

Metering for Software as a Service (SaaS) Vendors

If the application is designed to serve different customers, such as a multi-tenant application, you may want to implement metering both for forward planning, such as partitioning the tenants and data, and in order to bill customers for the features and services they actually use—especially if the users consume expensive resources. For example, you may want to bill customers for resources such as processing time, storage, or bandwidth. However, it is important to understand that there is a difference between how the platform is metered and billed, and how a SaaS vendor typically bills a user.

Many vendors immediately think that they should directly pass on all the costs to customers. However, detailed usage can be difficult to measure in a multi-tenant solution that shares many resources. Customers are likely to find the billing model difficult to understand, and it makes it hard for them to predict their costs. This approach may also fail to accurately match all vendor costs, such as development and maintenance costs, with income from customers. Instead, it is worth considering alternative approaches:

- Pay-per-use plans where customers are billed based on the resources they use, but with an overhead that covers the vendor's development, maintenance, and other fixed and ongoing costs. Specific instrumentation must be included in the application to support metering for billing. This plan has the advantage that it relates the customers' costs to their usage, but it may not be financially capable of supporting the vendor's investments during the early lifetime of the application when there are few customers. It may also result in complex bills that are hard for customers to understand and predict their ongoing costs.

- Fixed fee plans where customers pay a regular amount that covers all the vendor's fixed and ongoing costs. To make this more attractive to customers it may be possible to offer different levels of functionality or support, so as to maximize income from a range of small and large customers. One advantage of this plan is that it does not require specific instrumentation to support metering for billing purposes, but the application should still incorporate sufficient instrumentation for monitoring and debugging.

- Fixed fee plans with additional bolt-on features, where the customer is billed a fixed amount for using the application, and can opt for the availability of additional metered features such as extra storage or a higher limit on the number of requests per minute. This requires instrumentation to be included in the application that measures the usage of each bolt-on feature, and prevents the customer exceeding the preset limits.

- Combination plans where there is a fixed monthly fee with additional metered charges based on the usage of specific features, services, or resources in the application. This does require specific instrumentation to be included in the application to support metering for billing, but has the advantage that heavy use, especially of expensive resources, is accounted for and the vendor is protected against unexpected costs that might result. For example, a customer that exceeds a preset quota for storage could be charged extra for each additional gigabyte of data stored.

> For more information about building multi-tenant applications, see the p&p guide *Developing Multi-tenant Applications for the Cloud* on MSDN. The chapter *Hosting a Multi-Tenant Application on Windows Azure* discusses billing and costing in a multi-tenant application. Additional information and sample code is available from *Multi-Tenant Metering for Windows Azure* on the ISV Developer blog, the associated *Cloud Ninja Metering Block* on CodePlex, and *Meter and Autoscale Multi-Tenant Applications in Windows Azure* on the Windows Azure Insider blog.

CONSIDERATIONS FOR METERING

When planning to implement metering in your application, consider the following points:

- Why you want to include metering. It may be to plan future requirements; to gain an understanding of how applications are used; to enforce quotas; to bill customers or users; to understand your costs for specific operations; or to identify areas that could be optimized to increase profitability. These decisions should be driven by business requirements. A common challenge, especially for organizations unfamiliar with moving to or building in the cloud, is poorly defined business requirements. If it is not clear why you need to gather metering information, you are unlikely to collect the data you really need.

- The cost of collecting the metrics, and the balance between the value they provide and the impact on application operation. If metering code cannot be incorporated into existing components or roles, and you need to increase the number of instances of components or roles just to carry out metering, you might increase costs beyond the savings or income available from metering. For example, the cost of measuring storage transactions for small tenants may exceed the small fraction of the total operating costs that are incurred by the transactions. One possible solution is to use shared metering components for multiple applications, but you must be aware of any related security issues that this may introduce.

- The robustness of the metering system. If the metering system fails—even partially—or logs are lost, this may have a major impact on vendor profitability. One approach is to regularly checkpoint the logs and save intermediate totals elsewhere, perhaps using a background scheduled task. This is particularly useful where there are many small value transactions. Event log analysis utilities may be able to detect and even restart a failed metering system.

- Taking advantage of surrogate metrics, and metering on an end-to-end scenario or use case basis. For example, count the number of orders placed by a tenant instead of trying to measure transaction size, data storage size, and other intermediate operational factors. This simplifies the metering mechanism and reduces the load on the application while still providing a useful billing metric.

- Windows Azure billing is on a per-subscription basis. If you need to precisely bill a small set of users or customers for their actual usage, consider deploying the application into separate subscriptions; one for each user or customer where you need accurate billing totals. Alternatively, locate just the services you need to accurately bill, such as Windows Azure SQL Database or Windows Azure storage, in separate subscriptions and share the other services such as compute with all users. Note that using separate subscriptions for applications will prevent you from taking advantage of cost savings through better utilization of shared services, as well as considerably adding to the cost and complexity of maintaining and updating multiple deployments.

EXAMPLES

The following examples explore some of the ways that service metering may be relevant in different scenarios:

- **Project document storage**. Clients upload and store project documents for team collaboration. The application issues clients with a Shared Access Signature (SAS) token that they use to access the storage. To control costs, the application enforces a quota on the storage size by regularly checking the total amount used by each client. If it exceeds the quota, the application will no longer issue that client with a SAS that enables uploads. In this scenario the majority of the cost is storage, and so bandwidth usage and transaction counts are ignored. Important points are to consider how often to collect and save this metering data (daily, hourly, or when an upload occurs), and how long to keep each value. For operational purposes you need only the current size of each client's storage, but for identifying trends you might want to keep details of the storage use by each client at regular intervals over a longer period.

- **Processing and compute**. Analysis of a complex model in an engineering application may take between one and 60 minutes to complete, depending on the complexity of the model and the data required. The code is instrumented to record the time it takes to complete a successful analysis of a model, identified by the client ID, and this is used to track the total processing time per client for either quota enforcement or for highly accurate billing purposes. However, a simpler approach, if there is less variation in the processing time for each model, might be to count the total number of analyses performed by each client. Billing could then be based on a standard charge for each analysis performed. The average time taken for each analysis can be calculated from the totals, compared across all clients, and used to determine the individual average cost. The result would be monitored over time to detect changes.

- **Web application usage**. The application could be instrumented to track the number of requests and the time online for each user. If the load on the application has a direct relationship to the number of concurrent users, these counts or time periods can be used to allocate charges to a tenant or a department. This information can be used for billing purposes, or to better understand how customers use the application. This information could also be used when determining how to rebalance and partition tenants in a multi-tenant application.

- **Data transfer**. IIS web logs contain an entry for each request/response, and this entry contains information such as the number of bytes transferred as well as the time taken for the request to be processed. The tenant or client ID will often be a part of these entries. It may be included in the query string, or it may be part of the host name if the tenant is in a subdomain or uses a custom domain. Instrumentation is not necessary to collect the information; instead, existing log analysis tools can perform the required analysis. However, this technique will probably not be able to provide information about the internal operations within the application unless they are identified in the request path.

- **Storage**. Database storage in a multi-tenant solution can represent a significant cost. If each tenant has a separate database it is relatively easy to meter costs, but a shared database approach requires the application to monitor and meter database actions for each tenant, or even for each client. Typically, a large proportion of the data access and storage volume is represented by only a subset of the tables, reducing the amount of instrumentation required and consequent log size. Alternatively the metering code can simply count the number of rows in relevant tables, and associate a value or weighting to each table based on this.

RELATED PATTERNS AND GUIDANCE

The following guidance may also be relevant to your scenario when implementing metering in your cloud-hosted applications:

- **Instrumentation and Telemetry Guidance**. Service metering is typically implemented by adding instrumentation to applications, and for large solutions by using telemetry to collect and communicate this information to analysis tools. The Instrumentation and Telemetry Guidance explores the process of gathering remote diagnostics information that is collected by instrumentation in applications.

MORE INFORMATION

All links in this book are accessible from the book's online bibliography available at:
http://aka.ms/cdpbibliography.

- The chapter *Hosting a Multi-Tenant Application on Windows Azure* in the p&p guide *Developing Multi-tenant Applications for the Cloud* on MSDN.
- The article and sample code from *Multi-Tenant Metering for Windows Azure* on the ISV Developer blog.
- The *Cloud Ninja Metering Block* on CodePlex.
- The article *Meter and Autoscale Multi-Tenant Applications in Windows Azure* on the Windows Azure Insider blog.

Made in the USA
San Bernardino, CA
22 April 2014